LIVING WITH THE
HIMALAYAN
MASTERS

ALSO BY SWAMI RAMA

BOOKS
A Practical Guide to Holistic Health
Book of Wisdom (Ishopanishad)
Celestial Song/Gobind Geet
Choosing a Path
Creative Use of Emotion
Enlightenment without God (Mandukya Upanishad)
Exercises for Joints and Glands
Fearless Living: Yoga and Faith
Freedom from the Bondage of Karma
Happiness Is Your Creation
Indian Music
Inspired Thoughts of Swami Rama
Japji: Meditation in Sikhism
Living with the Himalayan Masters
Love and Family Life
Love Whispers
Life Here and Hereafter (Kathopanishad)
Meditation and Its Practice
Meditation in Christianity
Mystical Poems of Kabir
Path of Fire and Light
Path of Fire and Light, Volume 2
Perennial Psychology of the Bhagavad Gita
Science of Breath
Spirituality: Transformation Within & Without
Swami Rama Gift Book Set
The Art of Joyful Living
The Royal Path: Practical Lessons on Yoga
Wisdom of the Ancient Sages (Mundaka Upanishad)
Yoga and Psychotherapy

DVDs
Inner Peace in a Troubled World
Stressless Living
Spiritual Origins of Health
Finding Meaning in Life
How to Tread the Path of Superconscious Meditation

LIVING WITH THE
HIMALAYAN
MASTERS

Swami Rama

 HIMALAYAN INSTITUTE®

HimalayanInstitute.org

Himalayan Institute
952 Bethany Turnpike
Honesdale, PA 18431

HimalayanInstitute.org

Printed in the United States of America

25 24 23 22 21 20 19   6 7 8 9 10

ISBN-13: 978-0-89389-156-5 (paper)

Library of Congress Catalog Card Number: 80-82974

This paper meets the requirements of ANSI/NISO Z39-48-1992
(Permanence of Paper).

Contents

Introduction *by Pandit Rajmani Tigunait* xiii

At Thy Lotus Feet—Sri Swami Rama xviii

Map of Northern India xx

Map of Uttar Pradesh xxiii

I. Spiritual Education in the Himalayas 1
    The Sacred Himalayas 3
    My Gurudeva and Parents 23
    My Master and the Prince Swami 31
    Footprints of Delusion 34
    How We Live in the Caves 37

II. The Master Teaches 41
    Learning to Give 43
    How a Master Tests His Students 45
    An All-Night Journey Through the Forest 47
    Crossing a Flooded River 49
    My Offering to My Master 51
    Loneliness 53
    Maya, the Cosmic Veil 56
    Bitter Truth with Blessed Effects 59

You Teach Others but Deprive Me 62

Discipline Is a Must 65

Blessings in a Curse 69

III. The Path of Direct Experience 71

Direct Experience Alone Is the Means 73

Real Knowledge Removes Suffering 75

A Mantra for Happiness 79

A Mantra for Bees 81

Misuse of Mantra 85

I Receive a Beating 88

Unique Practice of Tantra 91

You Have Committed Many Thefts 94

A Firethrower Swami 97

An Astounding Mystic 99

My Mother Teacher 103

An Ageless Yogi 107

IV. Learning Humility 111

Ego and Vanity Are in Vain 113

My Swollen Ego 115

Cultivating Inner Qualities 117

I Thought I Was Perfect 121

Practice Makes Perfect 126

The Sage from the Valley of Flowers 128

V. Conquering Fear 133

The Devil 135

Mistaken for a Ghost 138

My Fear of Snakes 141

In a Tiger's Cave 147

VI. The Path of Renunciation 151
    My Whole Being Is an Eye 153
    My Experience with a Dancing Girl 155
    Transformation of a Murderer 159
    A Lesson in Non-attachment 163
    Taste the World and Then Renounce 166
    Jewels or Fire? 169
    My First Days as a Swami 171
    A Constant Persecution 175
    Living on a Mount of Pebbles 177
    Temptations on the Path 179
    Should I Get Married? 181
    Spiritual Dignity Is Also Vanity 185
    A Miserable Experiment 189
    Charms of the World 191
    Two Naked Renunciates 195
    In the World and Yet Above 197
    To Lose Is to Gain 199

VII. Experiences on Various Paths 201
    A Renowned Lady Sage 203
    With My Heart on My Palms and
       Tears in My Eyes 210
    Karma Is the Maker 213
    In the Ashram of Mahatma Gandhi 217
    "Not Sacrifice but Conquest"—Tagore 221
    Setting History Straight 227
    Maharshi Raman 235
    Meeting with Sri Aurobindo 239
    The Wave of Bliss 243
    Three Schools of Tantra 248

The Seven Systems of Eastern Philosophy 251

Soma 258

VIII. Beyond the Great Religions 263

A Christian Sage of the Himalayas 265

My Meeting with a Jesuit Sadhu 271

Jesus in the Himalayas 273

A Vision of Christ 278

Judaism in Yoga 283

I Belong to None but God 285

IX. Divine Protection 287

Protecting Arms 289

Lost in the Land of Devas 295

The Land of Hamsas 299

An Atheistic Swami 303

An Appointment with Death 308

X. Powers of the Mind 313

Lessons on the Sands 315

Transmutation of Matter 319

Where Is My Donkey? 325

Who Was That Other Gopinath? 329

An Experience with a Psychic 332

XI. Healing Power 335

My First Exposure to the Power of Healing 337

My Master Sends Me to Heal Someone 340

Unorthodox Ways of Healing 345

Healing in a Himalayan Shrine 349

At the Feet of the Masters 357

XII. Grace of the Master 361

   Guru Is a Stream and a Channel of Knowledge 363

   A Weeping Statue 366

   My Master's Photograph 369

   Who Can Kill the Eternal? 371

   Half "Here," Half "There" 373

   How a Young Widow Was Rescued 377

   My Master Saves a Drowning Man 379

   Shaktipata—Bestowing Bliss 381

   My Grandmaster in Sacred Tibet 385

   Preparing to Tear the Veil 402

XIII. Mastery over Life and Death 405

   Birth and Death Are but Two Commas 407

   Attitudes Toward Dying 414

   The Techniques of Casting Off the Body 419

   Living in a Dead Body 423

   My Master Casts Off His Body 428

XIV. Journey to the West 433

   A Doctor's Recurring Vision 435

   Transformation in the Cave 439

   Ways of East and West 443

   Our Tradition 447

Glossary 453

About the Author 457

Sri Swami Rama of the Himalayas

Introduction

◆

By Pandit Rajmani Tigunait, PhD

Sri Swami Rama took me under his wing in 1976, and from that time on every minute of the twenty years I lived with him was a time of learning. Now that he is no longer in his physical body, I look back and realize how skillfully he filled my every breath with the living presence of the masters who were such an integral part of his own life. In continuous waves he nourished my mind and heart with the perennial knowledge and love of the lineage of the sages. Today, with awe and gratitude, I ask myself: After having him as my master, is there anything yet to be achieved?

One of the most blessed and richest periods of my life was in 1985, when at Swamiji's behest I began to translate *Living with the Himalayan Masters* into Hindi, my native language. Every evening, when I showed him that day's translation, Swamiji told me the untold part of the story, and I soon realized he was using the translation as an excuse for me to glimpse the inner life of the sages he had written about, and to absorb their teachings. Every episode brought a revelation, which I was able to assimilate only through the grace of Sri Swamiji and the masters who speak through this book. *Living with the Himalayan Masters* is the embodiment of Swamiji's life, his spiritual journey, and his experiences with the masters of different traditions. He addresses the issues that all of us confront at least once in our lifetime, and shares his experiences in such a simple and loving manner that they become a part of us.

At the mundane level, this book shows us who we are and what steps we must take to be happy and successful. It inspires us to work hard and have faith in our own self-effort. At the spiritual level, it introduces us to our own mystical and esoteric self as we encounter the adepts hidden in the caves and monasteries of the Himalayas and other remote parts of India, Tibet, Nepal, Sikkim, and Bhutan.

Spiritual books, especially those of an autobiographical nature, often give the impression that the experiences and spiritual achievements of the masters are beyond our reach. Swamiji, however, puts miracles and mysticism in an entirely different light. Reading it, we feel that he is one of us. He is a young boy, full of mischief. He is a teenager, full of curiosity and adventurous zeal. He is a seeker, with certain strengths and weaknesses. Just like us, he sometimes fails to distinguish the fakes from genuine masters, mistaking magic for spiritual achievement. At one time, for example, attracted by the magical power and glamorous life of sorcerers and low-grade tantrics, he even considers abandoning his master for another teacher. His human traits are so familiar to us that in reading about them his journey becomes our journey.

The stories in this book infuse our hearts with overwhelming gratitude for the sages who selflessly share their boundless love and yet remain unrecognized by the multitude. Swamiji is one of them. While he lived among us he lectured, wrote books, and established large charitable organizations, but very few of us perceived his spiritual stature. In the last phase of his life those who were near to him and had "eyes to see" came to know that Swamiji was master of every esoteric practice he mentions in this book, but they never knew how and when he practiced them.

Swamiji discouraged a belief in miracles, yet every moment of his life was filled with miracles. No one who came near him ever went away empty-handed. His gifts were of different shapes, sizes, and weights—upon touching his feet, a businessman might be blessed with prosperity, a sick man with health, and a student with knowledge. Some understood what they had received; others did not. Now I look back and wonder at how beautifully he unveiled the spiritual mysteries while skillfully hiding his identity as one of the greatest sages from the Himalayan peaks.

Swami Rama was fully established in his own self-nature. A playful child, a carefree adolescent, a gentle sage, a tactful adult spontaneously manifested in him. For him past and future did not exist—he always lived in the present, and the circumstance of the moment called forth whatever persona would help and guide those who were with him. Transformative energy emanated from him. If he stayed for a time in a rocky, barren land, a beautiful rock garden would emerge; if he stopped to speak to a woman suffering from chronic depression, her face would light up and the years would drop away.

To Swamiji, nothing was useless; everything had purpose and meaning. He once put rocks and pebbles around an odd-looking septic vent pipe and artfully placed a few stumps around it; the resulting "sculpture" looked like a holy man sitting in meditation, and visitors kept a respectful distance. He was very fond of cactus. He had a huge collection in India and a smaller one in the States. One day I asked him, "Swamiji, why do you love cactus so much?" He said, "I am in the habit of tending those who are full of thorns and are discarded by everybody. It gives me great joy when I see them blossom."

I remember my own life. Before 1976 I was like a speck of dust drifting along the roadside. Then one day Swamiji picked me up and transformed me into living pollen. With his loving touch I became an integral part of that garden which the sages cultivate. Today I have been given the honor and privilege of writing an introduction to this classic work, but I hope you will understand that my attempt to do so is like a flower's attempt to describe the gardener and his work—work which far exceeds the flower's understanding. What I received directly from Swamiji and what I learned about him by visiting places where he did his sadhana, however, gives me the confidence to say that the stories in this book represent only the tip of the iceberg.

Living with the Himalayan Masters has its own spirit. I have read and pondered over it countless times. And each time I have found something new, something that was just what I needed at that level of my development. The book speaks to each reader at the personal level. I must not try to tell you what I think it is about, because by doing so I might put a veil between you and its message. In these pages you will experience Swamiji's presence and the presence of other great masters. May you bask in their grace and receive just what you need.

At thy lotus feet

This is not my life but the gift
of experiences which I gathered from
the sages of the Himalayas and from
Thee, my beloved master.

One lonely evening it seemed
to me as if a ray of light all of a
sudden broke through the mist and
I wondered what it might mean.

The same eve thou gavest me
a glimpse of the love divine.

And then I heard His name
uttered from thy lips shedding a
new light over my destiny.

In the dark chamber of my
heart the lamp was lit which always

goes on burning like the lamp on the altar.

who has, like thou, mingled the strains of joy and sorrow into the song of my life, enabling me to realise " the joy that sits still on the lotus of pains and the joy that throws every thing it has upon the dust and knows not a word "?

To those who understand thy message there shall be no fear left on the earth.

Therefore today the flower of undying gratitude offers its petals at thy lotus feet.

Swami Rama.

Hunza

JAMMU AND KASMIR

Sonamarg
Amarnath Cave
Pahlgam
SRINAGAR
Martand
Gulmarg
Tangmarg

KASMIR HIMALAYAN MTNS.

HIMALAYAN

Pathankot

TIBET

Amritsar

Indus River

SVEN HEDRIN MTNS.

Indus River

KAILAS

SIMLA

PUNJAB

CHANDIGARH

Mana Pass

Suttej R.

Manasarowar L.

Gangotri

KAMET

Rakas L.

Jamnotri

LAND OF HANSA

Badrinath

NANDA DEVI

Tibrikot

Muktinath

MANASL

Kedarnath

DHAULAGIRI

ANNAPURN

Mussoorie

Joshimath

Pithoragarh

Saharanpur

Dehra Dun

Almora

RĀGASTHĀN

Hardwar

Rishikesh

Lansdowne

Naini Tal

NEPAL

DELHI

GARHWAL

Bijnor

Rampur

UTTAR
PRADESH

LUCKNOW

Agra

Kanpur

Ganges River

Allahabad

INDIA

INDIA

N

INDIA

xx

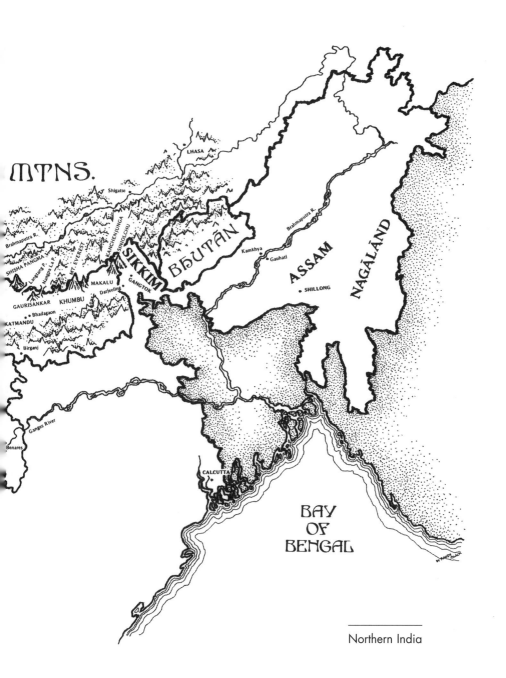

MTNS.

LHASA

Shigatse

Brahmaputra R.

SHISHA PANGMA

Langtang L.

Nangel La P.

MT. EVEREST

KANCHENJUNGA

SINIOLCHU

SIKKIM

BHUTAN

Kamkhya

Gauhati

ASSAM

NAGALAND

Brahmaputra R.

GAURISANKAR

MAKALU

KHUMBU

Darjeeling

GANGTOK

• SHILLONG

KATMANDU

• Bhadagaon

Birganj

Ganges River

Benares

CALCUTTA

BAY
OF
BENGAL

BY RANDY ASPLUND

Northern India

The State of Uttar Pradesh

I

Spiritual Education in the Himalayas

CHILDHOOD IS THE FOUNDATION STONE UPON which stands the whole life structure. The seed sown in childhood blossoms into the tree of life. The education which is imparted in childhood is more important than the education which is received in colleges and universities. In the process of human growth, proper guidance along with environmental learning is important.

The Sacred Himalayas

◆

The Himalayan ranges extend over almost 1,500 miles in length. Mount Everest, towering upward over 29,000 feet on the border of Nepal and Tibet, is the highest of all the mountains in the world. Persians, Indians, Tibetans, and Chinese have all written about the grandeur and beauty of these mountains. The word *Himalaya* comes from Sanskrit words: *hima*, meaning "snow," and *alaya*, meaning "home"—the home of snows. I would like to make you aware that the Himalayas are not merely the home of snow, but that they have also been a stronghold of yogic wisdom and spirituality for millions of people, regardless of their religious beliefs. This ancient and rich tradition still exists there today as these unique mountains continue to whisper their spiritual glory to all who have an ear to hear.

I was born and brought up in the valleys of the Himalayas. I roamed among them for more than four and a half decades and was educated by their sages. I met the masters who live and travel there, studied at their feet and experienced their spiritual wisdom. From the Punjab Himalayas to the Kumayun and Garhwal Himalayas, from Nepal to Assam, and from Sikkim

3

to Bhutan and Tibet, I traveled to those forbidden places which are virtually inaccessible to tourists. I climbed to a height of 19,000 to 20,000 feet without the help of an oxygen kit or modern equipment. Many times I did not have food and became unconscious, tired and sometimes wounded, but always, one way or another, I found help during such occasions.

For me, the Himalayas are my spiritual parents and living there was like living in the lap of a mother. She brought me up in her natural environment and inspired me to live a particular style of life. Once when I was fourteen years old, an unknown sage blessed me and gave me a leaf of *bhoja patra,* the paper made of bark on which the ancient scriptures were written. On it he inscribed, "Let the world be little with you. Let you be on the path of spirituality." It is still in my possession.

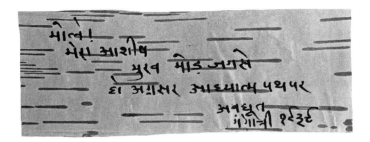

Let the world be little with you.
Let you be on the path of spirituality.
Awadhoot, Gangotri, 1939

The love I received from the sages is like the perennial snows which form the silvery glaciers of the Himalayas and then melt into thousands of streams. When love became the lord of my life, I became quite fearless and traveled from one cave to another, crossing streams and mountain passes surrounded by snow-blanketed peaks. In all conditions I was cheerful, searching for the hidden sages who preferred to remain unknown. Every breath of my life was enriched with spiritual experiences which may be difficult for many others to comprehend.

That gentle and amiable sage of the Himalayas had only one entrancing theme: love—for nature, love—for creatures, and love—for the Whole. The Himalayan sages taught me the gospel of nature. Then I started listening to the music coming from the blooming flowers, from the songs of the birds, and even from the smallest blade of grass and thorn of the bush. In everything lives the evidence of the beautiful. If one does not learn to listen to the music of nature and appreciate her beauty, then that which impels man to seek love at its fountain may be lost in the remotest antiquity. Do you need psychological analysis to discover in nature the source of so much happiness, of so many songs, dreams, and beauties? This gospel of nature speaks its parables from the glacial streams, the valleys laden with lilies, the forests covered with flowers, and the light of stars. This gospel reveals that emphatic knowledge through which one learns truth and beholds the good in all its majesty and glory.

When one learns to hear the music of nature and appreciate her beauty, then his soul moves in harmony with its entire environment. His every movement and every sound will surely then find its due place in human society. The mind of man should be trained to love nature before he looks through the corridor of his life. Then a revelation comes peeping through with the dawn. The pain and miseries of life disappear with the darkness and the mist when the sun rises. Mortality finds its way in the awareness of immortality. Then a mortal being suffers no more from the pangs and sorrows which death seems to shower upon him. Death has for ages been a constant source of misery, but at death man learns to become one with the infinite and the eternal.

When one learns to appreciate fully the profundity of

nature in its simplicity, then thoughts flow spontaneously in response to the appeals of his delicate senses when they come in contact with nature. This soul-vibrating experience, in its full harmony with the perfect orchestra of melodies and echos, reflects from the sound of the ripples of the Ganges, the gushing of the winds, the rustling of leaves, and the roar of thundering clouds. The light of the self is revealed and all the obstacles are removed. He ascends the top of the mountain, where he perceives the vast horizon. In the depth of silence is hidden the source of love. The eye of faith alone can unveil and see the illumination of that love. This music resounds in my ears and has become the song of my life.

This discovery of the sages binds the whole of humanity in the harmony of the cosmos. Sages are the sources from which mankind receives knowledge and wisdom to behold the light, truth, and beauty which show the path of freedom and happiness to all. They make humanity aware of the mere shadows and vain illusions of this world. With their eyes the unity of the entire universe is best seen.

"The truth is hidden by a golden disc. O Lord! Help us in unveiling so that we can see the truth." The gospel of love as taught by the Himalayan sages makes the whole universe aware of the fountainhead of light, life, and beauty.

At a young age I sat at the foot of Mount Kailas and drank the glacial waters of Lake Manasarowar. Often I cooked the vegetables and roots grown by Mother Nature at Gangotri and Kedarnath. Living in the Himalayan caves was very pleasant, and when I was there I was in the habit of roaming through the mountains during the day, taking notes in a haphazard manner, and returning to my cave before darkness would fall. My diary is filled with descriptions of my experiences with the sages, yogis, and other spiritual leaders of the Himalayas.

This is a land where Sandhya Bhasha was born. Several modern scholars have tried to interpret and translate Sandhya

Temple at Kedarnath

Bhasha by calling it "the twilight language." Actually, the way I was taught this language, it is entirely different from the concept the modern writers have of it. It is a purely yogic language, spoken by only a few fortunate yogis, sages, and adepts. Philosophically and ideally, it is very similar to Sanskrit, for every word of Sandhya Bhasha flows full of meaning from its root sound. Sandhya Bhasha can be used only for the discussion of spiritual matters and contains no vocabulary for the business affairs of the world. When the sun weds with the moon, when the day weds with the night, and when *ida* and *pingala* [the left and right energy channels of the human body] equally flow, that union is called s*andhya* or *sushumna*. *Sushumna* is the mother from whose womb was born the language Sandhya Bhasha or twilight. During that period of *sushumna* the yogi derives the greatest joy that anyone can consciously experience. When such a yogi speaks with other adepts, then they converse in this language, which is hard for others to understand. Knowledge of the appropriate way of chanting the Vedic verses is slowly diminishing because the grammar of the Vedas is different from the Sanskrit language. (The grammar of the Vedas is called *Nirukta*.) Similarly, the grammar of Sandhya Bhasha is completely based on sounds and is diminishing. As the musicians of classical music can make notes from sounds and their pitches, so the notes can be made from the sounds used in Sandhya Bhasha. It is called "the language of devas" [gods].

When one sits in the mornings and evenings on the tops of the mountains, he can see beauty all around. If he is a spiritual man, he can understand how this beauty is an inseparable aspect of the Lord, whose attributes are *Satyam, Shivam,* and *Sundaram*—truth, eternity, and beauty. This is the land of *devas*. In the Himalayas, dawn (*usha*) and twilight (*sandhya*— when the day weds the night) are not mere moments created by the rotation of the earth, but have a deep symbolic meaning.

Morning, afternoon, evening, and night each have their own beauty which no language can ever describe. Many times a day the mountains change their colors, because the sun is at the service of these mountains. In the morning they are silvery, at noon they are golden, and in the evening they look red. I thought that my own mother was dressing to please me in many different-colored saris. Do I have vocabulary to explain this beauty through the language of the lips? It is only the language of the heart in which I can speak, but the words do not roll down through my lips.

I can give you only a glimpse of these beautiful mountains. Their beauty is splendid and beyond description. The morning environment in the Himalayas is so calm and serene that it leads an aspirant spontaneously to silence. That is why the people of the Himalayas become meditators. Nature strengthened the schools of meditation. When I lived in my cave, Usha (dawn), holding the rising sun in her palm, would awaken me

Shivling, towering between Gangotri and Gomukh

every morning, as though my mother were standing before me. The rays of the sun penetrated gently through the entrance. (In the cave there lived several yogis studying the wisdom of the Upanishads at the feet of the master.)

In the evening when the weather clears and the sun breaks through the clouds, it seems as though the mighty Painter were pouring out millions of colors on the snowy peaks, creating paintings which could never be duplicated by the brushes and colors of the tiny fingers of artists. Any art that exists in Tibet, China, India, and Persia has some influence of the Himalayan beauty on it. A few times I too tried to paint, but I stopped using my brushes because my paintings seemed to be mere scribbles drawn by a child. Beauty remains bound within the limitations of human realms if it is not appreciated heartily. When one becomes aware of the higher level of beauty which projects itself through nature, he becomes a true artist. When an artist becomes aware of that fountain from which arises all beauty, then instead of painting, he starts composing poems. The brush and colors do not have access to that finest level of consciousness. Spiritual beauty needs to be expressed on increasingly deeper and more subtle levels.

The most ancient travelers of the Himalayas are the clouds which roll gently from the Bay of Bengal. Rising from the ocean, these monsoon clouds travel toward the snowy peaks of the Himalayas, hug them, and return roaring to the plains, laden with pure snowy waters. They shower their blessings and bestow them upon the soil of India. Kalidasa, a great Sanskrit poet known as "the Shakespeare of the East," composed many poems about these clouds. *Meghadoota* is a solitary example of an excellent collection of these poems. In these poems Kalidasa used the clouds as messengers to deliver his message to his beloved, who was captive in the Himalayas. The *Ramayana* and *Mahabharata*, famous Indian epics, are full of praises describing pilgrimages to the Himalayas. Even modern poets of

Hindi and Urdu like Prasad and Ickbal could not resist composing poems on the Himalayan beauty. Many Sanskrit poems, such as *Mahimna-stotra*, are sung as though a traveler were going up and coming down from the Himalayas. I also used to compose poems and sing, although I was not a good poet or singer. The classical music of India borrowed ragas like *Pahari* from the melodious tunes sung by the girls from the tops of the mountains. The Himalayas remain replete with mysteries for poets, artists, musicians, and travelers, but they reveal their most important message only to those who are prepared. Mystics alone can unveil the real secrets of these wondrous mountains.

I used to roam in the mountains with my pet bear, who was very loyal to me. He was fond of me and became very possessive. He wouldn't hurt anyone, but would knock down anyone who came near me. I called him Bhola and he was my finest company during those days. For eleven years he lived near my cave and would always wait for me to come out. My master did not approve of my growing attachment to this pet and used to tease me, calling me a bear charmer. In the morning, carrying a long staff to help me in climbing, I would go to the mountaintops which were four to six miles from my cave. I had my diary, a few pencils and the bear Bhola with me.

After the fifteenth of September it starts snowing in the Himalayas, but I continued my long walks to the nearby mountaintops, singing the hymns of the Divine Mother. Occasionally the thought would flash in my mind that my life belongs to those who follow our tradition. I did not care for my individuality, but was acutely conscious of the tradition of sages which I followed. Even though I broke the discipline many times and became rebellious, I was still forgiven. During those days many profound psychological and spiritual experiences occurred. Sometimes I felt like a king but without any burden of the crown on my head. Not having human company or communication brought me great peace and serenity. I realized that nature is very peaceful. She disturbs only those who disturb themselves, but she teaches wisdom to those who admire and appreciate her beauty. This is especially true in the Himalayas.

Many varieties of flowers are found in abundance in these mountains. Those with a poetic imagination say that viewed from the snow-covered mountain peaks, these slopes laden with flower beds look like a magnificent vase of flowers which a fully prepared disciple would reverently present to his gurudeva. I would sit next to these natural flower beds and gaze into the sky, searching for their Gardener.

Among all the flowers grown in the Himalayan valleys, the most beautiful are the lilies and the orchids. Hundreds of varieties of lilies bloom after winter is over and sometimes even before snowfall. There is one variety of lily which is pink and very beautiful. It grows in June and July at a height of 8,000 to 11,000 feet and is found on the banks of the river Rudra Garo that joins the Ganges at Gangotri. This same variety of lily also grows under the trees at Bhoja Basa.

The orchids in the Himalayas are more gorgeous than any other flower. They grow at a height of 4,000 to 6,000 feet. The heaviest orchid that I ever found was growing on an oak tree and weighed a little less than one and a half pounds. Some varieties of these orchids can be found in greenhouses a few miles from Katmandu, Nepal, but many still remain undiscovered by horticulturists. During the blossoming season of orchids, the buds, in their natural obstinacy, delay blooming and sometimes take six to seven days to open. Orchid flowers are amazingly beautiful and their blooming season lasts for at least two and a half months.

The mountain cacti bloom suddenly in the moonlit night. They are shy to the sun's rays, and before the sun rises their petals withdraw their blooming beauty, never to bloom again. I know of more than twenty-five varieties of succulents and cacti in the Himalayas which are used for medicinal purposes. I was told that the soma creeper comes from the succulent family and grows at the height of 11,000 to 18,000 feet.

Among the great variety of flowers in the Himalayas there are more than one hundred and fifty varieties of rhododendron. The most striking of this species is blue and white. Pink and red varieties are common, and there is another variety which has multi-colored petals. In the summer, sometimes an entire valley is laden with rhododendron flowers.

The king of all the Himalayan flowers is the *himkamal,* or "snow lotus," a very rare flower. One day as I was wandering through the mountains I saw a single blue *himkamal* as big as a saucer, growing from between two rocks and half-buried in snow. I started looking at it and my mind entered into a dialogue with this beautiful snow lotus. I said, "Why are you here all alone? Your beauty is meant to be adored. You should give yourself to someone before your petals fall and return to the dust."

As the breeze blew its stem, it shook and then bent toward me, saying, "Do you think I am lonely being all alone? All alone means all in one. I enjoy these heights, the purity, the shelter of the blue umbrella above."

I wanted to pick the flower and considered pulling it out and taking the whole plant to my master. I compared my own life to this lotus and said like an irresponsible, joyous child, "What will happen to you if I crush your petals?"

The lotus replied, "I will be glad, for my fragrance will radiate everywhere and the purpose of my life will be fulfilled."

I pulled the lotus out by its roots and took it to my master, but he was not appreciative. He had never liked to use flowers and their fragrance except on a few occasions when he instructed me to collect flowers from the forest for worship. That was the last day that I ever picked a flower. I felt that I had been depriving Mother Nature by snatching her child from her lap. I never picked a flower again. Beauty is to be admired and not to be used, possessed, or destroyed. Aesthetic sense develops when one starts appreciating the beauty of nature.

To satisfy and fulfill my desire to be all alone I wandered here and there, admiring nature just by being with her. Sometimes I would go down to the snowy streams and look at the ripples kicking each other as they moved forward. The rivers and streams running from the tops of the glaciers looked like many long locks of hair. The music created by the streams is quite exhilarating. I would compare the stream of life with these ever-flowing streams and watch how a mass of water running toward the ocean would not leave a gap. The currents would never turn back, but another mass of water would fill the gap. There was always continuity. Those streams are like the perennial flow of life. For hours I would watch these snowy streams flowing from the glaciers and waterfalls. Both banks of the streams glittered like silver on moonlit nights.

Living in that part of the Himalayas where the Ganges flows, I would stay seated on its rocky banks and gaze at the blue sky and the clear moon, which paled its light on the sands. I watched the twinkling lights coming from the small homes of the distant villages, and when the clouds parted I saw the sky glittering with the lamps of a million stars. This grand assembly and long procession of the stars is beyond human imagination. Below on the earth, the peaks of the Himalayas silently enjoyed this fair of stars. Some of them seemed as though they were playing hide and seek among the mountain peaks. In all directions, the mountain peaks and snowy streams were illuminated with that milky light emanating from the starry multitude which I remember even today. In the evenings mist formed a thick white quilt over the Ganges between the two ridges of snowy peaks, and before sunrise a layer of mist would cover the Ganges like a white blanket. It seemed as though a sleeping serpent were snoring from beneath it. The rays of the rising sun rushed to drink these holy waters as eagerly as I rushed to bathe in the Ganges every morning. The mountain water was crystal clear, soothing to the eyes, and stimulating to the senses.

There are many rivers that flow from the great Lake Manasarowar at the foot of Mount Kailas, but of all the rivers which have their source in the Himalayan mountains, the Ganges is unique. When the Ganges flows from its sources in the glaciers of Gangotri, it carries in its water a variety of minerals which have nutritional and therapeutic value. Skin diseases are rarely found among villagers who live on the banks of the Ganges. A bottle of Ganges water is kept in every home and practically all of the villagers give it to a dying person to drink.

When bottled, this water does not become stagnant, and bacteria do not survive in it, although they do in the water from other rivers. Long ago, sailors learned that drinking water from the Ganges carried by ships traveling from Calcutta to London did not stagnate, but water from the Thames carried

This glacier at the base of the Bhagirithi Peaks is the source of the Ganges

by ships traveling from London to India had to be replaced by fresh water along the way. The unique chemical components and minerals of this water have been analyzed by many scientists from all over the world. Dr. Jagdish Chandra Bose, a prominent Indian scientist, analyzed the Ganges water and concluded: "There seems to be no other river water like this anywhere in the world. Its mineral qualities have powers to cure many diseases."

When the Ganges comes down to the plains, however, it is fed by many polluted streams and rivers, and the merits of its water are lost. Some of the villagers throw the bodies of their deceased into the Ganges, believing that by doing so the souls of their loved ones will go to heaven. Personally I don't approve of polluting water and then drinking the same water and calling it holy. I was instructed by my master not to drink from or bathe in the water of the Ganges with any idea that by doing so my sins would be washed off. He taught me the philosophy of karma and said, "One has to reap the fruits of his karma. The law of karma is inevitable and is accepted by all the great philosophies of the world: 'As you sow, so shall you reap.' Learn to perform your duties skillfully without aversion or attachment, and do not believe that anything can wash off your bad karma. Taking a bath in a river and making pilgrimages from one shrine to another will not free you from the bondage of karma. Such belief is only superstition and has no logic."

The rivers flowing from the Himalayas enrich the soil of India and feed more than 600 million people today, yet some call these mountains poor. Writers dare say that the Himalayas are economically disappointing, having few mineral deposits and being unable to support enterprises on a large scale. I agree with them: economically these mountains are not rich. They are spiritual mountains and provide for renunciates, not for the materially wealthy. Those who have tried to explore the riches of the Himalayas from an economic viewpoint have met with failure, and those who will undertake such ventures in the future will be similarly disappointed. Himalayan villages have not received their share of modern education, technology, and medicine, even though the Himalayas are the reservoirs for the drinking and irrigation waters for the whole of India. Indian planners are unwise in not placing greater emphasis on this important resource. However, the Himalayan inhabitants prefer things to remain as they are. "Leave us alone without exploitation; just be grateful and respect us from a distance" are the words I hear from many villagers of the Himalayas.

The economy of the villages is supported by the nearby tiny terraced fields, where barley, wheat, and lentils are grown. Livestock include buffaloes, sheep, cattle, ponies, and goats. The villagers living in the Punjab and Kashmir Himalayas, in the Kumayun and Garhwal Himalayas, and in the Nepal and Sikkim Himalayas have many common characteristics. They

Terraced fields below a Himalayan village

are poor but honest; they do not steal or quarrel. In the villages high in the mountains, no one even locks his house—locks are not needed. There are places of pilgrimage there. If you go to a shrine high in the mountains and drop your purse on the path, it will still be there when you come back weeks later. No one will touch it. They consider it disrespectful to touch somebody else's things without permission. "Why should we need someone else's things?" they will ask. There is no greed, for their needs are few. They do not suffer from materialistic insanity.

The villagers are dependent on the plains only for salt and for oil to burn in their lamps. These village societies are less corrupt than most others in the world because of the people's simple, honest, and gentle habits. Life there is calm and peaceful. The people don't know how to hate anyone. They don't understand hatred. These people don't want to come down to the plains. When they leave the mountains they do not feel comfortable around the people of the plains, with their many tricks and games and pretenses. In the mountain areas most influenced by modern culture, however, lying and stealing have begun to occur much more frequently.

Modern society is considered to be advanced and cultured, but it is not genuine. It is cultured like a cultured pearl. Few value genuine pearls today. The modern human being has weakened himself and his human nature by culturing it again and again, losing touch with nature and reality. In modern culture we live for showing off to others, not for serving others. But if you go to the mountains, no matter who you are the first things they will ask you are, "Have you taken your food? Do you have a place to stay?" Anybody there will ask you these things, whether you are friend or stranger.

The people of the Garhwal and Kumayun mountains are intelligent, cultured, and hospitable. Kangra Valley art and Garhwal art are renowned for their unique pen and color work. Education in some of these mountain communities is better than in many other parts of India. The priests of the different communities know so much about astrology mingled with tantrism that it sometimes surprises travelers from the plains. The people here lead simple lives close to nature. They live in beautiful wooden houses and weave their own clothes. In the evenings they assemble for chanting, and sing their folklore in beautiful melodies. They dance in a group and sing folk songs which are harmonious and moving. The mountain drummers are excellent, and bamboo flutes and jaw harps are used by the shepherds and schoolchildren. As the girls and boys go to the mountains to fetch grass for cattle and wood for fuel, they spontaneously compose and sing poems. The children have their own way of enjoying life by playing hockey and soccer. Reverence for parents and elders is one of the striking features in the Himalayan culture.

Most of the trees which grow at heights of 4,000 to 6,000 feet are oaks, pines, and *devadaru* (fir) trees of various kinds. In the high mountains, *bhoja patra* grows and supplies bark paper, which the villagers use to record their experiences, their ways of worship, and the usage of the herbs. Every villager knows something about herbs, which are useful for many purposes in daily life. All the villages from Kashmir to Punjab, Nepal, and Sikkim have a reputation for providing strong and healthy soldiers for the Indian army. The life span of the people is often over one hundred years.

The Himalayan community which lives in the mountains of Pakistan is called Hunza. There they eat meat, but the community that lives in the Indian part of the Himalayas is called Hamsa, and is vegetarian. *Hamsa* means "swan," and it is a frequent symbol in Indian mythology. The swan is said to have the power of separating and drinking only the milk out of a mixture of milk and water. Similarly, this world is a mixture of two things: the good and the bad. The wise person selects and takes the good and leaves the bad.

Throughout these mountains, Shakti worship is prominent, and in every village there are at least one or two small chapels. The sages, however, travel and do not form communities such as the villagers do. These sages are treated very nicely by the villagers and are given free food and shelter. They come from different cultures and parts of the country (and world) and live in caves, under trees, or in tiny thatched huts. These dwelling places are considered temples and are situated outside the villages. There is always at least one wise man and sometimes several staying there whose bare necessities are maintained by the villagers. When any wandering *sadhu* [renunciate], yogi, or sage comes by, the villagers freely offer whatever food they have. They enjoy entertaining guests and easily establish friendship with them. As I traveled throughout the Himalayas I did not enjoy staying with the villagers or the officers stationed here and there, but preferred to stay in the hermitages, caves, and thatched huts of these sages.

Culturally the Himalayas are not obstacles, and do not create any barriers to the countries situated on either side. There are hundreds of communities and nationalities in these mountains which are conspicuous for the peculiarities in their ways of life, resulting from some unusual blend of Indian, Tibetan, and Chinese cultures. Different languages are spoken in different parts of the Himalayas. I could at one time speak Nepalese, Garhwali, Kumayuni, Punjabi, and some Tibetan, but I have never learned the Kashmiri language. Knowledge of these mountain languages helped me in communicating with the local spiritual leaders and herbalists.

The month of July is the finest month for traveling in the Himalayas. The snow and glaciers are melting then, and there are thousands of streams rushing all over. It is not unpleasantly cold, and those who know the nature of glaciers, avalanches, and landslides can travel comfortably if they are careful. The dangers of the Himalayan mountains are the same today as they have always been. Avalanches, fast-running streams and rivers, overhanging cliffs, and high, towering, snow-covered peaks will not change their ways for any traveler. Nonetheless, the spiritual heritage of the Himalayas has long motivated travelers to explore their unknown wisdom. Over a thousand years ago hundreds of Tibetan and Chinese travelers took Buddhist literature from India and translated it into their own languages, thereby disseminating Buddhist teachings to their own countries. The Great Vehicle of Buddhism, Mahayana, passed across the Himalayan borders, first to Tibet and then to China, greatly enriching Chinese culture and religion. The meditative traditions of Zen are aspects of this Buddhism that were then passed on to Japan. The original teachings were imparted by Indian teachers who traveled to Tibet and China ten centuries ago. The followers of Taoism and Confucianism adore the Himalayas and the Himalayan teachers, for they have received much wisdom from those who traveled and lived in these mountains. The principle of inaction emphasized by Taoism is found precisely formulated in the *Bhagavad Gita*. The concept of nirvana, clearly present in early Indian philosophy, has influenced all the religions of Tibet, Mongolia, China, and Japan. Today Tibet is a communist country and it appears that its ancient wisdom, and the culture based on it, have vanished. However, the Dalai Lama and a handful of his followers have migrated to the foothills of the Himalayan mountains in India.

These mountains were my playgrounds. They were like large lawns spread as though Mother Nature had personally looked after them so that her children who live in the valleys would remain happy, joyous, and aware of the purpose of life. It is there that one can come to understand that from the smallest blade of grass to the highest of mountain peaks, there is no place for sorrow in life.

My forty-five years of living and traveling with the sages of the Himalayas, under the guidance of my gurudeva, enabled me to experience in a few years that which normally would not be possible for anyone to experience in several lifetimes. I was able to do so because of the grace of my beloved master, who wanted me to experience, choose, and decide for myself. This series of experiences and my learning with the sages have helped me to attain and maintain a center of awareness within. I will tell you how I grew up and how I was trained, about the great sages with whom I lived and what they taught me, not through lectures and books but through experiences. The stories collected here are a record of some of these experiences.

Whenever I want to tell a story to the world, I think that the world itself is a story. I pray that others may benefit from these experiences also, and that is why I talk about them as I lecture and teach. I always say to my students, "What is that which is mine and what is that which I have not surrendered to thee?" From these spiritual stories, learn that which is useful for your growth, and start practicing it, and that which is beyond your grasp, leave it for now with the narrator. Memories of these experiences awaken me even today, and I feel the Himalayan mountains are calling me back.

My Gurudeva and Parents

◆

My father was a well-known learned Sanskrit scholar and a highly spiritual man. Mostly brahmins lived in his village and they would come to my father for consultation and to study with him. My parents were moderately wealthy and generous landowners. My father did not plow his fields himself, but would share the yields with the field-workers who did.

For six months no one had known where my father was, and his family had concluded that he was either dead or had taken a vow of renunciation. Actually, he had gone on a long retreat because he was having problems with his spiritual practices. He was meditating intensively in the forest at Mansa Devi, not far from Hardwar. My master, on a trip which took him by Mansa Devi, arrived one evening at the place where my father was staying. Upon seeing my master, he knew immediately that this was his gurudeva. Often in such initial contact between master and disciple, the two hearts respond and spontaneously open to each other. This can happen with only the contact of a single glance. Thereupon begins communication without action or speech. My master stayed there for a week, guiding my father and finally instructing him to return to his home, which was at the height of about 5,500 feet in the hills of Uttar Pradesh.

My mother had given up hope of her husband returning and had started an intensive practice of austerities. When my father returned, he told her about his experiences with the master who had initiated him at Mansa Devi. He told her that his master had said that although they were forty-three and sixty years old, they would have a son who would also follow him.

Two years later my master came down from the Himalayas to my parents' village and visited their home. My father was having dinner when my master arrived, and my mother answered his knock at the door. Without knowing who he was, she requested him to please wait because her husband was taking food and she was serving him. Upon hearing of a guest's arrival, however, my father left his meal and rushed to the door. My master said, "I have not come to eat or accept your hospitality. I want you to give me something."

My father replied, "Anything I have is yours."

My master said, "I need your son."

My parents responded, "For us to have a son at our ages would be a miracle, but if we can have him, he will be yours." Eighteen months after this meeting, I was born.

The day I was born, my master arrived at our house and asked my mother to hand me over to him. As a protective new mother, she was reluctant to comply, but my father asked her to do so. After holding me for a few minutes in his arms, my master handed me back and instructed, "Look after him; I will come again later and take him with me."

Three years later my master returned and initiated me by whispering a mantra in my right ear. I told him that I already knew the mantra and had been remembering it all the time. He said, "I know. I am only confirming that which you remember." As a young child I was not at all attached to my parents, but I remembered my master all the time and was constantly aware of his presence. I thought of him so much that sometimes my parents seemed to be strangers. I always used to think, "I do not belong to this place and to these people." From time to time my mother used to look at my right ear to see the hole which was there by birth. It was a mark that my master had predicted before I was born. At times my mother used to weep, saying, "One day you will leave us and go away." I loved my mother and father, but I really used to wait for that day. I remembered at an early age that the purpose of my life was the completion of the unfulfilled mission of my previous life. As a child I clearly remembered details of my past life.

I was awakened every night because my master would appear in my dream again and again. This upset and worried my parents and they consulted priests, doctors, and astrologers to discover what was wrong, but through a messenger my master told them not to worry for there was nothing wrong with me.

There were two old widows in the same village with whom I used to sit and talk about my future plan. They were very holy. They used to advise me to go to junior high for studies. Actually they persuaded me, but soon I left the school and did not go back. I thought it was useless for me to waste my time in such a school.

After a few years, my parents died and I went to my master. My master started disciplining me, although it was difficult for him. I rarely missed uttering the word "father" because I was not at all attached to my physical father. I never missed him because I was given more by my master than a father can ever give to a child. My master is not only like a father to me, but far more than that.

Any thought that came into mind, he knew. If I thought of not doing meditation, he would look at me and smile. I would ask, "Why are you smiling?" And he would reply, "You don't want to meditate."

This helped me, because I knew for sure that he was

guiding me not only in regard to my actions and speech, but also in organizing my thinking process and emotions. I was afraid of thinking undesirable things, but whenever I thought of something which seemed to be bad, he continued to love me nonetheless. He never controlled my thoughts, but would gently make me aware of my thinking process. The student is always loved by his teacher. A genuine teacher never condemns his student, no matter how bad the student may be. Instead, the teacher gently helps and corrects. However much a child misbehaves, a truly loving mother will continue to tenderly care for him. As a mother raises her child with love, gentleness, and guidance, so a master raises his student.

I did not know what a mother and father could give, but my master gave me everything, and he has never expected anything in return, nor had I anything to give. My love for him is immense, for he has done everything for me—educated me, trained me—and so far I have not been able to do anything for him. A master needs nothing. True spiritual leaders are like that: they take nothing and they give everything.

A real teacher is he who is very selfless and who loves his students even more than a father can love his child. A father usually imparts only worldly means, helps the children to grow, and trains them to live in the world. But a spiritual father selflessly gives that which cannot be given by a father or anyone else. I have not seen an example of this anywhere except in the spiritual tradition. Father and mother give birth, bring up, educate, and give their property, but a gurudeva gives to his disciples that knowledge which comes through his direct experience. Imparting such knowledge is a yoga tradition exactly like a father handing over his property to his sons. A master's divine love is not that of human love but is something which only the heart, and never the mind, is capable of understanding. In a true spiritual tradition the teacher gives so much to his student that the student's life is overwhelmed and transformed.

After staying with my master for a good while, I was sent to live with my brother disciple at Gangotri. He started teaching me scriptures. He loved me, but he did not understand my rebelliousness or condone my constant arguing with other sadhus. He would send adverse messages to my master about my behavior, and my master would then come and take me with him for a while. Later he would send me back to my brother disciple. I was also unhappy when I was in a situation in which I had to stay with a family as a guest, but fortunately this rarely happened.

One day I was curious to know about my brother disciple's life and I repeatedly asked him questions about his birthplace. I did not know that renunciates never discuss their past, but on my insistence he told me about his birthplace. Masters and sages do not want to recall their past, nor do they attach much importance to birthdays, age, or birthplace. They dislike talking about the members of their blood families. When the initiation ceremony is performed, the renunciate himself performs his last rites and then deliberately forgets about his birthplace and the people with whom he has previously lived. It is a custom in the renunciate orders to not discuss one's past. They call it the dead past and consider themselves reborn.

I posed the same questions to my master, and after persistent requests he did tell me something about his life. He reported that he was born to a brahmin family of West Bengal. The members of his family were initiates of a sage who used to come down from the Himalayas at times and travel in that area. My master was the only son of his parents, and he became orphaned at a young age. He was then adopted by this advanced sage. My master was about eighty years of age when he related this story to me. He has a Bengali accent, and although he did not use his native language, he did sometimes sing Bengali songs. He is a Sanskrit scholar and knows English and several other languages.

Swami Rama as a young brahmachari

Once during my travels in Bengal I visited my master's
birthplace. There was no trace of his house, and I thought of
building a memorial in his name there, but he instructed me not
to do so. In the village no one knew anything about him, except
two old ladies in their eighties. They reported that a master
from the Himalayas came and took him away when he was
fourteen years of age. "Indeed we do remember him," they
said, and were curious to know if he still lived, where he was,
and what he had done with his life.

My master lives in a cave, coming out only once in the
morning at sunrise and returning to his seat after an hour. Twice
a day he gets up from his seat. Sometimes he walks outside

the cave, but at other times he won't come out at all for days at a time. There are three to five advanced students with him all the time. For three months in the winter my master and his disciples come down to a height of 7,000 to 8,000 feet. He sometimes travels to Nepal and stays for a few months seven miles from Namcha Barwar.

He generally drinks goat's milk and at times the milk of a tiny black *shyama* cow, a pet who is looked after by the students there. From time to time I would give my master a drink of half water and half goat's milk. I gave it to him without his asking for it, and if I saw that he did not take it, I took it away. Later I would give him more. This was his only food.

My master remains in *sahaja-samadhi* [a constant state of deep meditation] and speaks very little. We once lived together for nine months and hardly talked at all. Most of the time we sat with closed eyes in meditation. I did my work and he did his work. There was no occasion for talking. Understanding was there, so oral communication was not necessary. When understanding is not present, then talk is needed in order to relate, but language is a poor means of communication. There was already communication on a deeper level, so there was no necessity for talking. My master and I believed more in silent communication. He answered my silly questions with a smile. He talked very little, but created an atmosphere for my growth.

Some people call my master Bengali Baba and some simply know him as Babaji. I call my gurudeva "master" because I have no word more suitable than this. My love for him is like an eternal law. I never found him unrealistic in what he taught me, and I never found him selfish in any way. All his teachings through his actions, speech, and silence were full of divine love. My words are inadequate to comprehend his greatness. I devoutly believe him to be a yogi of immortal wisdom and to be one of the greatest masters of the Himalayas. His reason for living is to enlighten those who are prepared, and to love, protect, and guide those who are still preparing. Anyone in difficulty who remembers him is helped. I know this, for many times it has happened to me and several others.

Whenever I find time from my busy schedule I have a strong desire to go back to him, for he is my only guide. With all possible reverence and devotion I pay homage to him wherever I am. If I commit mistakes they are mine, but if there is anything good in my life it comes from him.

My Master and
the Prince Swami

◆

My master is known throughout India because of this
historical event which I am going to relate. Apparently
many Indian lawyers, judges, and other educated people already
know of it.

There was a young man named Bhawal Sannyasi who was
the heir prince of Bhawal, a state in Bengal. After his marriage
he spent most of the time with his wife in his luxurious mountain resort at Darjeeling. His wife was already in love with a
doctor, and the two lovers conspired to poison the prince. The
doctor started giving him cobra venom injections in very small
dosages. The prince was told the injections were vitamins. The
doctor slowly increased the dosages, and one day after two
months, the prince was declared dead. A huge procession carried his body to a cremation spot situated at the edge of a
mountain stream. At the point when piles of wood had been
ignited and the body placed over the fire, torrents of rain began
to fall (Darjeeling is noted for the highest rainfall in the world).
The fire was extinguished by the torrents of rain, and the
stream flooded over and swept the body away.

Three miles downstream from the cremation site my master

was staying in a cave with some of his student swamis. He was in the process of traveling from the foot mountains of Kinchinjunga to our cave in the Kumayun Himalayas. When he saw the body tied with coffin cloth and bamboo sticks rushing down the stream toward him, he instructed his students to pull it out of the current and release it from the well-tied ropes. He said, "This man is not dead but is in a deep unconscious state without normal breath and pulsation. He is my disciple." They untied the ropes and brought the body before him. Within two hours the prince recovered his normal senses, but he completely forgot his past. He became a disciple of my master and was later initiated as a renunciate. He lived with my master for seven years. Then my master asked him to visit different places to meet other sages. He predicted that this prince swami would meet his sister and would recall his past. My master said, "There are going to be a lot of problems for us, so I had better leave for higher altitudes." He went to our ancestral cave in the Himalayas and stayed there for several years.

After wandering several months in the plains and meeting many sages, one day the prince swami unknowingly went to his sister's house to beg alms, and she immediately recognized him. It took him six hours to remember everything from his past. I was young at the time and remember accurately the details of the whole incident as they were then reported.

Influenced by the promptings of his family and remembering his past, the prince swami went to the court and claimed to be the prince of Bhawal. Numerous witnesses were called to testify for both sides of the case. During court proceedings it was proven that the doctor had obtained snake venom from a laboratory in Bombay. And it was proven beyond a doubt that the swami was the prince who had been poisoned by his wife and her doctor boyfriend. The prince swami told how he had been declared dead, his body carried to the cremation site near Darjeeling, swept away by a flood, and then picked up by a master of the Himalayas and his disciples. My master did not go to court, but sent two swamis to serve as witnesses. The case continued in the Calcutta court for several years and was one of the longest and largest cases tried in the history of the Indian judiciary. The prince eventually regained possession of his property and wealth, but ironically, he died a year later.

Through this case my master became known all over the country and people started searching for him. He has always avoided crowds and worked with only a chosen group of students to whom he provided constant and loving guidance. My master did not want to come into the limelight. Many times the people of India wondered who this great sage was, but my master preferred to remain away from the crowds. He still prefers to remain unknown, and says that the aspirant who genuinely wishes to follow the path of enlightenment should avoid crowds, publicity, and creating large followings.

Name and fame are the greatest barriers and downfalls for a spiritual man. Even after renouncing worldly positions, the desire to earn name and fame lurks in the unconscious mind. An aspirant should wash off this desire completely by dedicating his body, mind, and soul to the Lord, and by having no personal desires whatsoever. Such a sage can help, heal, and guide humanity even from a quiet and isolated corner of the Himalayas. Serving humanity becomes an important part of life for such sages. They do not expect anything from humanity, for they think that serving humanity is the expression of love for God.

Footprints of Delusion

◆

Westerners have been hearing many stories about the existence of yetis (snowmen) and Shangri-la. Although these stories are based on fantasies and fallacies, curiosity-mongers from the West are drawn by them and have tried to search the secret Himalayas. They are helped by the community of Sherpa porters, who are traditionally trained to climb the mountains and who earn their living by guiding these travelers to the various mountains of the Himalayas. These Sherpa guides have knowledge of the prominent mountain peaks and are very helpful in guiding the climbers and expeditioners, but they have no knowledge of the spiritual tradition of any part of the Himalayas.

Many foreigners have gone to these mountains in search of Shangri-la, but Shangri-la does not exist in reality. The myth of Shangri-la is based on the existence of two ancient cave monasteries hidden in the Himalayas. These caves are described in our traditional scriptures and have a long heritage of meditation and spiritual practices. One is situated on the Mount of Kinchinjunga at the height of 14,000 feet and the other, where I lived, is in the deep Himalayas on the borders of Tibet and

Garhwal. This cave monastery accommodates many practitioners comfortably. It is situated at a height between 11,500 and 12,000 feet above sea level. Very few people have been to this place. This monastery still exists, and there are many Sanskrit, Tibetan, and Sandhya Bhasha manuscripts preserved there.

Foreigners go to the Himalayas, and especially to Darjeeling, to climb the mountains with the help of the Sherpas. During their expedition they talk and think of Shangri-la and yetis. They carry cameras, tents, respirators, and tinned foods, and even litter some of the places in the Himalayas. But there is an unknown part of the Himalayas, and those who are not prepared and who cling to their lives should not make an attempt to go there.

I once met a rich man from the West along with a team of Indians who were in search of snowmen. I could not convince them that the so-called yetis or snowmen did not exist, and they spent four months and $33,000 in search of them. But they returned to Delhi disappointed. This rich American wanted to film a yeti and even published a photograph of a Nepalese sadhu, calling that sadhu a snowman. I also met a Western woman with two Sherpa guides in Sikkim. She was suffering from severe frostbite. She said her mission in life was to search for snowmen. She stayed in Darjeeling and made three attempts to find the snowmen, but she never found one.

Though I have been roving in the Himalayas since my childhood I have never met a snowman, but I have often heard stories about them. Grandmothers in the Himalayan villages tell such stories to their grandchildren. The story of the snowmen is as ancient as the human mind's ability to fantasize. In the deep snows, one's vision becomes blurred and white bears, which are rarely seen in the mountains, are mistaken for snowmen from the distance. These bears live high in the mountains and steal the food of expeditioners. They leave long footprints which are similar to those of human beings.

The word *yeti* is misused for "snowman." It is a Sanskrit word which means a renunciate, an austere person, and is the name of a group of renunciate sadhus who belong to one of the orders of Shankaracharya. How strange to use this word for a snowman; yetis are human beings and not snowmen!

The human mind remains under the influence of delusion until ignorance is completely dispelled. If there is no clarity of mind, the data that is gathered together from the external world is not perceived in a coordinated manner, and the clouded mind conceives a false vision. This is one of the modifications of the mind, like fancy, fantasy, symbol, and ideas. Maya is cosmic illusion, and *avidya* is individual ignorance which comes from a lack of knowledge about objects and their nature; it is also an illusion. The story of Bigfoot is based on the belief of a fantasy and discoordinated perception. When a bear runs fast in the snow, climbs upwards or runs downwards, the size of the foot of the bear looks very large. When I had a pet bear, I myself was surprised to see the big footprint it created. It is usually large and similar to a human foot.

Alas! the world, under the influence of illusion, is still searching for the shadows and the large foot. I call it "Himalayan maya." I was born and lived in these mountains and I have nothing to say to those who are delighted to believe in these myths and who are still searching for something which never existed. God help those misguided souls. These are not the footprints of snowmen or yetis, but of delusion.

How We Live in the Caves

◆

Those who are really committed to a life of austerity can live conveniently in certain parts of the Himalayas, where there are small caves to accommodate four to five people. There are also a few cave monasteries in the Himalayas in which the traditions are unbroken. The monastery in which I grew up is one of these. In our cave monastery the tradition goes back four or five thousand years, and it is well-remembered. We have records of who the first masters were and how the tradition began.

Our cave monastery is a natural cave with many compartments. Over the centuries the rocks have been slowly carved away to enlarge it more and more so that it can accommodate many students. Generations of dwellers have worked to make the cave comfortable and peaceful, but it is not very modern. There are no bathrooms, kitchens, or other conveniences, and yet the monasteries function very well.

For light inside the cave there is a stick of incense called *dhoop,* which is made of herbs. When it burns it gives light, and when it is extinguished it gives fragrance. Dhoop is crushed raw and then made four inches long and one inch thick. It burns well and one can read the scriptures in its soothing light. When it is extinguished it gives fragrance and works like incense. Branches of pine and *devadaru* trees are also useful for making good torches. They both have natural resin, which helps them to burn without any difficulty. The cave is kept quite warm by the *dhooni*, a fire which is never extinguished. This fire is constantly supported by huge wooden logs, and is regularly and vigilantly fed additional fuel. Sufficient fuelwood is collected in the summer for winter use. Nutritious vegetables are also grown during the summer on the banks of nearby streams. Varieties of mushrooms and *lingora* and *ogal*, two common vegetables which grow wild, are also used there. There are several varieties of roots; two are called *tarur* and *genthi*; others look and taste like sweet potatoes. In our cave we live comfortably on barley, potatoes, wheat, gram, and corn, which is grown up to 6,500 feet in the mountain villages. Every village maintains a cottage industry which produces high-quality woolen blankets, carpets, and warm cloth. A narrow, perennial stream of water flows from our mountain cave. During November and December, when the water freezes, we simply melt the snow. In other caves where I have lived, such as the cave in Manali, fresh water is not easily available. We would fetch water from a distance of three to four miles.

There are certain hermitages where masters still teach their students in the ancient manner. There, the teacher lives in a natural cave and the disciples come from various places to study and practice with him. Most would-be students do not reach these caves, however, for there is something about the Himalayas which protects the teachers from those who are merely curious or who are not prepared for the higher teachings. If one leaves his home and starts searching for a teacher only because of curiosity or emotional problems, he will not reach these higher elevations. He will not have the intense determination and

Nanda Devi is among the most spectacular peaks in the Himalayan range

drive required to go on to those places hidden deep in the Himalayas where the great sages dwell.

Teaching is often done by demonstration, and goes on at certain fixed times. The students are then asked to show their own progress by demonstrating their skills. Sometimes the teaching is done in silence, and when a certain level of attainment is reached, the teachers ask, "How will others learn from yogis if you spend your whole life in a cave?" Consequently most of the students leave after a few years.

It is important to make one's life creative and helpful, but before doing so one should make contact with his own potentials deep within by disciplining himself and gaining control over his mind, speech, and action. If discipline such as that taught in the cave monasteries is practiced even for a few years, the flower of life will bloom forever. A person who has gained such self-mastery lives in the world and yet remains above it, unaffected by worldly fetters and problems.

II

The Master Teaches

YOUNG AGE IS THE BUDDING PERIOD OF THE FLOWER of life. It needs protection so that the diverse opinions of others do not create confusion in the mind. A tender mind can be bent easily. Loving guidance and right communication is important. Parents who pay proper attention to their children can help them to pass through the adolescent period. This is the period of shaping the habits of the mind.

Learning to Give

$\diamond$

Nearly all children are quite selfish by nature. They do not want to give anything to others. I was trained to reverse this tendency.

In the mountains I used to take only one meal a day. I would have one chapati, some vegetables, and a glass of milk. One day when it was almost one o'clock I washed my hands, sat down, and the food was given to me. I said grace and was about to start eating when my master came in and said, "Wait!" I asked, "What's the matter?" He answered, "An old swami has come. He's hungry and you must give him your food."

"No," I argued, "I'm not going to, even if he is a swami. I'm also hungry and I won't get any more food until tomorrow." He said, "You won't die. Give it to him. But don't give it just because I am ordering you. Give it as an offering of love." I said, "I'm hungry. How can I feel love toward someone who is eating my food?" When he could not convince me to offer my food to the swami he finally said, "I order you to offer your food!"

The swami came in. He was an old man with a white beard.

With only a blanket, a walking stick, and wooden sandals, he traveled all alone in the mountains. My master said to him, "I'm so glad that you have come. Will you bless this child for me?"

But I said, "I don't need your blessing. I need food. I am hungry."

My master said, "If you lose control in this weak moment, you will lose the battle of life. Please offer your food to the swami. First give him water and then wash his feet."

I did as I was told, but I did not like it, nor did I understand the meaning of it. I helped him wash his feet and then I asked him to sit down and I gave him my food. Later I found out that he had not had any food for four days.

He took the food and said, "God bless you! You will never feel hunger unless food comes before you. This is my blessing to you."

His voice still echoes in my ears. From that very day, I have been free from that urge which had so often led me to childish cravings.

There is a narrow barrier between selfishness and selflessness, love and hatred. After crossing it one enjoys doing things for others, without seeking anything in return. This is the highest of all joys, and an essential step in the path of enlightenment. A selfish man can never imagine this state of realization, for he remains within the limited boundaries built by his ego. A selfless man trains his ego and uses it for higher purposes. Selflessness is one common characteristic that we find among all great men and women of the world. Nothing could be achieved without selfless service. All the rituals and knowledge of the scriptures are in vain if actions are performed without selflessness.

How a Master
Tests His Students

◆

Teachers often test their students. I was asked to meditate punctually at a certain time. One day during this time my master came and stood before me while I was sitting with my eyes closed. I was not very successfully meditating or I would not have been conscious that he was there.

He said, "Get up!" I did not respond. Then he asked me, "Do you hear me and know that I am here?"

I said, "Yes."

He asked, "Are you meditating?"

"No."

"Then why did you not get up?" he asked.

I was only pretending to meditate, actually, and I had been fully conscious of his presence.

The teacher often does such things to test our attitudes, our honesty, and our discipline. He will tell you one secret and then whisper another to another student, saying to both, "Don't tell this to anyone."

Then, rather than keep the secrets, you exchange them with one another. In this way he finds out that you are not prepared to keep a greater secret. He says, "I told you not to tell. Why did you?"

Teachers also impose more severe tests. Sometimes they will say, "Stand here!" and they will not come back for three days. It may be cold and raining, but only after days do they come back and get you. They have many such tests.

A person's strength needs to be tested often so that he learns to be self-reliant. Teachers, by testing their students, teach self-discipline and promote self-reliance. In order to gauge a student's progress, testing is important. Testing also helps students to evaluate their own progress, and to uncover errors of which they may not have been consciously aware.

An All-Night Journey Through the Forest

O n the way to Nepal from Tanakpur we stayed in a forest. My master said, "Let us eat something." It was two o'clock in the morning. He said, "Go to the shop in Tanakpur. It is twelve miles away along the forest path."

There was another swami with us. He also had a disciple. He asked my master, "Why are you sending him at night? I would not send my boy who is with me."

My master said, "Be quiet. You are making him a sissy and not a swami. I am training this boy. He must go."

Then he said to me, "Come here, son. Hold this lantern; it has enough oil. Keep matches in your pocket; have a staff in your hand; wear your shoes. Go to the food grain shop and get enough groceries for three or four days." I said, "Okay," and left.

Many times during that long night tigers and snakes crossed the path in front of me. The grass on both sides, elephant grass, was very tall, much higher than I. I heard many noises in the grass, but I couldn't know their cause. With my small lantern I walked twelve miles to the shop and then came back with the supplies at seven in the morning.

A Himalayan sage

My master asked, "How are you?" And I began to tell him all that had happened on the way. Finally he said, "That's enough. Let us prepare the food."

Fearlessness is also an essential prerequisite for attaining enlightenment. Great are those who are always fearless. To be completely free from all fears is one step on the path of enlightenment.

Crossing a Flooded River

◆

Students are many; disciples are few. Many students came to my master and requested, "Please accept me as your disciple." They all showed their faithfulness by serving him, by chanting, by learning, and by practicing disciplines. He did not respond. One day he called everyone to him. There were twenty students. He said, "Let's go." Everyone followed him to the bank of the Tungbhadra River in South India. It was in full flood, very wide and dangerous. He said, "He who can cross this river is my disciple."

One student said, "Sir, you know I can do it, but I have to go back to finish my work." Another student said, "Sir, I don't know how to swim." I didn't say anything. As soon as he said it, I jumped. He sat down quietly as I crossed the river. It was very wide. There were many crocodiles, and huge logs were rolling with the currents of water, but I was not concerned. My mind was one-pointed on completing the challenge I was given. I loved to be challenged, and I always accepted a challenge joyfully. It was a source of inspiration for me to examine my own strength. Whenever I was tired I would float, and in this way I succeeded in crossing the river.

My master said to the other students, "He didn't say that he was my disciple, but he jumped."

I was close enough to him to know his power. I thought, "He wants his disciples to cross the river. Here I am. I can do it. It's nothing, because he is here. Why can't I do it?" So firm were my faith and determination.

Faith and determination, these two are the essential rungs on the ladder of enlightenment. Without them the word "enlightenment" can be written and spoken, but never realized. Without faith we can attain some degree of intellectual knowledge, but only with faith can we see into the most subtle chambers of our being. Determination is the power that sees us through all frustrations and obstacles. It helps in building willpower, which is the very basis of success within and without. It is said in the scriptures that with the help of *sankalpa shakti* (the power of determination) nothing is impossible. Behind all the great works done by the great leaders of the world stands this *shakti*. With this power behind him, such a leader says, "I will do it; I have to do it; I have the means to do it." When this power of determination is not interrupted, one inevitably attains the desired goal.

My Offering to My Master

What did I offer my master? I will tell you. When I received my second step of initiation, at the age of fifteen, I had nothing with me. I thought, "All these rich people come with baskets of fruit, flowers, and money to offer to their teachers, but I have nothing to give."

I asked my master, "Sir, what is the best thing for me to offer?" He said to me, "Bring me a bundle of dry sticks."

I thought, "Surely if someone brings such sticks to his teacher, his teacher will kick him." But I did as he instructed. I brought him a bundle of dry sticks, and he said, "Offer it to me with all your heart, mind, and soul."

I looked at him and thought, "He is so wise and educated. What has happened to him today?"

He said, "This is the greatest gift that you can ever give me. People want to give me gold, silver, land, a house. These valuables mean nothing to me." My master explained that when you offer a bundle of dry sticks to a guru he understands that you are prepared to tread the path of enlightenment. It means "Please relieve me from my past, and burn all my negative thinking in the fire of knowledge."

He said, "I will burn these dry sticks so that your past karmas do not affect your future. Now I am giving you a new life. Do not live in the past. Live here and now and start treading the path of light."

Most people brood on the past and do not know how to live here and now. That is the cause of their suffering.

Loneliness

◆

I am never lonely. A lonely person is one who is not aware of the complete fullness within. When you become dependent on something outside without having awareness of the reality within you, then you will indeed be lonely. The whole search for enlightenment is to seek within, to become aware that you are complete in yourself. You are perfect. You don't need any externals. No matter what happens in any situation, you need never be lonely.

One day when I was sixteen years old I was standing outside our cave in the Himalayas and saw several people approaching. When they came closer, I recognized them to be a ruling prince of India with his secretary and guards. He came up to me and arrogantly said, "*Brahmachari* [young swami], I have come to see your master!"

In the very same tone I said, "You cannot see him!"

His secretary asked, "Don't you know who he is?"

I replied, "I don't care, I am the protector of this cave! Go away!" So they departed. They returned several times, but to no avail, because I seldom allowed anyone to see my master. I wanted to shield him from disturbance, and we had no inclination to see arrogant people. Sometimes I would say to my master, "These rich people come from far and wide and you say you don't want to see them. Is this good?" He would smile and answer, "I am happy with my Friend within me. Why do I need to see these people? They are not genuine seekers; they want something worldly. One wants to have a child, another to have a high position. They don't want spiritual food. Why do you ask me to see them?"

Finally the ruler prince recognized that I didn't care about his status, so he changed his attitude. When he came again he politely asked, "Sir, may I please see your master?" I took him inside the cave, where my master was sitting quietly.

That prince wanted to be polite and to show his manners and Western breeding. He said, "Sir, you seem to be lonesome." My master said, "Yes, because you have come. Before

A fog-enveloped hermitage high in the mountains

you came I was enjoying the company of my Friend within. Now that you have come I am lonesome."

It is true that the highest of all companionship is the company of the real self. Those who learn to enjoy the real self within are never lonely. Who makes us lonely? Those who claim to know and love us, or those whom we love, create loneliness and make us dependent. We forget the eternal Friend within. When we learn to know our real self we do not depend on externals. Dependence on external relationships is ignorance that needs to be dispelled. Relationships and life are synonymous and inseparable. Those who know the Friend within love all and are not dependent. They are never lonely. Loneliness is a disease. Being alone happily means enjoying the constant company—the constant awareness—of the Reality.

After learning this lesson, the ruler returned to his palace and pondered over the teachings. He then started practicing meditation. He soon realized that it is possible for everyone to be free from the self-created misery of loneliness and to enjoy life.

Maya, the Cosmic Veil

O ne day I said to my master, "Sir, I have been taught that avidya [ignorance] and maya [illusion] are one and the same. But I do not really understand what maya is."

He often taught by demonstration, so he said, "Tomorrow morning I will show you what maya is."

I could not sleep that night. I thought, "Tomorrow morning I am going to meet maya."

The next day we went for our morning ablutions as usual. Then we met again afterwards. We bathed in the Ganges. Afterwards I did not feel like I could sit for meditation because I was so excited by the prospect of the mystery of maya being unveiled.

On our way back to the cave we came upon a big, dry trunk of a tree. My master rushed up to the tree and wrapped himself around it. I had never seen him run so fast before.

He called out, "Are you my disciple? Then help me!"

I said, "Huh? You have helped so many people, and today you need my help? What has happened to you?" I was afraid of that tree. I wouldn't go near it because I feared it would also entrap me. I thought, "If the tree also entraps me, then who will help us both?"

He cried, "Help me! Take hold of my foot and try your best to pull me away." I tried with all my might, but I could not separate him from the tree.

Then he said, "My body has been caught by this tree trunk." I exhausted myself trying to pull him from the tree.

Finally I stopped to think and I said to him, "How is this possible? The tree trunk has no power to hold you. What are you doing?"

He laughed and said, "This is maya."

My master explained *anadi vidya*—cosmic illusion—to me just as Shankara had described it. He said that avidya means individual ignorance, while maya is both individual and cosmic illusion. *Ma* means "no" and *ya* means "that": that which is not self-existent, yet appears to exist, like a mirage, is called maya.

Then he explained another school of philosophy, which maintains that maya is universal illusion and also the mother of the universe. He told me that in tantra philosophy maya is considered to be both cosmic *shakti* and the primal force, or kundalini—the latent force in all human beings. By focusing one's awareness on the Absolute, this sleeping force is awakened within and directed toward the center of consciousness. When one comes in touch with this power he can easily attain the highest level of consciousness. Those who do not awaken this force of *shakti* remain forever brute and ignorant.

After describing the philosophies of maya he said, "When we devote our mind, energy, and resources to believing in that which is non-existent, then it appears to exist, and that is maya. Don't contemplate on evil, devils, sins, avidya, or maya and thereby put yourself in a state of stress and worry. Even spiritual people become preoccupied with blaming the world for their lack of progress. This weakness is significant in creating obstacles. For lack of sincerity, honesty, faithfulness, and truthfulness we do not realize that which we are. We project our weaknesses and think that the objects of the world are the source of our obstacles."

He told me to practice non-attachment and constant awareness. He said, "The strongest of bondages is created by attachment, which makes one weak, ignorant, and unaware of the absolute Reality. Maya, or illusion, is deeply rooted in attachment. When we are attached to or have a desire for something, it becomes a source of illusion for us. Those who are free from attachments and have directed their desires toward spiritual growth are free from the bondage of maya— illusion. The less attachment, the more inner strength; the more inner strength, the nearer the goal. *Vairagya* and *abhyasa*— non-attachment and constant awareness of absolute Reality— are like two wings of a bird which can fly from the plane of mortality to the height of immortality. Those who do not allow their wings to be clipped by the illusion of maya can attain perfection.

"Many people confuse attachment with love. But in attachment you become selfish, interested in your own pleasure, and you misuse love. You become possessive and try to gain the objects of your desires. Attachment creates bondage, while love bestows freedom. When yogis speak of non-attachment they are not teaching indifference, but are teaching how to genuinely and selflessly love others. Non-attachment, properly understood, means love. Non-attachment or love can be practiced by those who live in the world as well as those who are renunciates."

The message which I received on the sands of the Ganges in the Himalayas helped me to understand that illusion is self-induced. By imparting this knowledge my beloved master made me aware of the nature of cosmic illusion and the individual barriers we create.

Bitter Truth with Blessed Effects

◆

I remember an occasion when I was traveling with my master. The stationmaster in a town we were passing through came to me and said, "Sir, give me something to practice, and I promise I will follow it faithfully."

My master said to me, "Give him something definite to practice."

I said, "Why should one fool misguide another? It will be better if you instruct him."

So my master said, "From this day on, don't lie. Practice this rule faithfully for the next three months."

Most of the employees of the railroad in that area were dishonest and took bribes. But this man decided that he would not take bribes or lie any more.

That very same week a supervisor from the head office came to investigate him and his assistants. The stationmaster answered the probing questions of the supervisor honestly. This inquiry brought serious trouble to his staff. All the employees who had been taking bribes, including the stationmaster himself, were prosecuted. He thought, "It has been only thirteen days, and look at the difficulty I am in. What is going to happen to me in three months' time?"

Soon his wife and children left him. Within a month his life had crumbled like a house of cards from a single touch.

That day the stationmaster was in great agony, and we were some three hundred miles away on a bank of the Narmada River. My master was lying under a tree when he suddenly began laughing. He said, "Do you know what is happening? That man whom I instructed not to lie is in jail today." I asked, "Then why are you laughing?" He answered, "I am not laughing at him, I am laughing at the foolish world!"

Twelve people in that man's office had gotten together and said he was a liar, although he had been speaking the truth. They accused him of being the only one guilty of taking bribes. He was put in jail and all the others were released.

When the stationmaster went to court the judge looked down at him from the bench and asked, "Where is your attorney?"

"I don't need one."

The judge said, "But I want someone to help you."

"No," said the stationmaster, "I don't need an attorney; I want to speak the truth. No matter how many years you put me behind bars, I won't lie. I used to share in bribes. Then I met a sage who told me never to lie, no matter what. My wife and children have left me, I have lost my job, I have no money or friends, and I am in jail. All these things have happened in one month. I have to examine truth for two more months no matter what happens. Sir, put me behind bars; I don't care."

The judge called a recess and quietly called the man to his chamber. He asked, "Who is the sage who told you this?" The man described him. Fortunately the judge was a disciple of my master. He acquitted the stationmaster and said, "You are on the right path. Stick to it. I wish I could do the same."

After three months that man did not have anything. On the exact day that the three months were up he was sitting quietly under a tree when he received a telegram saying, "Your father had a huge plot of land that was taken long ago by the government. The government now wants to give you compensation." They gave him one million rupees [about $100,000]. He had not known about the land, which was in a different province.

He thought, "Today, I have completed three months of not lying and I have been rewarded so much." He gave the compensation to his wife and children, and they happily said, "We want to come back to you."

"No," he said. "Until now I have only seen what happens by not lying for three months. Now I want to find out what will happen if I do not lie for the rest of my life."

Truth is the ultimate goal of human life, and if it is practiced with mind, speech and action, the goal can be reached. Truth can be attained by practicing non-lying and by not doing those actions which are against one's own conscience. Conscience is the best of guides.

You Teach Others
but Deprive Me

◆

One day I told my master, "You have been cheating me." When we are inadequate ourselves but our ego is strong, we tend to blame others.

He asked, "What's the matter?"

I said, "You think I am still a child, and you are withholding things from me."

"Tell me, what am I withholding?"

"You are not showing me God. Perhaps you cannot, but can only teach me about God. If that is the limit of your powers, then you should be honest."

He answered, "I will show you God tomorrow morning."

I asked, "Really?"

He replied, "Most certainly . . . are you prepared?"

I used to meditate regularly before going to bed, but that night I could not. I was sure that in the morning I would get to see God, so what was the point of meditating? I was so restless and excited I did not sleep the whole night.

Early in the morning I went to my master. I did not even bathe. I thought, "When my master is showing me God, why take time for a bath?" I just slapped my face, patted down my hair, and presented myself to him.

He said, "Take your seat." I thought, "Now he is going to show me God." I was seldom humble, but I became extraordinarily humble that morning. I bowed before him many times. He looked at me and said, "What has happened to you? What is this funny business? Why are you abnormally emotional?"

I said, "Did you forget? You promised that you would show me God."

He said, "Okay, let me know what type of God you are prepared to see."

I said, "Sir, are there many types?"

He asked, "What is your concept and definition of God? I'll show you God exactly according to your conviction and definition. Everyone wants to see God without having any firm conviction of God in their minds and hearts. If you are searching and are not firm and sure regarding the object of your search, what will you find? If I tell you that whatsoever you see is God, you are not going to be satisfied. If I say God is within you, still you won't be satisfied. Suppose I show you God and you say, 'No, that's not God.' What am I going to do then? So you tell me the way you think about God and I will produce that God for you."

I told him, "Wait a moment. Let me think."

He said, "God is not within the range of your thinking. Go back to your meditation seat and when you are ready, let me know. Come to see me anytime you want after you have decided what type of God you want to see. I don't lie—I'll show you God. That is my duty, to show you God."

I tried my best to imagine what God would be like, but my imagination could not go beyond the human form. My mind ranged over the kingdom of plants, then the kingdom of animals, then human beings. So I imagined a wise and handsome man, who was very strong and powerful. And I thought, "God must look like this." Then I realized that I was making a foolish demand. What could I experience when I didn't have clarity of mind?

Finally I went to my master and said, "Sir, show me that God who can free us of miseries, and who can give us happiness."

He said, "That is a state of equilibrium and tranquility which you must cultivate for yourself."

Without having clarity of mind, a mere desire to see God is just like groping in the dark. I found out that the human mind has its boundaries and can visualize only according to its limited resources. No human being can possibly explain what God is, or conceive of God mentally. One can say God is truth, a fountain of love, absolute Reality, or the One Who manifested this universe. But these are all abstract ideas which do not satisfy the desire to see God. Then what is there to be seen? Those who believe God is a being can imagine and see a vision, but in reality God cannot be seen through human eyes. God can only be realized by realizing the real self and then the self of all.

So when a student has the attitude "I want to see God; my teacher is not showing me God; my teacher is not giving me what I want," he must finally realize that it is not a matter of the teacher's duty. Find out if you are making inappropriate demands, and instead of demanding from the teacher, transform yourself from within. God is within you, and that which is within you is subject to self-realization. No one can show God to anyone else. One has to independently realize his real self; thereby he realizes the self of all, which is called God. In the state of ignorance, the student thinks that God is a particular being, and he wants to see that being exactly as he sees something in the external world. It never happens. But when he realizes that God is truth and practices truth in action and speech, then his ignorance about the nature of God disappears and self-realization dawns.

Discipline Is a Must

◆

I would often go to the Ramgarah Forest, where my friend Nantin Baba lived [*nantin* means "child"]. He had been practicing austerities and spiritual disciplines from the age of six. We both were very mischievous. We would often sneak into a village and go into someone's kitchen, eat whatever we found, and then return to the forest. That created a mystery among the villagers; some thought that we were divine incarnations, while others thought that we were devils.

There were many apple orchards in that area owned by the rich people of Nanital; one day we left our place to live near a small creek which flowed through an orchard. In the evening we collected wood for a fire. The forest-preserve officers were concerned about fires, so we made our fire in the orchard. The owner saw us and thought we were stealing the golden apples and other rare varieties. He was very stingy and miserly and never allowed anyone to pick up apples off the ground like the other orchard owners did. He ordered his watchmen to come with bamboo sticks. Five men ran toward us to beat us up. When they came closer, they saw that we were not thieves but those two young yogis who lived in the forest.

The village of Toli in the Himalayas

When I returned to my master after three months he said, "You create problems for me by doing silly things."

I replied, "I haven't done anything."

But he continued, "I have to protect you as an infant is protected by its mother. When will you grow up? Why did you trespass on someone's property?"

I answered, "All things belong to God. They can be used by those who are in the service of God."

To this my master replied, "This type of thinking is a misuse of the scriptural sayings for your own convenience. Your thinking should be corrected." Then he gave me these instructions:

1. See the ultimate Reality as all-pervasive throughout the universe.
2. Do not be attached to the pleasures received from the objects of the world. Treat them as means for spiritual progress.
3. Do not covet anyone's property, woman, or wealth.

He said, "Don't you remember these sayings of the Upanishads? In the future if you commit any social crime and disturb the householders I will not talk to you anymore."

At times he would punish me by refusing to speak to me. The difference between his rebuking silence and the positive silence which was filled with love and understanding was very apparent to me. I was sixteen years of age then, and had tremendous energy. I was very active and would constantly annoy him. But he often said, "This is my karma and not your fault, my boy. I am reaping the fruit of my own deeds." I would feel sad and promise not to repeat that which was against his instructions, but soon I would misbehave again. Sometimes I was consciously irresponsible and at other times I acted wrongly unconsciously through inattentiveness. But this great man always loved me under all circumstances, in spite of my misbehavior.

When one becomes mature he starts knowing the real philosophy of life. Then he starts becoming aware of his thoughts, speech, and actions. Spiritual practice needs constant vigilance. Discipline should not be rigidly imposed, but students should learn to commit themselves and accept the discipline as essential for self-growth. Imposing rigidity and following it doesn't seem to be helpful: through this approach one might know what to do and what not to do, but can never know how to be.

Blessings in a Curse

◆

Whenever I became egotistical, I fell down. This is my experience.

My master said, "Try your best, but whenever you feed your ego, whenever you try to do anything selfish, you will not succeed. This is my curse on you."

I looked at him in surprise. What was he saying?

Then he continued, "This is my blessing to you, that whenever you want to become selfless, loving, and without ego, you will find a great force behind you, and you will never fail to achieve some good."

A selfish man always thinks and talks about himself. His selfishness makes him self-centered and miserable. The shortest cut to self-enlightenment is to cut through the ego; surrender before the Highest One. *Satsanga*—company of the sages—and constant awareness of the center within help one in going beyond the mire of delusion. The ego is also purified by cultivating selflessness. Unpurified ego is an evil which obstructs one's own progress. But the purified ego is a means in discriminating real self from not-self—real self from mere self. No one can expand his consciousness if he remains egotistical. Those who build boundaries around themselves because of their ego problems invariably create suffering for themselves, but those who try to be constantly aware of their unity with others can remain happy and fearless, enjoying every moment of life. Those who are selfless, humble, and loving are the true benefactors of humanity.

III

The Path of
Direct Experience

◆

DIRECT EXPERIENCE IS THE HIGHEST OF ALL WAYS
of gaining knowledge. All other means are only
fragments. In the path of self-realization purity,
one-pointedness, and control of the mind are
essentials. An impure mind hallucinates and
creates obstructions, but an orderly mind is an
instrument for direct experiences.

Direct Experience Alone
Is the Means

◆

One day my master told me to sit down. He asked, "Are you a learned boy?"

I could say anything to him, however outrageous. It was the only place where I could be completely frank. I was never sorry, no matter what I told him. He used to enjoy my foolishness. I replied, "Of course I am learned."

He asked, "What have you learned and who taught you? Explain it to me! Our mother is our first teacher, then our father, and then our brothers and sisters. Later we learn from the children with whom we play, from teachers at school, and from the writers of books. No matter what you have learned, you have not learned a single thing independently of others. So far all that you have learned is a contribution from others. And from whom have they learned? They have also learned from others. Yet as a result of all this you call yourself learned. I pity you because you have not learned anything independently. You have apparently concluded that there is no such thing as independent learning in the world. Your ideas are the ideas of others."

I said, "Wait a minute, let me think." It was a shocking realization that whatever I had learned was nothing of my own.

If you put yourself in my place you may well have the same feeling. The knowledge on which you depend is not at all your knowledge. That is why it is not satisfying, no matter how much of it you possess. Even if you have mastered an entire library, it will never satisfy.

"Then how can I be enlightened?" I asked.

He said, "By experimenting with this knowledge that you have acquired from outside. Find out for yourself, with the help of your direct experience. Finally you will come to a conclusive and fruitful stage of knowledge. All knowing is in vain if it is not direct. Indirect knowledge is of course informative, but not fulfilling. All wise people throughout history have gone through great pains in order to know truth directly. They were not satisfied by the mere opinions of others. They were not frightened off from this quest by the defenders of orthodoxy and dogma, who persecuted and sometimes even executed them because their conclusions were different."

Since that time I have tried to follow his advice. I have found that direct experience is the final test of the validity of knowledge. When you have known truth directly, you have the best kind of confirmation. Most of you go to your friends and give your viewpoint. You are seeking confirmation in their opinions. Whatever you think, you want others to confirm it by agreeing with you, to say, "Yes, what you think is right." But somebody else's opinion is no test of truth. When you know truth directly you do not need to ask your neighbors or your teacher. You don't have to seek confirmation in books. Spiritual truth does not need an external witness. As long as you doubt, it means you have yet to know. Tread the path of direct experience until you attain that state where everything is clear, until all of your doubts are resolved. Direct experience alone has access to the source of real knowledge.

Real Knowledge
Removes Suffering

◆

Self-reliance is important. It comes when you start receiving experiences directly from within. No doubt you need a teacher, you need a guide—I am not telling you that you should not learn things from other people, or that you need not study books. But I have met people who did not even know the alphabet, and yet whenever we had difficulty in understanding some profound truth or scripture, they alone could give us a solution.

Once I was teaching the *Brahma Sutras*. It is one of the most abstruse books in Vedantic literature. Aphorisms which I myself did not really understand I explained to my students, and they seemed satisfied. But I was not. So in the evening I would go to a swami who had not actually studied scriptures. He couldn't even sign his name—yet his knowledge was unmatched. He said, "You will never understand these terse aphorisms if you do not have direct experience." Then he told me this story to help me understand the difference between direct and indirect knowledge.

Swami Rama in Uttarkashi, Himalayas

A master had a student who had never seen a cow nor tasted milk. But he knew that milk was nutritious. So he wanted to find a cow, milk it, and drink the milk. He went to his master and asked him, "Do you know anything about cows?"

The master answered, "Of course." The student requested, "Please describe a cow to me." So the master described a cow: "A cow has four legs. It is a tame, docile animal, not found in the forest but in villages. Its milk is white and is very good for your health." He described the type of tail and ears it has, everything.

After this description the student went in search of a cow. On the way he came across a statue of a cow. He looked and thought, "This is surely what my master described to me." By chance that day some people who lived nearby were whitewashing their house and there was a bucket of whitewash near the statue. The student saw it and concluded, "This must be that milk which they say is so good for you to drink." He gulped down some of the whitewash, became terribly ill, and had to be taken to a hospital.

After he recovered he went back to his master and angrily charged, "You are no teacher!" His master asked, "What's the matter?" The student replied, "Your description of a cow was not at all accurate."

"What happened?" He explained, and the master asked, "Did you milk the cow yourself?" "No." "That is why you suffered."

The cause of suffering among intellectuals today is not because they don't really know. They know a little. But what they know is not their own knowledge, and that is why they suffer. A little or partial knowledge is always dangerous, like partial truths. A partial truth is not truth at all. So is the case with partial knowledge. The wise directly perceive truth.

The sage who did not even know the alphabet of any language would always remove my doubt. Systematic study under a self-realized and competent teacher helps in purifying the ego; otherwise scriptural knowledge makes one egotistical. He who is called an intellectual man today only collects facts from various books and scriptures. Does he really know what he is doing? Feeding intellect with such a knowledge is like eating a food with no food-value. One who constantly eats such a food remains sick and also makes others sick. We meet many teachers and they all teach well, but a student can assimilate only that which is unalloyed and comes directly from self-experienced teachers.

A Mantra for Happiness

◆

M antra is a syllable, a sound, a word, or set of words found in the deep state of meditation by the great sages. It is not the language in which human beings speak. Those sounds which are received from the superconscious state lead the seeker higher and higher until he reaches the perfect silence. The more awareness is increased, the more mantra reveals new meaning. It makes one aware of a higher dimension of consciousness. Exploiting the noble tradition by selling mantras in the marketplace is absurd.

Mantra is exactly like a human being having many sheaths: gross, subtle, more subtle, and subtlest. Take, for example, *Aum*. These three letters actually represent the three states (waking, dreaming, and sleeping) or the three bodies (gross, subtle, and more subtle). But the fourth state or the finest body of the mantra is formless, soundless, and indefinable. A student, if he understands the process of *laya* yoga (dissolution), can know the formless body and superconsciousness of mantra. Mantra is very powerful and essential, a compact form of prayer. If remembered constantly, it becomes a guide.

I used to collect mantras like people collect material objects, hoping that some new mantra I was about to receive would be better than what I already had. Sometimes I would compare myself to other students and think, "My mantra is better than his mantra." I was very immature. I call it crazy spirituality.

There was a swami who lived quietly deep in the Himalayas between Uttarkashi and Harsil. I went to see him, and when I arrived he asked, "What is the purpose of your coming?" I told him, "I want to receive a mantra." "You will have to wait," he replied. When Westerners go to someone for a mantra they are prepared to spend a lot of money, but they don't want to wait. I tried the same thing. I said, "Swamiji, I am in a hurry."

"Then come next year," he said. "If I stay now, how many days will I have to wait?" I asked. "You will have to wait as long as I want you to wait," he replied.

So I waited patiently, one day, two days, three days. Still the swami wouldn't give me a mantra. On the fourth day he said, "I want to give you a mantra, but promise that you will remember it all the time." I promised.

He said, "Let us go to the Ganges." Countless sages have done spiritual practices on the banks of the sacred Ganges and have been initiated there. I stood by the river and said, "I promise I will not forget this mantra." I repeated this promise several times, but he still delayed.

At last he said, "No matter where you live, live cheerfully. This is the mantra. Be cheerful at all times, even if you are behind bars. Anywhere you live, even if you have to go to a hellish place, create heaven there. Remember, my boy, cheerfulness is of your own making. It only requires human effort. You have to create cheerfulness for yourself. Remember this mantra of mine."

I was both very happy and very sad, because I had expected him to give me some unusual sound to repeat. But he was more practical. I apply this "mantra" in my life and find it successful everywhere. His spiritual prescription seems to be the best of physicians—a real key for healing oneself.

A Mantra for Bees

◆

There is a type of mantra called *apta* mantra which belongs uniquely to the particular sage who imparts it. I want to tell you about an experience I had with such a mantra.

There once was a swami who lived in a small hut across the river from Rishikesh. In order to get there you had to cross the Ganges on a swinging rope bridge. At that time Rishikesh was not overly populated. Wild elephants sometimes came at night and ate the straw from the walls and roof of our huts. While we were sitting inside they would come in big herds of thirty or forty, and would sometimes eat half of a hut. Tigers also roamed about. It was still quite primitive.

Following my master's directions, I went to stay with that swami across the river. Early in the morning Swamiji would go for a dip in the Ganges, and I would go with him, for I was expected to follow the customs wherever I stayed. After our baths we would take the twig of a tree, crush its end, and make it into a brush to clean our teeth. We would do this every day. Swamiji's disciple would climb up a tall tree and pull off a branch to make the toothbrushes.

One day Swamiji climbed the tree himself. He didn't usually

Tat Wala Baba of Rishikesh

do that, but this time he wanted to show me something. He was over seventy years old, but he climbed the tree easily. There was a hive of wild bees in that tree, but he made no effort to avoid it. On the contrary, he climbed up to that very branch and started talking to the bees. From down below I shouted, "Swamiji, please don't disturb the bees!" I covered my head because I thought, "If they are disturbed, they will also sting me." They were large and dangerous bees, so dangerous, in fact, that if ten or twenty were to sting you, you might not survive.

The swami pulled off a branch right by the hive, but the bees were not aroused. He came down safely and said, "Now you go up and pluck a branch for yourself."

I replied, "I don't need one. I can live without it." Then I added, "If you want me to climb the tree, first tell me the mantra that protected you." During that time I was fascinated with mantras, and I wanted to know his mantra because I wanted to show people what I could do. That was my purpose.

The swami said that if I climbed the tree he would tell me the mantra, so I climbed up to the hive. He said, "Go nearer and talk to them face to face. Say, 'I live here alongside you and I don't harm you. Don't harm me!'" I said to Swamiji, "That is not a mantra."

He replied, "Do as I say. Talk to the bees. Your lips should be so close you can whisper to them." I asked, "How do they know Hindi?" He answered, "They know the language of the heart, so they know all the languages—just talk to them."

I was skeptical, but I did exactly as he instructed, and I was surprised that the bees did not attack me. I said, "Swamiji, are they tame?" He laughed and said, "Don't impart this mantra to anyone, for it will work only for you. Don't forget what I am telling you."

Later when I traveled to more populated areas I would usually stay outside the city in a garden, and people would come to see me there. I was young and immature, and wanted to boast. I would climb the tree and casually take some honey from the hive without incurring a single sting. It was always a surprising feat.

When I was in Bhiwani, Punjab, a goldsmith whom I knew well requested, "Please give me the mantra." I agreed, forgetting that the swami told me it would not work for anyone else. I told him how to talk to the bees. He climbed up to a hive and repeated the mantra, but it didn't work. The bees attacked him—hundreds of bees at once. He fell from the tree and we had to rush him to the hospital, where he remained in a coma for three days. I was worried, thinking, "Suppose I have killed this poor man." I prayed continuously that he would be spared.

On the third day I was astonished to see the swami who had given me the mantra appear at the hospital. He said, "What have you done? Through your showing off you have nearly killed someone. Let this be a final lesson to you. The man will recover in the morning, but I am withdrawing the power of this mantra from you. You can never use it again." Since that time I have been more cautious.

Sometimes the words of a great man can have the effect of a mantra. Whenever any great man speaks to you, you should accept his words as mantras and practice them.

Misuse of Mantra

◆

There are some manuscripts in the monastery to which access is strictly prohibited. No one is allowed to read them except the head of the monastery. They are called *Prayoga Shastras;* they describe very advanced practices.

My master used to say, "You are not to experiment with those manuscripts." But I was obstinate and eager to know what was written in them. I was eighteen years old, fearless but somewhat irresponsible. I thought, "I am quite advanced. Why did they write these manuscripts if they are to be left unused? I should do experiments with the practices in these manuscripts. My master is very powerful; he will protect me if anything goes wrong."

My master gave me one of these manuscripts to carry for him on a journey. He said, "Do not open it." I was very curious and resolved, "If he leaves this manuscript with me and I find myself alone, I am going to read it."

One evening we came upon a small dwelling on a bank of the Ganges. My master went inside the hut to rest. I thought, "Here is my chance to study the manuscript." There were no windows and only one door in the little dwelling. I locked the door from the outside. I thought that I would spend the whole night discovering what was in the manuscript. It was a moonlit night and I could see clearly. The manuscript was wrapped and tied with a string. I took my time to unwrap it and then started reading. It described a certain practice and the effects it would produce.

After reading for an hour I thought, "Why not try it?" So I put the manuscript aside. It said that only very advanced yogis should do this practice and that if it were not done properly it was very dangerous. At that young age I thought I was very advanced, so I commenced doing it. It involved the repetition of a special mantra in a particular style, with certain rituals. That mantra awakens a power outside of a person as well as inside.

The book said that the mantra had to be repeated one thousand and one times. I repeated it nine hundred times and nothing seemed to be happening. I concluded there would be no effect. But when I came to nine hundred and forty, I saw a huge woman nearby. She gathered some wood and started making a fire. Then she put water in a big vessel and put it on the fire to boil. By then I had counted to nine hundred sixty-three. The last I counted was nine hundred seventy, and after that I lost track because I saw a huge man coming from the same direction. At first I thought, "This must be the effect of the mantra. I'll not look at him, and complete the one thousand and one repetitions." But he started coming toward me. I had never before seen or even imagined such a gigantic man, and he was completely nude.

He asked the woman, "What have you cooked for me?"

She said, "I have nothing. If you give me something, I'll cook it."

He pointed at me and said, "Look at him sitting over there. Why don't you cut him into pieces and cook him?"

When I heard that, my teeth clenched and the *mala* I was

counting with fell from my hand. I fainted. I don't know how long I remained unconscious. When I regained consciousness my master was standing in front of me. He slapped me on the cheek and said, "Hey, wake up." I would become conscious momentarily and exclaim, "Oh, that giant is going to carve me up!" and then lapse into a faint again. This happened three or four times, until finally my master kicked me, became more insistent, and said, "Get up! Why have you done this? I told you not to practice these mantras. And you locked me in, you foolish boy."

From this experience I came to realize the power of mantra. I started practicing the mantra which my master had given me and I began to count on it even for little things. I did many foolish and silly things when I was young, but my mantra, which created awareness for me, always helped me to come out of those situations.

If mantra is not properly used with spiritual discipline, it can lead to hallucinations, as it did for me. Hallucinations are the products of an impure and untrained mind. Mantra becomes helpful when the mind is purified and directed inward. Without knowing the meaning of the mantra, the proper feeling cannot be aroused, and without strong feeling, mantra and its technical repetition is not of much use.

I Receive a Beating

$\blacklozenge$

Once I was maintaining silence in order to watch my inner feelings and observe my behavior. I was living on a bank of the Saryu River outside of Ayodhya, the birthplace of Rama. People there knew that I was practicing silence and could not ask for food, so they brought me a meal once a day. It was summer and I did not have any shelter. Suddenly one evening thundering clouds appeared and it started raining heavily. I had only one long blanket with which to cover myself, so I started going toward one of the temples to get out of the rain. It was already dark. When I entered through the back side of the temple and sat under the portico, three temple guards came with bamboo sticks and asked what I was doing there. They thought I was a thief. Since I was keeping silence, I did not respond to them. Then they started hitting me very hard with their sticks. I was knocked unconscious by their blows. The temple priest came with a lantern to see who the intruder was. My head was bleeding and there were many bruises all over my body. The priest, who knew me well, was shocked to see my horrible condition. When I became conscious again, he and the servants of the temple began apologizing for their serious

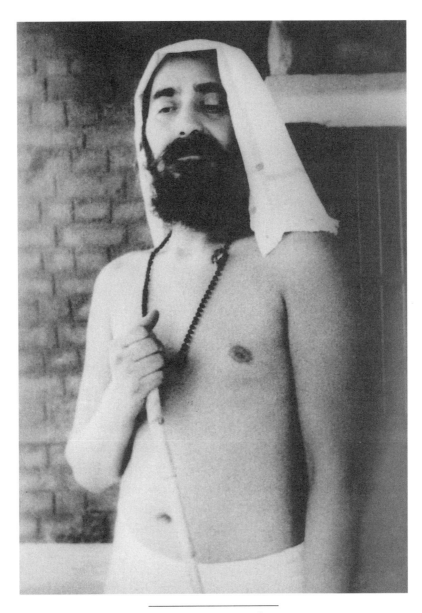

Swami Rama in Ayodhya

mistake. That day I realized that practicing austerity is not easy. I continued in my path of self-training, but I stopped roaming in the cities.

Among all the methods for training and therapies, the highest of all is that of self-training in which one remains conscious of one's mind, actions, and speech. I used to build up my *sankalpa* (right determination) and always kept track of my feelings, thoughts, speech, and actions. During those days I found that whenever I would calm down my conscious mind in meditation, the bubbles of thoughts would suddenly come up from the unconscious mind. In learning to control the mind and its modifications, it is essential to go through the process of self-observation, analysis, and meditation. Learning to control the mind and careful study of the relationship between the conscious mind and the unconscious mind took me a long time. Many times I thought, "Now I have conquered my thoughts. My mind is under my control." But after a few days some unknown bubble would arise from the bottom of the unconscious and would control my conscious mind, thus changing my attitudes and behavior. At times I was disappointed and depressed, but I always met someone who helped and guided me.

As an aspirant, it is always wise to be vigilant and firm in practicing meditation, without expecting much in the beginning. I was told that there is no instant method of meditation. Modern students expect immediate results from meditation, and this expectation causes them to fantasize, imagine, and hallucinate many things which they think are spiritual experiences but are actually products of their unconscious minds. As a result the frustration imbalances them and either they stop meditating or they start following strange methods harmful to their progress.

Unique Practice of Tantra

◆

My brother disciple, whose father was a learned Sanskrit pandit, was from Medanipur, Bengal. When he was eighteen years old, before I had met him, his family forced him to get married. The marriage ceremony was being performed in the evening, and this suited his plans well. During a Hindu wedding the bride and groom participate in a fire ceremony and take seven steps around the fire. On the fourth step he jumped out of the ritual and ran into the fields. The people in the wedding party did not understand his behavior. They began to chase him, but could not catch him. He walked for several days until he reached the banks of the Ganges and started following the river in search of a spiritual teacher. For six years he went through many experiences, but did not find a teacher. Then he met my master at Shrinagar, in the Himalayas. When they met, my master embraced him and knew that they had known each other before. My brother disciple lived with my master for three months and then was instructed to go to Gangotri, where we stayed in a cave together.

One day he began talking about his hometown, Medanipur, and told me that if ever I visited there I should tell his family that he had become a renunciate and lives in the Himalayas. Soon after that I visited his home and met the woman to whom he was to have been married. She was waiting for him to come home. I suggested to her that she get married to someone else because the marriage ceremony had not been completed. On hearing such advice from me, she said, "You and your brother disciple are the worshippers of the devil and not of God." She was in a fit of anger.

I went back to my hut, which was situated outside the village. In that area tantra was practiced. Practically all the homes of this area worshipped Mother Divine, calling her Ma Kali. I had heard much about tantra and had read a few scriptures. I wanted to meet someone who could really demonstrate the practices so that I would have no doubts of their validity. One of my brother disciple's cousins in that village introduced me to a Mohammedan tantric who was ninety-two years of age. I went to see him and we talked for three hours. He was famous there as a *maulavi*, a priest who leads the prayers in the mosques and knows the Koran, the sacred bible of Islam.

The next morning the maulavi took me to a pond outside the village. He also brought a chicken. First he tied this chicken with a string and then he tied the other end of the string to a banana plant. He told me to sit down and watch attentively. He was muttering something and throwing black-eyed peas on the string. The chicken fluttered and became lifeless. He said, "The chicken is dead."

I thought, "This is not being creative. It is a very bad power. It's black magic." He asked me to make sure that the chicken was dead. I said, "Can I put the chicken under water for some time?" He said, "Go ahead."

I kept the chicken under water for more than five minutes, and then took it out. To my knowledge the chicken was dead. Then he brought the chicken back to life by performing that same ritual of throwing black-eyed peas and muttering something. This really shook me up. He said, "Now tie one end of the string on the banana plant and tie the other end to your waist. I'll show you something different."

Instead of doing what he said, I ran as fast as I could toward the village, leaving the old maulavi and his chicken far behind me. When I arrived I was breathless and the villagers did not know why I was running so fast. I told them that the old maulavi wanted to kill me, but no one believed me, for in that area he was considered to be a very holy man. I thought, "I'd better leave this place and tread my path instead of seeking such miracles."

From this place I went to Calcutta to stay a few days with the chief justice, R. P. Mukharji. When I told him of my experience and asked if I had imagined it or hallucinated, he said, "No; such things happen." Later I asked some sages how such a miracle was accomplished. They could not explain it, but acknowledged that Bengal was famous for such practices. When I related this story to my master, he laughed at me and said, "You need exposure to all sorts of things, although you should not attempt to practice yourself. You should follow only that discipline which has been given to you."

This sort of tantra is not the real science of tantra, but is an offshoot of tantrism. The power of the mind can be used in many ways. Without knowledge of the goal of life, mental faculties can be directed negatively for harming others. But ultimately this misuse of mental powers destroys the person who practices it. There still exist a few people with such tantric powers. But out of a hundred, one is genuine and the other ninety-nine are magicians.

You Have Committed
Many Thefts

In my youth I was searching for miracles. Once when I saw a person lying on a bed of nails, I said to him, "I wish I could do that. Can you teach me?" He said, "Of course. But first you will have to beg alms for me and bring money to me. If you promise that you will give me whatever money you have, I will teach you!"

One after another I met many such people and they despised each other, saying, "He is nothing. I will teach you something better." One of them had a big steel needle, and he pushed it through his arm. He said, "See, there is no bleeding. I will teach you this, and you'll be able to make money by demonstrating it to others. But you will have to become my disciple and give me a part of what you earn."

I left him and went to another person. Many people respected this man. I wanted to know why so many people followed him around. I wondered, "What exclusive knowledge does he have? Is he wise; is he a great yogi?" I stayed with him until everyone went away. When I was all alone with him, he asked, "Which is the most luxurious hotel that you know of?" I said, "The Savoy Hotel in London."

He said, "You pay me one hundred rupees and I will get you some delicious food from the restaurant of that hotel." I gave him a hundred rupees and suddenly some food appeared before me, exactly as it was prepared at that hotel. Next I asked for some food from Hamburg, Germany. Again I paid him seventy rupees and he got the dish I requested. It appeared along with the bill.

I thought, "Why should I go back to my master? I'll stay with this man and all my needs will be taken care of. Then without any botheration, I can quietly meditate and study."

He asked, "What type of watch do you want?" I replied, "I already have a good watch." But he said, "I will give you a better watch," and he did it.

When I looked at the watch I thought, "This watch is manufactured in Switzerland. He is not creating these things; he is only doing a trick, transporting them from one place to another."

Two weeks later I went to him again and bowed before him. I gave him an oil massage and helped him cook food. He was pleased with this and he instructed me, so I could do things similar to those he had done. I practiced until one of the swamis from our monastery came and slapped me, saying, "What are you doing?" He took me to my master, who said, "You have committed many thefts." I asked, "What thefts?"

He answered, "You ask for sweets and they come to you from someone's shop. They disappear from the shop and the owner does not know what has happened to them." I promised my master that I would never do it again.

Later I met a man who worked as a salesman in a store that sold sewing machines in Delhi. I told him about the *haji* and his powers. The salesman said, "If he can get a Singer sewing machine from my store in Delhi, I will consider him to be the greatest man alive and follow him for the rest of my life."

So we both went to him and requested him to perform the

miracle. He said, "I will get it immediately"—and it appeared! Then the salesman became concerned that it would be missing from the store and he might be accused of stealing it. The *haji* tried to send it back, but he could not do so. He started weeping and crying, "I've lost my powers!"

When the salesman returned to Delhi he took the machine with him. In the meantime at the store they had discovered the machine was missing, and they reported the matter to the police. The police found it in the salesman's possession and he was taken to the court. No one believed his story and the salesman was punished.

I had many such experiences and I insulted my master many times by saying, "There are people who have powers greater than yours, so I like to follow them." He said, "Go ahead! I want you to grow and be great. You don't have to follow me!"

Later I realized that mostly such phenomena are tricks. Wherever they are found to be genuine, they are black magic. Spirituality has nothing to do with these miracles. The third chapter of the *Yoga Sutras* explains many methods of attaining *siddhis* [powers], but these siddhis create stumbling blocks in the path of enlightenment. One person in millions does indeed have siddhis, but I have found that such people are often greedy, egotistical, and ignorant. The path of enlightenment is different from the intentional cultivation of powers. The miracles performed by Buddha, Christ, and other great sages were spontaneous and for a purpose. They were not performed with selfish motives or to create a sensation.

On the path of yoga sometimes one comes across the potentials of siddhis. A yogi without having any desire for a siddhi might get one, but one who is aware of the purpose of his life never misuses them. Misuse of siddhi is the downfall of a yogi.

To commit a theft is accepted to be a crime socially and morally. Jugglery is not any part of yoga. Siddhis do exist, but only with adepts.

A Firethrower Swami

I once met a swami who could produce fire from his mouth. The flame would shoot out several feet. I tested him to see if the phenomenon was authentic. I asked him to wash out his mouth, to be sure he was not secreting something like phosphorus in it. I also had my friends examine him. He seemed genuine, so I concluded, "This man must definitely be more advanced than my master."

That swami said to me, "You are wasting your time and energy staying with your master. Follow me and I will give you some real wisdom. I will show you how to produce fire."

I was so swayed by him that I decided to leave my master. I went to my master and said, "I have found someone more advanced than you, and I have decided to become his disciple."

He said, "I am delighted. Go ahead, I want you to be happy. What does he do?" I replied, "He produces fire from his mouth. He is a very powerful swami." My master requested, "Please take me to him."

The next morning we went. The swami was staying twenty-three miles away in the mountains and it took us two days to get there. When we arrived, the swami bowed before my master!

I was surprised and asked my master, "Do you know him?" He replied, "Of course. He left our monastery some time ago. Now I know where he has been hiding."

My master asked him, "What have you been doing here?" He said, "Sir, I have learned to produce fire from my mouth."

When my master saw the flame come from his mouth, he laughed gently. He instructed me, "Ask him how many years it has taken to learn this." That swami was proud of his accomplishment. He bragged, "I have practiced twenty years to master this."

Then my master said to me, "A match will produce fire in a second; if you wish to spend twenty years to produce fire from your mouth, you are a fool. My child, that is not wisdom. If you really want to meet masters, I'll give you directions to where they are staying. Go and have the experiences."

Later I realized that all such siddhis are but mere signs on the path. These powers have nothing to do with spirituality. I later found out, after experiencing and examining, that these psychic powers have little value. To the contrary, they can create serious obstacles on the path. Sometimes psychic powers develop: you start telling the fortunes of others, you start knowing things. These are all distractions. Do not allow them to obstruct your path. Too many people, including swamis, have wasted time and energy on such distractions. Anyone who wants to develop siddhis can do so and can demonstrate certain supernatural feats; but enlightenment is an entirely different matter.

An Astounding Mystic

◆

Selflessness is one of the prominent signs of a spiritual man. If this quality is missing in the character of one who is supposed to be spiritual, he is not really a spiritual person. There was a well-known master, Neem Karoli Baba, who befriended me when I was still quite young. He lived in Nanital, one of the hill resorts in the Himalayas. He was a man who lived "half here and half there." When someone came to him he would say, "Okay, now I have seen you, you have seen me, *ja, ja, ja, ja . . .* " which means, "go, go, go, go . . . ." That was his habit.

Once we were sitting and talking when one of the richest men in India came to see him with quite a big bundle of Indian currency. The man said, "Sir, I have brought this for you."

Baba spread the notes out and sat on them. He said, "They are not very comfortable as a cushion, and I don't have a fireplace, so I cannot burn them for heat. They are of no use to me; what shall I do with them?"

The man said, "Sir, it's money!" Baba returned the money and asked him to get some fruit with it. The rich man said, "Sir, there is no market here." "Then how can you say it is money?" asked Baba. "If it doesn't buy fruit it isn't money for me."

Then Baba asked him, "What do you want from me?" The man said, "I have a headache." Baba replied, "That you have created for yourself. What can *I* do for you?" He protested, "Sir, I have come for your help."

Baba relented. "All right: henceforth there will be no headache—but from now on you'll be a headache to other people. You will be so miserably rich that you will be a headache to the whole of your community." And he is indeed a headache to his whole community, even today.

It is true that some amount of money is one of the necessary means of making oneself comfortable in the world. But it is also true that having more than necessary can be a source of misery. Hoarding money is a sin, for we are depriving others and creating disparity in society.

Neem Karoli Baba loved Lord Rama, an incarnation of God, and was always muttering a mantra which no one understood. This sage was adored by many people in northern India. People did not give him rest. They traveled with him from one mountain and village to another. He was very mysterious in his ways.

I had many more delightful and funny experiences with Neem Karoli Baba which you wouldn't believe, but a few Americans who have met him will understand what I am talking about. If someone came to see him he would say, "You were talking against me with such and such a person under such and such a tree." He would give the exact date and time of day. Then he would say, "Now you have seen me, go, go, go." Then he would cover himself with a blanket.

One day a pharmacist was delivering some powder from Talital to Malital. He was a devotee of Neem Karoli Baba, so he stopped to see him on the way. I was also there.

Baba said, "I'm hungry. What is that you are carrying?" The pharmacist said, "This is arsenic. Wait and I will bring some food for you." But Baba snatched the powder from him and ate a handful. Then he asked for a glass of water. The pharmacist thought he would die from the poison, but the next day he was quite normal.

He was not aware of the external. If you asked him, "Have you eaten your food?" he would answer "No" or "Yes," but it would have no meaning. If your mind is somewhere else, you can eat many times a day and still remain famished. I saw this with him. Five minutes after eating he would say, "I am hungry," because he didn't know that he had already eaten. I would say, "You have taken your food." And he would answer, "All right, then I am not hungry."

If I wouldn't tell him, "You have now eaten," he would not stop. One day I thought, "Let me see how many times he can eat." That day he took forty meals at various houses. He was eating the whole day. We wanted to know about his powers, and he knew what we wanted. So when anyone brought food before him, he ate.

They would ask, "Will you eat?" And he would say, "Okay." He went on eating all day. Finally I came and said, "You have eaten enough." He said, "Oh, have I?" I said, "Yes!"

In such a high state one becomes like a child. He is not fully aware of mundane things, but he is constantly aware of the Truth.

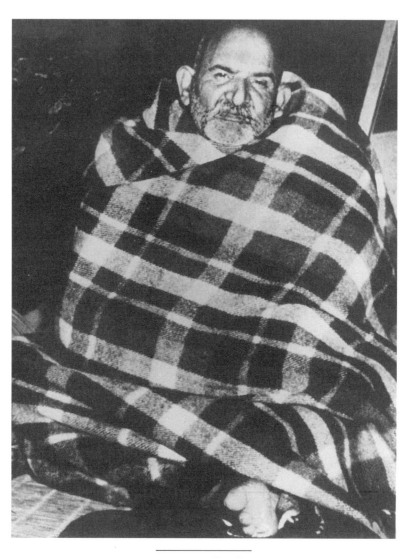

Neem Karoli Baba

My Mother Teacher

◆————————◆

I once went to Assam to meet Mataji, a great lady yogi who was then ninety-six years of age. She was living next to a famous Shakti temple called Kamakhya. Everyone aspires to go there but very few are able to visit that place, because it is in a far corner of India. From Calcutta I went to Gohati and then on foot to Kamakhya. I reached the temple late in the evening, stumbling in the darkness and stubbing my toes many times. At that time there were three or four small wooden houses near the temple. I was asked by the temple priest to stay on the second floor of the same building in which the famous woman was living. My room had many holes and cracks through which mice and snakes would crawl in. It was terrible, but I was helpless. I would close the holes with pieces of cloth which I found here and there. I managed to live in that room for two months. My experiences there were shocking and surprising in the beginning, but very pleasant toward the end of my stay.

It was the twentieth year in which this old woman had not come outside during the daytime. However, she regularly visited the temple at midnight and at three o'clock in the morning. For the first four nights I remained inside my room, but on the fifth night I came out and went to the temple. It was a moonlit night. When I reached the temple gate I could hear someone chanting mantras inside. It was that old woman sitting all alone with an oil lamp burning beside her. When she sensed me outside the north gate she shouted very assertively, "Don't come in! You will kill yourself! I am the Mother Divine! Get out of this place!"

I was frightened, but at the same time I was curious to know what was happening inside that small temple. I peeped in and she rushed toward me. She was completely naked—a bag of bones wrapped inside shining skin. Her eyes were glowing like bowls of fire. She shouted, "Go away! Why are you watching what I am doing?" I bowed in reverence and out of fear, thinking she would calm down, but she whipped me with her cane and drove me away. I went back to my room.

The next morning this mother teacher called me to her room and began to talk to me. I said, "I need your blessings." She was in silence for a few seconds and then muttered my nickname, which was not known to anyone except my gurudeva. She hugged me and put me on her lap. I don't know what happened to me then, but if there is any seventh heaven, I can tell you, I was there.

Stroking me on the head, she blessed me and said, "Although you will find many obstacles on the path, all will be crossed. Go with my blessings." But I said, "I want to stay here for some time," and she consented.

When I asked this mother teacher what she was doing all alone in the temple at three o'clock in the morning, she said, "I do Shakti worship, and I do not want anyone near me at midnight and at three in the morning." From midnight to two o'clock and from three to four-thirty, nobody visits that temple.

She permitted me to sit with her for half an hour every evening. When I sat in front of her my whole consciousness would rise exactly as if I were sitting before my master. In my heart I accepted her as my mother teacher. I had many questions I wanted to ask her, but she told me to remain silent. I followed her instruction and received answers to my questions without either of us speaking. This silence was more communicative than any other type of teaching. The most advanced teachers impart their knowledge in silence.

She was a very powerful and yet gentle old woman, with tremendous willpower. I observed that whatever she said would always come true. When someone came to ask her help, she spoke very little and always in a brief sentence. "Go." "It will happen." "Bless you." "Pray to Mother Divine." Then she would go to her room.

When I heard that this mother, whom I called Mother Teacher, did not lie down to sleep, but would remain sitting in her meditation posture throughout the night, I started observing her by peeping through the crack in her door. I spent three days and nights watching her, and found that it was true that she never slept.

One day, I said to her, "Mother, if you lie down, I will give you a gentle massage which will help you to fall asleep."

She giggled and said, "Sleep! That is not for me. I am beyond sloth and inertia. I enjoy sleepless sleep, for which I do not need to lie down. One who enjoys yoga sleep, why does she need the sleep of pigs?"

I asked, "What is that?"

She said, "Pigs eat beyond their capacity and then lay themselves down snoring. I wonder how they can sleep so much." She explained to me the whole anatomy of sleep, and asked me if I knew that mechanism in which a human being goes from the conscious state to the dreaming state and then to the deeper state of sleep. She started giving me accurate and systematic lessons. After that I was able to understand the *Mandukya Upanishad*, which explains the three states of mind—waking, dreaming, sleeping—and the fourth state, *turiya*, which is termed as "the state beyond." The *Mandukya* is considered to be the most important and difficult of all the Upanishads. I filled up seventy pages of my diary taking down the notes as she talked. In her gentle, slow speech, there were no repetitions and no mistakes. She gave a systematic commentary on this Upanishad, which I intellectually understood but did not understand in reality until I started to practice remaining conscious during these four states.

After two and a half months, the day of parting came. I was very sad, but she said, "Don't be attached to the mother image in my physical body and personality. I am the mother of the universe, who is everywhere. Learn to raise your consciousness above and beyond my mortal self." With tears in my eyes I looked at her and she said, "Be fearless. I am with you." I bade goodbye to her and came back to my Himalayan abode again. My master spoke very highly of this old woman. She had lived by that temple area since she was 12 years old and stayed there up to the age of 101, when she left her mortal body.

An Ageless Yogi

$\blacklozenge$

Practically every summer Devraha Baba, who lives in East Uttar Pradesh, comes to a shrine in the Himalayan mountains for a few months. He is said to be quite aged. I do not know this directly, but I have heard Dr. Rajendra Prasad, the first president of India, say that from his own experience he can attest to the fact that Devraha Baba is more than 150 years of age. He said that in his childhood his father took him to this baba, who was then a very old man. At the time he gave the statement, Dr. Prasad was more than seventy years of age. This statement aroused my curiosity, and I made it a point to meet this baba when he stopped in Rishikesh on his way to the mountain shrine. We conversed often there. He was living in a temporary pinewood hut which was constructed for him wherever he went. Sometimes he also lived in tree houses. He looked quite healthy and appeared to be in his seventies. Although he is very austere and gentle and doesn't allow any student to touch him, he sometimes gives discourses on divine love. He is very famous in North India. Huge crowds assemble to have his *darshan* [glance]. He has a large following, and the police and other government officers often visit him with the desire to be

The Ageless Sadhu, Devraha Baba

blessed. Several of my American students visited him during Kumbha Mela [a great fair which is held every twelve years in India] at Hardwar in 1974.

I tried to find out the secret of how he lived to be so aged. I discovered that he practices certain aspects of yoga regularly, and that he eats only fruits and vegetables. There are many specific practices in yoga; individual aspirants choose those which suit them.

During my conversation with Baba he said, "Happiness is the greatest wealth of all. Punctuality is essential. Practicing advanced methods of breathing is equally important. The technique of agelessness is a technique of pranayama." This Devraha Baba is a symbol of love.

IV

Learning Humility

TO CULTIVATE THE QUALITY OF HUMILITY IS ONE
step toward enlightenment. By being humble we
gain much and lose nothing. Prayer and contemplation strengthen our willpower in cultivating
this inner quality.

Ego and Vanity Are in Vain

◆

Once my master lived in a holy place of the Himalayas called Tungnath. On the way to see him I stopped at a mountain shrine called Karnaprayag. A great, renowned swami, named Prabhat Swami, lived in a cave near the shrine, so I went to visit him. I was being trained to be a swami at that time. I greeted him according to our tradition. He was seated on a blanket which had been folded into quarters, and a few villagers were seated before him. I expected him to offer me a seat beside him. I was still suffering from an inflated ego, at least partly because people in the villages of India respect and bow before a swami. This feeds the ego and creates many problems for a swami in training.

Prabhat Swami knew my problem; he smiled and said, "Please take your seat."

I asked, "Could you please unfold your blanket so I can sit next to you?" I insisted, but he just laughed at me. I asked, "Why won't you let me sit next to you?" I was quite conceited and impolite.

He quoted the dialogue between Rama and Hanuman in the *Yoga Vasishtha* and said, "'Eternally we are one and the same, but as human beings, you are still a servant and I am your master.' Modern man tries to have the position of a master without attaining anything."

Then he gave me a lesson, saying, "A man went to see a master who was seated on a high platform teaching many people. The man held a distinguished position in society, so he chafed at being treated like all the rest of the students, without getting special attention. He went up to the master and asked, 'Sir, can I sit on the same platform with you?'

"The master said, 'You should know the role of a student as well as the role of a master.'

"The man asked, 'Sir, what are the duties of a student?'

"The master explained, 'A student cleans, serves, washes dishes, cooks food, prepares and purifies himself, and serves his master.'

"Then the man asked, 'And what does a master do, sir?'

"'A master teaches—he doesn't do any of the menial work.'

"'Why can't I become a master without doing all of this?' asked the man. 'The menial work has nothing to do with my learning how to teach.'

"The master said, 'No, you will be hurting yourself and hurting others. You have to understand from the very beginning that the spiritual path can tolerate everything but ego.'"

Ego places a veil between the aspirant and the process of learning. When one becomes egocentric he isolates himself and thus is not able to communicate with his teacher and conscience and doesn't follow the instructions of the teacher. Such an ego needs immense austerities and modifications, without which all knowledge drains away.

My Swollen Ego

◆

During the rainy season swamis do not travel, but stay in one place for four months. People then come and learn the scriptures from them. Although I was still being trained as a swami, I too would teach every day. Students often create problems for a teacher. For instance, the first thing they do is place him high above them so that there is limited communication. My students built a high platform on which I was asked to sit. I was inordinately proud that I had a large following. That happens when you are a neophyte and hanker after name and fame. The more one's followers increase, the more egotistical one becomes.

I remained under the notion that one particular swami among my students was not very knowledgeable. During my lectures he used to sit quietly in a corner. This swami was actually an advanced adept, although I was not at all aware of it. He came because I used to pray to the Lord, "Lord, enlighten me. Help me, Lord." I sincerely cried and prayed, so the Lord sent that man to me. And what did I do? I used to give my loincloth to him for washing, and I would order him to do things for me all day. He was with me for two months before deciding to teach me a lesson.

One morning we were both sitting on a rock on a bank of

the Ganges. While brushing my teeth, I ordered, "Go and fetch me some water." He had had enough of my swollen ego. He said, "Go on brushing." I lost awareness of what was happening to me after that.

Two days later some people found me lying there. My face was horribly swollen. I had dropped the brush but was still rubbing my finger in my mouth continuously. I was doing it unconsciously. My master appeared and said, "Get up!" I opened my eyes but could not lift my face, it was so heavy. My gums were swollen and I could not move my jaw.

Then my master told me, "That swami is a great sage. God sent him to you. You do not know to be humble and behave properly with the men of God. Now I hope you have learned a lesson. Do not commit this mistake again." Then he said, "Get up; look at the sky and start walking."

I protested, "If I keep on looking at the sky and continue walking, I will stumble and fall down." He said, "Bow your head and then you will be able to walk without stumbling. For going through this hazardous journey of life, you should learn to be humble. Ego and pride are two stumbling blocks on this journey. If you are not humble, you cannot learn. Your growth will be stunted."

When one begins to tread the path of spirituality it is essential to be humble. Ego creates barriers, and the faculty of discrimination is lost. If discrimination is not sharpened, reason does not function properly and there is no clarity of mind. A clouded mind is not a good instrument on the path of enlightenment.

"There must be renunciation, there must be action: in reconciliation of the two, the crown of life resides." It is not action that ought to be renounced, but the fruit of action. Be sure that the ego has been annihilated in the ocean of consciousness. Be sure that it is not lurking somewhere in the inner dark chamber of your heart. Its ways are various and its forms are numerous. Action greased with love gives a glimpse of eternity and perpetual joy.

Cultivating Inner Qualities

———◆———

When I was in Shrinagar, Kashmir, I met a great scholar of Vedanta who was head of the department of philosophy in a renowned university. He said, "If I can answer your questions, I will be glad to do so."

So I put these questions to him: "The Upanishads appear to be full of contradictions. In one place they say that Brahman is one without a second. Somewhere else they say that everything is Brahman. In a third place they say this world is false and Brahman alone is truth. And in a fourth place it is said that there is only one absolute Reality beneath all these diversities. How can one make sense out of these conflicting statements?"

He replied, "I don't know how to answer a swami's questions. You are learning to be a swami of the Shankaracharya order. You should know the answers better than I."

I went to many other learned people, but nobody could satisfy me. They could give me commentaries on different Upanishads, but no one could resolve these apparent contradictions. Eventually I went to a swami near Uttarkashi, 135 miles deep in the Himalayas. His name was Vishnu Maharaj. He was always naked, having no clothes or any other possessions.

Sadhus on the shores of Shesnag Lake in Amarnath, Kashmir

I said to him, "I want to know something about the Upanishads."

He said, "Bow down first. You are asking about the Upanishads with a swollen ego. How can you possibly learn these subtle truths?"

I did not like to bow down before anyone, so I left his place. After that, whenever I inquired about the Upanishads I was told, "Go to Vishnu Maharaj. No one else can answer you." But I was afraid because he knew that my whole problem was my ego, and he immediately tested my ego by saying, "Bow down and then I will answer your question." I wouldn't do that. I tried my best to find other swamis who could answer these questions, but everyone I asked referred me to Vishnu Maharaj.

Every day I would approach the cave where he lived on a bank of the Ganges. I would think, "Let me see how he answers my questions." But when I got near I would become very fearful of the impending confrontation, so I would change my mind and go back.

One day he saw me nearby and said, "Come, sit down. Are you hungry? Do you want to eat with me?" He was very pleasant and gracious. He gave me food and drink and then said, "Now you should go. I have no more time to spend with you today."

I said, "I have come with certain questions, sir. Food and drink I can get elsewhere. I want spiritual food."

He said, "You are not prepared. In your mind you want to examine me; you want to know whether I can reply to your questions or not; you don't want to learn. When you are prepared, come to me and I will answer you."

The next day I became very humble and I said, "Sir, the whole night I prepared myself, and now I'm ready!"

Then he taught me, and all my questions were resolved. Answering my questions systematically, he said that there are no contradictions in the teachings of the Upanishads. These teachings are received directly by the great sages in a deep state of contemplation and meditation. He explained, "When the student starts practicing, he realizes that this apparent world is changeable, while truth never changes. Then he knows that the world of forms and names which is full of changes is false, and that behind it there exists an absolute Reality that is unchanging. In the second step, when he has known the truth, he understands that there is only one truth and that truth is omnipresent, so there is really nothing like falsehood. In that stage he knows that reality which is one and the same in both the finite and infinite worlds. But there is another, higher, state in which the aspirant realizes that there is only one absolute Reality without second, and that that which is apparently false is in reality a manifestation of the absolute One.

"These apparent contradictions confuse only that student who has not studied the Upanishads from a competent teacher.

A competent teacher makes the student aware of the experiences one has on various levels. These are the levels of consciousness, and there is no contradiction in them." He continued: "The teachings of the Upanishads are not understood by the ordinary mind or even by the intellectual mind. Intuitive knowledge alone leads to understanding them."

In fact I wanted to strengthen my knowledge which I had received from my master, and knowingly used to pose such questions to others. Such questions posed without being humble are never answered by the sages. The questions are resolved by humility itself. This great man taught me to rise above argumentation and instructed me to allow intuition to flow uninterruptedly to solve such subtle questions.

I Thought I Was Perfect

◆

As a young man I thought I had perfected myself and that I didn't need any further teaching or study. I felt there was no swami in India as advanced as I because I seemed to be more intellectually knowledgeable than others, and I was myself teaching many swamis. When I conveyed to my master this inflated opinion of myself, he looked at me and asked, "Are you drugged? What do you mean?" I said, "No, really. This is the way I feel."

He returned to the subject a few days later. "You are still a child. You only know how to attend college. You have not mastered four things. Master them and then you will have attained something.

"Have a desire to meet and know God. But have no selfish desire to acquire things for yourself. Give up all anger, greed, and attachment. Practice meditation regularly. Only when you have done these four things will you become perfect."

Then he told me to visit certain sages. He said, "When you are with them you should be very humble. If you become obstinate or aggressive, you will be deprived of their knowledge. They will just close their eyes and sit in meditation." He said this because he knew that I was very obstinate and impatient.

He gave me a list of sages of different orders. They were his friends who had known me from my young age because I had been with my master when he visited with them. I had been quite mischievous. I used to pester them and throw things so that they would know I was around. Whenever they came to visit my master they would ask, "Is he still with you?"

First I went to see a swami who was renowned for silence. He had withdrawn from worldly concerns. No matter what happened around him, he never looked up. On my way I talked with villagers nearby. They told me, "He doesn't talk to anyone or look at anyone; he doesn't even eat. This is the third month he has been in the same place without getting up. We have never seen such a man." This state is called *ajagar-vritti,* which means "python's tendency." Just as a python remains in a dormant state for a long time, some sages do not move for many days, but remain in a deep state of meditation.

When I went to see him he was lying on a hillock under a banyan tree, smiling, with his eyes closed, as though he were a lord of the universe. He never wore anything, whether it was summer, winter, or the rainy season. His skin appeared weatherproof, like that of an elephant. He did not own a thing, but he was utterly content.

When I first saw him lying that way, I thought, "At least he should have a little decency." Then I thought, "My master told me to visit him, and I know that my master would not waste my time. I am only seeing his body." I touched his feet. [According to our custom, when we touch the feet of great men, they bless us.]

He was not sensitive to external stimuli; he was somewhere else. Three or four times I said, "Hello, sir; how are you?" But he did not respond. There was no movement, no answer. Then I started massaging his feet. When our teachers are tired we often do that. I thought he would be pleased, but he kicked me.

That kick was so strong that I was thrown backward all the way down the hill, which was quite steep, and into a lake below. I fell against many trees and rocks on the way down and ended up with many painful bruises. I was vindictive. "What reason has he to do this? I came to him in reverence, started massaging his feet—and he kicked me! He's not a sage. I'll teach him: I'll break both his legs! I'll give him double what he gave me!" I really wanted to retaliate. I decided that perhaps my master sent me to him to teach him a lesson.

When I returned to the hill to vent my anger, he was sitting up and smiling. He said, "How are you, son?"

I said, "How am I? After kicking me and knocking me down the hill, you're asking how I am?"

He said, "Your master told you to master four things, and you have even destroyed one. I kicked you to test your control of anger. Now you are so angry that you cannot learn anything here. You are not tranquil. You are still very immature. You don't follow the spiritual teaching of your master, who is so selfless. What could you possibly learn from me? You are not prepared for my teachings. Go away!"

Nobody had ever talked to me like that. When I thought about what he said, I realized that it was true; I was completely possessed by my anger.

He asked, "Do you know why we touch the feet of a sage?" Then he recited something beautiful, a Persian belief: "A sage gives the best part of his life, surrendering it at the lotus feet of the Lord. People ordinarily recognize you only by your face—but the face of the sage is not here; it is with his Lord. People find only feet here, so they bow to the feet."

He said, "You should have that humility when touching someone's feet. Now you cannot stay here. You will have to go."

I wept and thought, "A few days ago I thought I was perfect, but surely I am not." Then I said, "Sir, I will come back to you when I have really conquered my ego." And I departed.

All the kicks and blows of life teach us something. No matter whence they come, they are blessings in disguise if we but learn their lesson. Buddha said, "For a wise man, there is nothing to be called bad. Any adversity of life provides a step for his growth, provided he knows how to utilize it."

I visited another swami and determined that no matter what he did, I would not get angry. He had a beautiful farm. He said, "I'll give you this farm. Would you like it?" I said, "Of course."

He smiled. "Your master told you not to be attached, and yet you are very quick to tie yourself to a farm." I felt very small. My mind seemed bent toward anger and attachment and not toward higher things.

Later I was sent to still another swami. He knew that I was coming. There was a small natural fountain on the way where we used to go and wash. He left some gold coins there. I stopped there and I found three of them. For a second I entertained the thought of picking them up. I did so, and tucked them inside my loincloth. Then I reconsidered: "But these coins are not mine. Why do I need them? This is not good." I put them back.

When I went to the swami, he was annoyed. I bowed before him and he said, "Why did you pick up the coins? Do you still have lust for gold? Get out. This is not the place for you."

I protested, "But I left them there."

He said, "You left them later on. The problem is that you were attracted to them and picked them up in the first place."

From the experiences that these sages gave me I began to realize the difference between book knowledge and experiential knowledge. I began to see my many weaknesses, and I did not find it pleasant. Finally I returned to my master. He asked, "What have you learned?"

"I have learned that I have intellectual knowledge, but I do not behave in accord with that knowledge."

He said, "This is the problem all intellectuals have. They

become overly proud of their knowledge. Now I will teach you how to practice, so that you will know."

A human being knows enough, but that knowledge needs to be brought into daily life. If this is not done, the knowledge remains limited within the boundaries of knowing only. We all know what to do and what not to do, but it is very difficult to learn how to be. Real knowledge is found not in knowing but rather in being.

Practice Makes Perfect

◆

Once when I was teaching about life and death a swami quietly came in and sat with my students. I thought that he was a beginner, so I treated him as I treated the others. I was annoyed because he only smiled, constantly smiled, while the others were very conscientiously taking notes. I finally asked, "Are you listening to me?"

He said, "You are only talking, but I can demonstrate mastery over life and death. Bring me an ant."

A large ant was brought. He cut it into three pieces and separated them. Then he closed his eyes and sat motionless. After a moment the three parts moved toward each other. They joined together, and the revived ant scurried away. I knew it was not hypnosis, or anything like that.

I felt very small before that swami. And I was embarrassed before my students because I only knew the scriptures without a firsthand understanding and mastery of life and death. I asked, "Where did you learn that?" He said, "Your master taught me."

At that I became angry with my master and immediately went to him. Seeing me he asked, "What happened? Why are you once again allowing anger to control you? You are still a slave to your violent emotions." I said, "You teach others things which you don't teach me. Why?"

He looked at me and said, "I have taught you many things—but you don't practice. That is not my fault! All these achievements depend on practice, not just on verbal knowledge of them. If you know all about the piano but don't practice, you will never create music. Knowing is useless without practice. Knowing is mere information. Practice gives direct experience, which alone is valid knowledge."

The Sage from
the Valley of Flowers

◆

There was not much literature on the flowers and ecology of the Himalayas, but whatever was available, I tried my best to go through. One of the British writers wrote a book on "the Valleys of Flowers of the Himalayas." After reading this book a flame of burning desire arose in my heart. In the Himalayas there are countless varieties of lilies, rhododendrons, and other flowers, but I specifically was anxious to see one of the two valleys.

There lived a sage constantly traveling in that region of the Himalayas where this Valley of Flowers exists. I knew him well. He was very strong and healthy, about eighty years of age, but quite unusual. He used to carry a unique blanket all the time. It was very heavy. The weight of this blanket was approximately eighty to one hundred pounds. You might wonder how he made this blanket so heavy. Any piece of cloth which he found during his wide travels, he would patch onto the blanket. It was a blanket of a thousand patches. He called it *gudari*, which means "blanket of patches," and people called him Gudari Baba.

On my request he said, "If you would really like to see the

Valley of Flowers and want to follow me, you will have to carry this blanket."

I agreed, but when I put the blanket on my shoulders I stumbled under its weight. He asked, "How is it possible for a young man like you to be so weak when you are apparently so healthy?" He picked up the blanket and said, "See how light it is?" Then he put it on my shoulder again. He knew my master and so he allowed me to follow him to the Valley of Flowers.

As I was following him this sage said, "No one can retain his memory when he goes through the Valley of Flowers during the blooming season. We should bring all the obstinate kids like you here and set them right. Those who try to be intellectual and argue with us should be brought here so that they understand their worth."

I said, "But I am following you."

He said, "Oh yes. You argue all the time and don't listen attentively. You are very proud of your intellectual knowledge.

The Valley of Flowers

I do not know how to read and write. You are more educated than I. You have education, but I have control of mind."

I told him, "I also have control." He replied, "We shall see."

I said, "Sir, first of all, please take away your blanket from my shoulders because it is difficult to carry." He lamented, "Oh, the children of this modern age!"

He took his blanket from me and started conversing with it: "O my beloved blanket, nobody understands anything about you. No one knows that you are a living blanket." I looked at him and thought, "This man is really crazy!"

The next morning a Japanese monk joined us. He was equally anxious to see the Valley of Flowers. This Japanese monk also thought that Gudari Baba was a crazy man. He asked me, "Rama, can you explain why this man is carrying such a heavy load?" We started talking and I thought it would be nice to share these experiences with each other.

This monk was afraid of going to the Valley of Flowers all alone. Someone had told him that if any traveler goes to see this valley, he forgets everything and his senses do not coordinate in perceiving sense objects. The traveler loses his memory and smiles all the time. He said that this baba was the right person to guide us because he traveled in this region and knew all the trails.

The next day this Japanese monk started shivering with fever. He had lived in the jungles of Burma and had suffered from malaria. He had a temperature of 103 to 104 degrees and his pulse rate was very high. The baba said to him, "You told this boy that I was crazy. Do you want to see the living power of my blanket? Do you know that this blanket is not a mere blanket, but a living force? Do you want to get well? Then kneel down and be humble!" The baba covered the Japanese monk with the blanket.

The monk said, "I will be flattened! It's too heavy and I am a small man."

The baba said, "Keep quiet!" After a few minutes he took the blanket away from the monk. When he removed the blanket, it was shivering. The baba asked the monk, "What happened to your fever?"

He said, "Sir, I don't have a fever anymore."

The baba said, "This blanket is very generous and kind and has taken away your fever." The baba looked at me and said, "Do you want his fever to be cured forever?"

I said, "Yes, please."

The baba said, "But he calls me crazy. I don't think he deserves my help."

I said, "The sages are kind and great and they always forgive others."

The baba smiled and said, "Of course I will help him." We traveled together for fifteen days and the Japanese monk did not suffer from the fever again.

Nine miles outside of Badrinath there is a side trail which leads to the Valley of Flowers where there is a small *guru dwara* (temple of Sikhs). We took our meal there. The people of this temple knew Gudari Baba very well. We rested that whole day in the temple and started our journey to the Valley of Flowers toward Hemkund the next day.

The flowers were in full bloom as far as the eye could see. For the first few hours it was soothing to the senses and stimulating to the mind. But slowly I started noticing that my memory was slipping away. After five or six hours the baba asked, "Hey you! Can you tell me your name?"

We were both so disoriented that we could not remember our names. We had completely forgotten them. I was only aware of my existence and had a hazy idea that I was with two other people. That's all. The fragrance of those flowers was so strong that we could not think rationally. Our ability to reason wouldn't function. Our senses were anesthetized. We had a faint idea of our existence and that of the things around us.

Our talk to each other did not make any sense. We lived in this valley for a week. It was highly enjoyable. The baba made fun of us all the time and said, "Your education and strength have no value."

After we came out of the Valley of Flowers, the baba said, "Your joy was because of the influence of the fragrance of the flowers. You were not meditating. That's what marijuana and hashish do to people, and they think that they are in meditation. Look at me. I was not affected or influenced by the fragrance of those wild flowers. Ha, ha, ha! You have gone to college and have read many books. You have lived on the opinions of others so far. Today you had a good chance to understand and compare direct knowledge and the so-called knowledge which is really imitation. So far the opinions that you have are actually the opinions of others. Those who live on the opinions of others do not ever have the ability to decide and express their own opinions. Boys, this informative knowledge is not considered by us to be real knowledge. Even if you understand that direct knowledge alone is valid, you don't have control over the mind. The education given to modern children is very superficial. Without any discipline, control over the mind is not possible—and without control of the mind, direct experience is impossible."

The Japanese monk left for Bodhi Gaya, and I lived with the baba for another fifteen days. He is a free wanderer of this region, and all the pilgrims have heard about him. For practical schooling it is important for the renunciate to live with such sages who have direct knowledge of the values of life with its currents and crosscurrents.

V

Conquering Fear

FEAR IS THE GREATEST OF ALL FOES. IT IS A DEVIL residing within. Fearlessness is the first rung on the ladder of freedom.

The Devil

◆

One evening after my brother disciple and I had walked thirty miles in the mountains, we stopped to rest two miles beyond Kedarnath. I was very tired and soon fell asleep, but my sleep was restless because of my extreme fatigue. It was cold and I did not have a blanket to wrap around me, so I put my hands around my neck to keep warm. I rarely dream. I had dreamt only three or four times in my life, and all of my dreams had come true. That night I dreamt that the devil was choking my throat with strong hands. I felt as though I were suffocating.

When my brother disciple saw my breath rhythm change and realized that I was experiencing considerable discomfort, he came to me and woke me up. I said, "Somebody was choking my throat!" Then he told me that my own hands were choking my throat.

That which you call the devil is part of you. The myth of the devil and of evil is imposed on us by our ignorance. The human mind is a great wonder and magician. It can assume the form of both a devil and a divine being any time it wishes. It can be a great enemy or a great friend, creating either hell or heaven for us. There are many tendencies hidden in the

The trail to Kedarnath

unconscious mind which must be uncovered, faced, and transcended before one intends to tread the path of enlightenment.

Dreaming is a natural state of mind. It is an intermediate state between waking and sleeping. When the senses are prevented from receiving the sense perceptions, the mind starts recalling the memories from the unconscious. All the hidden desires also lie in the unconscious, waiting to find their fulfillment. When the senses are not perceiving the objects of the world and the conscious mind is at rest, then recalled memories start coming forward and they are called dreams. Through dreams we can analyze a level of our hidden personality. This analysis is sometimes helpful in curing certain ailments. With the help of meditation we can consciously recall these memories, observe them, analyze them, and resolve them forever.

There are various types of dreams. In addition to the painful and pleasant dreams which we ordinarily experience, there are another two categories of dreams which need to be analyzed. One is a prophetic dream, and the other is a mere nightmare. Sometimes prophetic dreams are guiding. Nightmares are the signs of intense agony created by frustrations. The latter can occur if someone is very tired or if he has bad digestion.

I have never heard anyone claiming to have seen a devil in the daytime. My brother disciple, with the help of a simile, told me, "A rope in darkness can be mistaken for a snake. A mirage in the distance can be mistaken for water. Lack of light is the main cause of such a vision. Does the devil exist? If there is only one existence, which is omnipresent and omniscient, then where is the place for the existence of the devil? Those who are religiously sick believe in the existence of the devil by forgetting the existence of God. A negative mind is the greatest devil that resides within the human being. Transformation of the negativity leads toward positive or angelic visions. It is the mind which creates hell and heaven. Fear of the devil is a phobia which needs to be eradicated from the human mind."

Mistaken for a Ghost

When I was staying in the Nanital forests in the Himalayan foothills I would sometimes come down to a small city which is situated at the height of 6,000 feet. People there used to chase after me for blessings and advice, as they do with most of the yogis and swamis. In order to have time to do my practices I found it necessary to protect myself from visitors. I found out about a cemetery in which Britishers were buried which was quiet and very neatly kept. Wearing a long white gown made from a blanket to protect myself from the cold, I would go to the cemetery to meditate at night.

One night two policemen who were patrolling that area walked through the cemetery, flashing their lights here and there to see if there were any vandals. I was sitting in meditation on the broad monument of a British military officer. My whole body, including my head, was covered with the blanket. The policemen flashed their lights in my direction from some distance away and were startled to see a human-like figure covered with a blanket. They went to the police station and told the other policemen and officers that they had seen a ghost in the cemetery. This rumor spread all over the city and many people were frightened.

The superintendent of police came to the cemetery the next night with several armed policemen and flashed light on me once again. In that state of meditation I was not aware of them, so I did not stir. They all thought I was a ghost. They drew their revolvers to shoot at me because they wanted to see if bullets would affect a ghost. But the superintendent of police said, "Wait, let us challenge the ghost first. Perhaps it is not a ghost, but some person." They came closer and surrounded the monument on which I was sitting. But they still could not figure what was inside the blanket. Then they fired a shot into the air. Somehow I became aware of them and came out of my meditation. I uncovered myself and asked, "Why are you disturbing me here? What is it you want of me?" The superintendent of police, who was British, knew me very well. He apologized for disturbing me and ordered the policemen who patrolled that area to supply me with hot tea each night. Thus the myth of the ghost which frightened many people was unveiled.

Mr. Peuce, the superintendent of police, then started visiting me regularly. He wanted to learn meditation from me. One day Mr. Peuce asked me about the nature of fear in man. I said that among all the fears, the fear of dying seems to be very deep-rooted in the human heart. The sense of self-preservation leads one to many hallucinations. A human being is constantly haunted by fears. He loses his balance and starts imagining and projecting his ideas the way he wishes. He deepens this process in repeating it again and again. Fear is the greatest enemy of man.

Mr. Peuce was very much afraid of ghosts and wanted to know if I had ever seen one. I said, "I have seen the king of ghosts—and that is man. A man is a ghost as long as he identifies himself with the objects of his mind. The day he becomes aware of his essential nature, his true self, he is free from all fears."

Soon many people started coming to see me. My friend Mr.

Peuce for some reason decided to resign and go to Australia. I left the city and went to the Almora mountains. I came to the conclusion that it is of no use to live under the pressures of fear, for there is no joy in being afraid in every step of life. Without encountering the fears, we only strengthen them. On the path of spirituality, fear and sloth are the prime enemies.

My Fear of Snakes

◆

Let me tell you about my fear. In my young age I was usually fearless. I could cross the swollen Ganges River and go into the forest without the slightest fear of tigers—but I was always very much afraid of snakes. I have had many encounters with snakes, but I concealed my fear from everyone, even my master.

Once, in September of 1939, my master and I came down to Rishikesh. We were on the way to Virbhadra, and camped at a spot where my ashram stands today. Early in the morning we took our bath in the Ganges and sat down on its bank for meditation. By that time I had already formed the habit of sitting for two or three hours without a break. It was about seven-thirty when I opened my eyes—and saw that I was face to face with a cobra. The lower half of its body was coiled on the ground, and the upper half was raised. It was sitting very still, just about two feet in front of me, looking toward me. I was terrified, and immediately closed my eyes again. I did not know what to do. After a few seconds, when I opened my eyes again and found that it had not moved, I jumped up quickly and ran away. After running for a few yards I looked back and saw that the cobra was just starting to crawl back toward the bushes.

I went back to my master and explained what had happened. He smiled and told me that it is natural for any living creature to be in a state of meditation near someone who is in deep meditation.

Another time, after experiencing many kinds of training, I had another frightening experience with snakes. I had been asked to go to South India, which is considered to be the home of Indian culture, and on one cold and rainy evening I went to a temple to ask for shelter. At first they said, "If you are a swami, why do you need shelter?" But then a lady came from the temple and said, "Come with me. I will give you shelter."

The woman took me inside a small six-foot-square thatched hut and told me to stay there. Then she left. I had only a deerskin on which to sit, a shawl, and a loincloth. There was no light in the hut, but I could see a little bit from the light which came through the entrance. After a few minutes I saw a cobra crawling in front of me—and then another one at my side. Soon I was aware that there were several cobras in the room. I realized that I had come to a snake's temple! It was a very dangerous situation, and I was afraid. The woman wanted to test whether I was a genuine swami or not, and I was actually just learning to be a swami. I was very much afraid—but I thought, "If I run away at night, where could I go? And if I do leave, that woman will never give alms to swamis in the future." I decided, "I will remain here. Even if I die, at least the principles of renunciation will not have been found wanting."

Then I thought, "That woman does not appear to be enlightened, and yet she can come into this hut. So why can't I remain here without being harmed?" Remembering my master's words, I said to myself, "If I sit still, what will the cobras do to me? I have nothing that they want." I sat there the whole night watching, and the only thing I lost was my meditation. I could only meditate on the cobras.

Despite these two experiences, however, my fear of snakes continued. As a young swami many people, even high government officials, came and bowed before me and I blessed them. But within me was an obsessive fear of snakes. I would teach the *Brahma Sutras,* the philosophy of fearlessness, to my students, but fear was there inside me. I tried my best to remove the fear by intellectualizing it, but the more I tried, the stronger the fear became. It became so strong that it started creating problems. With any sudden noise the thought of snakes would come into my mind. When I sat for meditation I would often open my eyes and look about. Wherever I went I would look for a snake. Finally I said to myself, "You must remove this fear even if you die in the process. It is not good for your growth. How can you lead people who love, respect, and depend on you? You have this fear and yet you are guiding people—you hypocrite."

I went to my master and I said, "Sir?" He said, "I know what you want. You are afraid of snakes."

"If you knew, why didn't you tell me how to get rid of that fear?" I asked. He said, "Why should I tell you? You should ask me. Why did you try to hide this fear from me?" I had never kept any secret from him, but somehow I did not tell him about this fear.

Then he took me to the forest and said, "We are observing silence starting tomorrow at dawn. At three-thirty in the morning you will get up and collect leaves and wild flowers for a special worship that we will do."

The next morning I found a big heap of leaves. As I picked up the heap in the darkness, I realized that there was a cobra in it. It was in my hand, and there was no escape. I did not know what to do. I was so frightened that I was on the verge of collapsing. My hands were trembling. My master was there and he said, "Bring it to me." I was shaking with fear. He said, "It will not bite you."

The unconscious fear welled up nevertheless. My mind said, "It is a death that you are holding in your hand." I believed my master, but my fear was stronger than my belief.

He said, "Why do you not love the snake?"

"Love?" I cried, "How can you love something when you are under the influence of fear?" This is a familiar situation in the world: if you are afraid of a person, you cannot love him. You will be unconsciously afraid of him all the time. The cause of fear grows in the unconscious.

My master said, "Look, it's such a beautiful creature. It roams all over, but look how clean and neat it is. You do not remain clean; you have to take a bath every day. A snake is the cleanest creature in the world."

I said, "It is clean, but it is also dangerous."

He told me, "Man is more unclean and poisonous than a snake. He can kill and injure others. Each day he projects poison in the form of anger and other negative emotions on those with whom he lives. A snake never does that. A snake bites only in defense."

He went on: "When you are fast asleep, does your finger prick your own eyes? Do your teeth bite your tongue? There is an understanding that all your limbs belong to one body. The day we have a like understanding that all creatures are one, we will not fear any creature."

I continued to hold the snake as he talked, and gradually my fear subsided. I began to think, "If I don't kill snakes, why should a snake kill me? Snakes don't bite anyone without reason. Why should they bite me? I am nobody in particular." My mind gradually began to function normally. Since that experience I have not again been afraid of snakes.

Animals are instinctively very sensitive and are receptive to both hatred and love. If one has no intention to harm animals, they become passive and friendly. Even wild animals would like to associate with human beings. In the valleys of the Himalayas

I observed this tendency in animals over several years. They come near the villages at night and return to the forest early in the morning. They seem to want to be near human beings, but are afraid of the human's violent nature. A human being, with all his selfishness, attachments, and hatred, loses touch with his essential nature and thus frightens the animals, who then attack in self-defense. If a person learns to behave gently with animals, they will not attack him. I often remember the way Valmiki, St. Francis, and Buddha loved animals, and I try to follow their example.

Fear gives birth to insecurity, which creates imbalance in the mind, and this influences one's behavior. A phobia can control human life and finally lead one to the insane asylum. If a fear is examined it will usually be found to be based on imagination, but that imagination can create a kind of reality. It is true that fear creates danger, and human beings then must protect themselves from that self-created danger. All of our dreams materialize sooner or later. Thus it is really fear that invites danger, though we usually think that danger brings on the fear. Fear is the greatest sickness that arises from our imagination. I have seen that all fears and confusion need only to encounter some practical experience and then they can easily be overcome.

The first ten commitments of the *Yoga Sutras* are preliminary requisites for attaining samadhi—and the first is *ahimsa*. Ahimsa means non-killing, non-harming, and non-injury. By becoming selfish and egotistical, human beings become insensitive and lose the instinctual power. Instinct is a great power, and if properly used can help one in following the noble path of ahimsa.

In all my years of roaming in the mountains and forests of India I have never heard that any sadhu, swami, or yogi was ever attacked by any wild animal. These people do not protect themselves from the animals or natural calamities like avalanches. It is inner strength that makes one fearless, and it is the fearless one who crosses the individual consciousness and becomes one with the universal consciousness. Who can kill whom? For Atman is eternal, though the body must return to dust sooner or later. This strong faith is enjoyed by the sages of different orders in the lap of the Himalayas.

In a Tiger's Cave

◆

Once I was traveling all alone in Tarai Bhavar toward the
mountains in Nepal. I was on my way to Katmandu,
which is the capital of Nepal. I walked twenty to thirty miles
each day. After sunset I would build a fire, meditate, and then
rest. I would begin walking again at four o'clock the next
morning and walk until ten o'clock. Then I would sit near
water under a tree through the middle part of the day, and
travel again from three-thirty until seven in the evening. I
walked in my bare feet carrying a blanket, a tiger skin, and a
pot of water.

At about six o'clock one evening I became tired and
decided to take a short nap in a cave which was about two
miles from the nearest road. I spread my blanket on the floor
of the small cave because it was a little damp. As soon as I lay
down and closed my eyes I was pounced on by three little tiger
cubs, who made gentle little cries and pawed at my body. They
were hungry and thought that I was their mother. They must
have been only twelve to fifteen days old. For a few minutes I
lay there petting them. When I sat up, there was their mother
standing at the entrance to the cave. First I feared that she

147

would rush in and attack me, but then a strong feeling came from within: I thought, "I have no intention to hurt these cubs. If she leaves the entrance of the cave, I will go out." I picked up my blanket and pot of water. The mother tiger backed off from the entrance and I went out. When I had gone about fifteen yards from the entrance, the mother tiger calmly went in to join her babies.

Such experiences help one to control fear and give a glimpse of the unity that lies between animals and human beings. Animals can easily smell violence and fear. Then they become ferociously defensive. But when animals become friendly they can be very protective and help human beings. One human being may desert another in danger, but animals rarely do so. The sense of self-preservation is of course very strong in all creatures, but animals are more dedicated lovers than human beings. Their friendship can be relied upon. It is unconditional, while relationships between people are full of conditions. We build walls around ourselves and lose touch with our own inner being and then with others. If the instinctive sensitivity for our relation to others is regained, we can become realized without much effort.

Swami Rama during the journey to Nepal

VI

The Path of Renunciation

◆

THE PATH OF RENUNCIATION IS THE PATH OF THE razor's edge. It is for a fortunate few, and not for all. Non-attachment and knowledge of the self are two important prerequisites on this path.

My Whole Being Is an Eye

I regularly visited a swami near Shrinagar over a period of two years. I would serve and wait on him, but he never talked to me and he rarely opened his eyes. His name was Hari Om. For two whole years he never once looked at me! One day I told my master, "I am fed up with that swami. It's like visiting and waiting on a log of wood or a rock."

My master said, "Don't say that. Although you may not be aware of it, he sees you indeed."

I said, "How could he see me? His eyes are closed."

That day when I went to see him, Hari Om smiled and giggled. Then he said, "Am I a log of wood or a rock? Don't you know I am in such great joy that I have no reason to open my eyes? Why should I open my eyes when I am already with that One who is the fountain of beauty and glory? The partial enjoyment which most people seek can no longer satisfy me. That is why I keep my eyes closed. You will have to open the eye of your mind to see that perennial beauty, for the senses have only a limited capacity. They perceive only the limited beauty of limited objects."

I was inspired by his beautiful words. After that when I

went to see him, he opened his eyes ever so slightly. When his eyes were a bit open, it seemed as though wine were overflowing the cup. You could experience the joy flowing from within.

He muttered the Sanskrit verse "During that which is night to others, the enlightened one keeps awake." Then he explained: "The finest hours are the hours of night, but very few know how to utilize their worth and silence. Three categories of people remain awake at night: the yogi, the *bhogi* [sensualist], and the *rogi* [sick person]. The yogi enjoys bliss in meditation, the bhogi enjoys sensual pleasures, and the rogi keeps awake because of his pain and misery. All three remain awake, but benefited is he who is in meditation. The bhogi experiences momentary joy—and with a desire to expand that moment, repeats the same experience. Alas, it can never be expanded this way. In meditation real joy expands into everlasting peace.

"Closing the eyes unconsciously, without having any content in the mind, is sleep. Closing the eyes consciously is a part of meditation. A yogi closes his eyes and withdraws his senses from the sense perceptions. He remains free from the pair of opposites of pain and pleasure. Closing the eyes is for him the opening of the inner eye. Ordinary people see the objects of the world with the help of two small eyes—but do you know that my whole being has become an eye?"

My Experience
with a Dancing Girl

◆

My master often told me, "This whole world is a theatre of learning. You should not depend on me alone to teach you, but should learn from everything." One time he instructed me: "Now, my boy, go to Darjeeling. Outside the city there is a stream and on the bank of that stream is a cremation ground. No matter what happens, for forty-one days you should do a particular *sadhana* [spiritual practice] which I am going to teach you. No matter how much your mind attempts to dissuade you from completing the sadhana, you should not leave that place." I said, "Very well."

Many people are afraid of staying at such a place. They have funny notions. But it didn't bother me. I went there and lived in a small thatched hut, where I made a fire for cooking. I was going to the University in those days and it was summer vacation. I thought, "It's very good for me to spend my vacation in sadhana."

I followed the practices he had assigned to me for thirty-nine days and nothing happened. Then some powerful thoughts came into my mind: "What a foolish thing you are doing, wasting your time in a lonely place, cut off from the world. You are wasting the best period of your youth."

My master had said, "Remember, on the forty-first day you will definitely find some symptoms of improvement within yourself. Don't give up before that. Don't be swayed by the suggestions of your mind—no temptations."

I had said, "I promise," but on the thirty-ninth day my mind advanced reason after reason against this thing I was doing. I thought, "What difference can two more days possibly make? You have not experienced anything after thirty-nine days. You promised your friends that you would write to them, and you haven't written a single letter. You are living among the dead! What type of teaching is this? Why should your master have you do this? He can't be a good teacher." So I decided to leave.

I poured a bucketful of water on the fire and I destroyed the small thatched hut. It was a cold night, so I wrapped myself in a woolen shawl and walked toward the city. I was going down the main street when I heard some musical instruments being played. There was a woman singing and dancing. The theme of the music was "There is very little oil in the vessel of life, and the night is vast." She repeated the phrase again and again. That stopped me. The sound of the tabla drums seemed to call to me: "Dhik, dhik! Fie on thee, fie on thee! What have you done?"

I felt so dejected. I thought, "Why don't I complete the final two days? If I go to my teacher, he will say, 'You have not completed your practice. You are expecting fruit before the plant has matured.'" So I turned back and continued my sadhana for the remaining two days. On the forty-first day, the fruit of the practice appeared just as he had predicted.

I then walked back to the city once again and went to the house of the singer. She was a beautiful and famous dancing girl. She was considered to be a prostitute. When she saw a young swami coming toward her house she called out, "Stop, don't come here! You are at the wrong place! Such a place as this is not for you!" But I kept right on. She closed her door and told a servant, a large and powerful man with big moustaches, not to let me in. He commanded, "Stop, young swami! This is the wrong place for you!"

I said, "No. I want to see her. She is like my mother. She has helped me and I am grateful to her. Had she not alerted me with her song, I would not have completed my practices. I would have failed and I would have condemned myself and felt guilty the rest of my life." When she heard this, she opened her door and I said, "Really, you are like a mother to me."

I told her what had happened and we talked for some time. She had heard of my master. When I got up to go, she said, "I promise to live like your mother from now on. I will prove that I can be not only mother to you but to many others as well. Now I am inspired."

The next day she left for Varanasi, the seat of learning in India, where she lived on a boat on the Ganges. In the evening she would go ashore and chant on the sand. Thousands of people used to join her. She wrote on her houseboat, "Don't mistake me for a sadhu. I was a prostitute. Please do not touch my feet." She never looked directly at anyone's face and never talked to anyone. If someone wanted to talk to her she would only say, "Sit down with me and chant God's name." If you asked, "How are you?" she would chant, "Rama." If you asked, "Do you need anything? Can I get you something?" she would respond, "Rama," nothing else.

One day before a huge crowd of five or six thousand people she announced, "I am leaving early in the morning. Please throw this body in the water, where it will be used by the fishes." And then she kept silence. The next day she cast off her body.

When awakening comes we can completely transform our personalities, throwing off the past. Some of the greatest sages of the world had been very bad—like Saul who later became St. Paul. Suddenly the day of awakening came for Saul on the way to Damascus, and his personality was transformed. Valmiki, the author of the *Ramayana*, one of the ancient epics of India, had a similar experience. Don't condemn yourself. No matter how bad or how small you think you have been, you have a chance to transform your whole personality. A true seeker can always realize the reality and attain freedom from all bondage and miseries. In just one second you can enlighten yourself.

Transformation of a Murderer

◆

There are four well-known shrines in the Himalayas: Gangotri, Jamnotri, Kedarnath, and Badrinath. From June to September people from the cities and the villages of the plains go to the mountains for a month or two. This ancient tradition of Indian life is followed even today. You meet all kinds of aspirants on the mountain paths. Once while on a pilgrimage to these shrines with two of my friends I met a sadhu who was in his mid-fifties. He was from Banda district of Uttar Pradesh. He was very humble, calm, and serene, and he joined our party. We avoided the usual paths and took shortcuts whenever we could. In the evening we stayed in a cave, where we made a fire and started roasting potatoes. This was the only food we had. The sadhu, who had nothing in his possession, shared the food with us. We all said grace before taking our meal. The grace is: "This is all Brahman, being offered by Brahman and taken by Brahman." Such affirmations are very helpful in maintaining God-consciousness. In the course of our conversation, the sadhu told this story to us.

When he was about eighteen years old there was a land dispute between his father and another landlord of the same village.

His father was murdered by the villagers because of their jealousy. Jealousy is an evil which grows in the womb of ego and is nourished by selfishness and attachment. This young man was away in school when his father was murdered. When he came home he took revenge for his father, murdering five people. Then he fled to the mountains, where he lived at the feet of the yogis and sages of the Himalayas. By constant *satsanga* and by visiting sadhus at one place or another, he tried to free himself from his feeling of guilt. He started practicing austerities and always confessed to the sadhus with whom he lived. He did vigorous spiritual practice and tried to wash the stains from his conscience. For thirty-six years he lived in the mountains, and many times he thought of surrendering to the police. During this thirty-six-year period he became well-known all over as Naga Baba—he who doesn't have anything, not even a loincloth. Many a time during his discussions with the people he would openly say that he was a criminal, and describe how he transformed his inner self. He would say, "I know I was a murderer, but now I am totally changed." Such a change of heart is described in many scriptures of the Hindus, Sufis, Christians, and Buddhists.

We remained talking with him, and we finally came to the conclusion that he should surrender to the police and present himself to the court. So instead of going with us toward the shrines, the next morning he started back to his old village. He went to the police station and told them the whole story. They took him into custody and presented him before the judge, but the judge asked them, "Where is the charge sheet? What are the charges against him?" The police told the story of the crime committed thirty-six years ago, but there was no file or any record attesting to these facts. After questioning him and finding out what he had done and how he had lived since then, the judge acquitted him. The sadhu then returned to the Himalayas.

Criminologists explain that all crimes are committed in a

Devprayag, on the way to Badrinath and Kedarnath

specific state of imbalance. I agree that the law should take its own course, but isn't there any way to reform and educate these people who commit such crimes? Do people commit crimes because they are sick, or do we compel them to commit crimes? Both these aspects should be carefully examined. Spiritual practices if introduced to those who have committed crimes can help them to become aware of the existence and rights of others. If crime is seen as a disease, then we should also try to find the way to cure it. Thinking how free we are, my heart often goes out to those people who are in prison in all the countries of the world. What a tragedy it is! In my opinion a favorable atmosphere for self-improvement and reformation can be created to help these fellow men.

Humanity is not yet fully civilized. There is no nation in the world which provides free education, medical care, equality, and justice under the law for all her people. We have yet to build a society which provides those essential needs to all human beings and which creates an atmosphere to attain the next step of civilization for which we are still waiting.

A Lesson in Non-attachment

◆

My master has given me everything, and I could not give anything to him. His devotees used to give him so much money that he did not know what to do with it. I, on his behalf, used to distribute it to others and spent it the way I wanted.

Once I told him, "I want to go to Bombay." He said, "Take money, as much as you want." I took 5,000 rupees and I purchased many things, including three gramophones. He only said, "Wonderful, my boy; play them all at the same time." When I played them all together, I could not understand a thing.

Lust and greed never satisfy anyone. Desires for possessions increase incessantly and finally become a whirlpool of miseries. Such ignorance cannot be dispelled by going to the temple, worshipping in the church, listening to sermons, or performing rituals. For centuries human beings have been fulfilling their desires, yet they are still miserable. To attain the ultimate Reality it is necessary to free oneself from the desire for non-essential encumbrances.

Possessing more than necessary only creates obstacles for oneself. It is a waste of time and energy. Fulfilling wants and desires without understanding needs and necessities deviates one from the path of awareness. Desire is the mother of all misery. When the desires for worldly attainments are directed toward attaining self-awareness, then the same desire becomes a means. At this stage the desire, instead of becoming an obstacle, becomes a useful instrument for self-realization.

This can be explained by a simple simile. A candle light is extinguished by the breeze very easily, but if that light is protected and allowed to catch the forest, it will grow into a forest fire. Then the breeze helps that fire instead of extinguishing it. Similarly, when an aspirant, with the help of discipline, protects the flame of desire burning within, it grows more and more. Then all the adversities, instead of becoming obstructions, in fact start becoming means. The obstacles which are supposed to obstruct the path of self-realization are not really obstacles. Our weaknesses and the values we impose on the objects of the world create these obstacles for us. Attachment is one of the strongest obstacles created by us. With the help of non-attachment we can overcome such obstructions.

There are four ways of removing these obstacles. First, if there is no object, the human mind cannot become attached to it. Renouncing the object is one way, but it seems to be quite difficult for ordinary people. Second, while having all the objects of the world, if we learn the technique of using them as means, then the objects are not able to create obstacles for us. On this path, attitudes need to be transformed. One who has transformed his attitudes can change his bad circumstances into favorable ones. The third way is the path of conquest, in which one learns to do his actions skillfully and selflessly, surrendering the fruits of his actions for the benefits of others. Such a person becomes detached and safely crosses the ocean of life. Fourth, by self-surrender one surrenders himself and all that he owns to the Lord and leads a life of freedom from all attachments. This path seems to be easy but is really rather difficult.

My master, instead of correcting me, used to make me aware of the fact that the human mind and heart have changed because of human weaknesses. I used to ponder over any weaknesses and then meditate for self-transformation. He never said, "Do this, and don't do this," but he showed me the path, which I started treading all alone. "Learn to walk all alone" was a lesson for me.

Taste the World
and Then Renounce

◆

In my youth I had the disgusting habit of wearing expensive suits. I would choose the material myself from the market, and then go to the tailor and get fitted. I would wear a tie and a hanky of complementary colors. This confused several followers of my master, and they always grumbled about the way I lived. I lived like this for five years, but my master was not concerned. I was learning a lesson which was essential for my growth. When I stood before my master he used to say, "Your taste is very poor." But I protested, "Sir, this is the best material available."

One day I lost my interest in dressing up. I went to him in my simple kurta and pajamas. He said, "You look beautiful." He wanted me to taste the things of the world, to come to understand their worth, and to analyze and then renounce them.

Simple living and elevated thoughts help in creating an aesthetic sense. It takes a long time to create this aesthetic sense and to incorporate grace and beauty into our lives. Costly dresses have no power to hide our ugliness—stylish clothes do not have the power to make us beautiful. Instead of focusing on externals we should learn to cultivate and express our inner beauty. This inner beauty will shine for all to see.

Renunciation is a path of fire, and should be followed only by those who have burned their worldly desires. On the spur of the moment many students become emotionally disturbed and disappointed by worldly gains and losses and consequently think of retiring from the world. Even though they may find an external situation that is very pleasant, the unstable world inside is still carried by such students no matter where they go. Disappointments, greed, lust, hatred and love, anger and jealousy cannot be renounced without spiritual discipline. A frustrated and dissatisfied soul is not fit to tread the path of renunciation. Sitting in the cave and thinking of worldly pleasures is misery.

My master wanted me to lead a normal childhood rather than a frustrated one. During those years I used to buy the best cars and trade them in twice a year. I used to live better than any prince of India. Many of my relatives and friends and even the police department wondered where I obtained so much money to lead such a luxurious life. The secret was that my master used to give me whatever I needed. He never kept or used anything. When I realized the value of the things of the world, I calmed down and acquired that peace of mind which helped me to meditate properly. Latent lust is very dangerous because it manifests more in meditation than in active life. The desire for worldly gains creates barriers in fulfilling the desire for enlightenment.

My master once said, "Let's go to the bank of the Ganges. I have yet to give you another lesson." I said, "What is that?" He said, "Why do you live in the Himalayas?" I said, "To practice spirituality." "Why do you want to practice spirituality?" he asked. I said, "To be enlightened and become perfect."

My master replied, "Then why do you desire worldly things—why do you need the world? Being a renunciate and living in the cave and yet thinking of the world means you have a latent desire to fulfill. It is a headache that cannot be cured by any other means than self-discipline. Self-discipline leads to self-training, and self-training leads to direct experience. Through direct experience you expand your awareness. Expansion is the purpose of life."

It is true that the charms, temptations and attractions of the world are very powerful, but a burning desire for enlightenment does not allow an aspirant to be distracted from his path.

Jewels or Fire?

◆

My master never insisted that I renounce the world and become a swami. He wanted me to experience and decide things for myself. He always said, "Whatever you want to learn from me, learn—but grow independently. Whenever you need my help, I am here." If I asked him a question he would say, "Are you tired? Can't you find the answer for yourself? Why should you come to me again and again with questions? I'll teach you the method of resolving questions, but I will not simply give you answers."

He tried his best to tempt me with worldly things. He said, "Go into the world; become a high government official. If you are attached to me and only want to be with me, that is not good. I want you to settle in the world. I will bestow wealth on you." I told him, "That is not what I want."

He asked, "Are you sure?" And what he did then you might not believe. He took me into the mountains and said, "You love jewels, don't you?" It was indeed true; I was inordinately fond of beautiful things. He knew my hidden desire, so he said, "Here, look at this." I was surprised to see a huge heap of jewels before me. I blinked my eyes in disbelief. I wanted to test whether it was a mirage or something real. He said, "It's not an illusion. Go on, pick them up. I assure you they're genuine. Take them. They're for you. You'll be the richest man in India. Now son, let me go. I want to go to the mountains far away."

My tears started flowing and I said, "Are you throwing me off? Are you telling me to accept these jewels instead of you? I don't want them. I want to be with you."

Then he said, "If you want to be with me, look over there. Do you see that lofty flame?" I looked—and was astonished to see huge walls of fire. He continued: "If you can go through that fire you can follow me. Which do you choose? You must decide: how much desire do you have for the world, and how much for the light?"

I said, "I prefer fire to temptations. I want to be reborn. There is no other way." And thus I chose to follow the path of renunciation.

The path of renunciation is like walking on the razor's edge. It is so difficult that with every step there is a chance of falling. Selfish desire is the strongest of all the obstacles one encounters. Only those who are fearless and free from the charms, temptations, and attractions of the world can tread this path. One who has directed all of his desires one-pointedly, strengthening only the desire for enlightenment, can succeed.

The path of renunciation is rarely chosen; it is not meant for everyone. But those who enjoy life in renunciation are blessed. The path of action, however, is equally helpful, provided one knows how to do one's actions selflessly and skillfully, living in the world yet remaining above. The goal of both remains the same.

My First Days as a Swami

The first day after I was ordained in the swami order, my master said, "Do you know that to be a swami you have to beg alms?" I said, "Huh?"

He said, "The ego in you says that you exist independently of others. You have to purify this ego, and you cannot do so without becoming humble. I will send you begging to houses where the people are poor, and then you will come to know who you are." I said, "Okay."

I'll never forget what happened then. I was healthy and was wearing silken garb. Can you believe it, a beggar in silk? I used to walk freely with no cares. According to yoga you should stand and walk straight—but then people are likely to think you unduly proud. I went to beg alms early in the morning, and came upon a woman who was milking a cow. She was singing and milking and had an earthen pot between her knees.

I said, "Narayan Hari." [This is the name of the Lord which swamis use to announce themselves.] She was so startled that she jumped up and the pot fell and broke. I thought, "Oh, Lord."

She was so angry she started shouting. "Such a strong,

Swami Rama after taking sannyasa

healthy man begging! You are a burden to the nation and a burden to yourself! Who taught you this begging? You have money to wear a silk garment, and yet you are begging!"

I felt very small. I implored her, "Please don't call me names."

She said, "This was an antique pot given to me by my mother-in-law! You parasite! Get out of my sight!" She was so attached to the pot that she went on and on.

I went back to my master. It had been his custom to ask me every day, "Have you taken your food?" I expected him to ask me that day as usual, but he didn't. The whole day I remained quiet, and so did he. He was quiet by nature all the time. In the evening I complained, "Today you did not ask me if I have taken food."

He said, "I did not, because you are a swami now."

I asked, "What do you mean by that?"

He answered, "A swami is master of himself and master of all his appetites."

I said, "So, this swami business means you will not take care of me?"

He told me, "Now you are a swami and I am a swami. What is the difference between you and me? You wanted to become a swami. Now take care of yourself. Why should you use me as a crutch?"

I became very sad and pensive and decided that I should be independent now. I said, "I promise that from this day on I will never beg alms, no matter what happens. If God wants me to live, I will live and meditate—but I will never beg alms."

He said, "If you want to stick to your promise, that's your choice. I have nothing to say. You are a swami."

With this vow I went and sat on a bank of the Ganges. People came to see me there and everybody assumed that someone else was caring for me. Many brought flowers and bowed before me, but no one brought fruit or anything to eat. For thirteen days nobody asked me whether I had eaten. I became so weak that I could hardly walk. I thought, "Why did I ever do such a silly thing as become a swami?"

After thirteen days I started weeping. I began talking to the Divine Mother. I said, "I have taken a vow to follow this path righteously, but there is not even a loaf of bread for me." Suddenly I saw a hand coming out of the water—only a hand holding a bowl filled with food. It started coming toward me, and I heard a woman's voice saying, "Here, this is for you." I took the bowl and ate. No matter how much I ate, the bowl did not empty.

I kept that bowl for three years. I used to distribute the food from it to many people and it wouldn't be exhausted. If you put sweets in it, you could not fill it. This was witnessed by thousands of people who used to come and see it. They would continue to pour milk in it, but it never overflowed. I became a slave to that bowl. People did not learn anything from me; they came just to see the miraculous bowl. My master advised, "Throw it in the Ganges." And I followed his advice.

God presents many temptations to you when you are on the path. Only when you reject all the temptations will you have arrived. When a little child weeps, what does the mother do? The mother may first give the child candy. If the child goes on crying, the mother tries several other bribes—a doll, a cookie. If the child still does not stop, then the mother picks up the child and holds her. It is some time before the mother holds the child; first she tries several other attractions. The same thing happens to us on the path of self-realization.

Begging alms is a must for a monk, but a humiliation to others. I realized that those who totally live on the grace of the Almighty receive the necessary food to eat and shelter to live. Worrying for food and shelter is not complete faith. I will believe till the last breath of my life that God alone is my property and depending on any other thing except God will bring disaster in my life. I find my Lord always walking before me providing all the things that I need.

A Constant Persecution

At the age of twenty-one I lived in a thatched hut on a bank of the Ganges five miles from Rishikesh. Because I lived alone many people thought I was a great sage. If you isolate yourself, wear funny garb, have some scriptures near you (even though you never study them), and ignore everyone who comes to see you, then people conclude that you must be a great swami.

People would arrive to see me all day long. I did not even have time to do my practices. From morning till evening they would bow before me and offer flowers, fruit, or money. For a while I exulted in it! But slowly it began to repel me. I thought, "What is all this? It's a sheer waste of time." I started getting angry with visitors.

The people reacted, "How is it possible for a swami to get angry? He is just pretending to be angry to avoid us." And they came in even greater numbers. That really irritated me. I completely lost my calm and balance and started calling visitors bad names. But they would respond, "Sir, your bad names are like flowers for us; they are blessings." I had to run away from that place. I thought to myself, "I still have not conquered my anger."

This happens to many renunciates. They are constantly disturbed and distracted by visitors. A swami must learn not to create attraction and not to live in such a way that his practice is interrupted. A swami's life is a constant persecution. People believe he is high above any ordinary human being. In India "swami" means one who is all-powerful, a healer, a preacher, a doctor, and much more. A swami is put in such a difficult situation that it would drive an ordinary person crazy. People do not realize that some swamis are still beginners on the path, that others have trodden the path a bit, and that only very few have attained the goal. This lack of differentiation creates expectations which confuse both the people and the swamis.

It is not easy to extricate oneself from this confusion. Whenever I was truthful in telling people, "I am still practicing; there is nothing to share. Please leave me alone," they would interpret these words in whatever way suited them and come to me more and more. When I lived far in the woods I was still disturbed. Sometimes I became fed up with this swamihood.

It is not necessary for one to wear the garb of a renunciate to attain enlightenment. What actually matters is the constant spiritual sadhana of disciplining mind, action, and speech. How wonderful it is to be a swami—but how difficult it is to be a real one.

Living on a Mount of Pebbles

◆

If you are a seeker after enlightenment doing your practice and people repeatedly come and disturb you, you will not be able to complete your practice successfully. Yet in India it is a custom that if you are a swami you have to answer the questions of all those who come to you. Many people think that swamis have the remedies for all the ills of life. Such people sometimes benefit from this belief and are healed. The result is likely to be exaggerated stories and the acceptance of a beginner as an accomplished healer. This poor creature cannot continue his practice, and forgets his goal. He wastes his time and life, remaining a swami, but unrealized. One of the best ways to escape from such problems is to remain in disguise and to do one's sadhana. There are many mystics who are really great in their actual life, but pretend to be imbalanced so that they are not disturbed.

I know of one instance where people kept bringing food and money to a swami. He did not want them to do this because they kept disturbing him. So he made a sign which said "Anybody who loves me will bring only a pebble." People concluded that the swami loved pebbles, and each day many people would bring him pebbles. One pebble, two pebbles, three pebbles—they collected pebbles from the road according to their whims. After some time there was a veritable mount of pebbles, and the swami lived on top of that. People started calling him Kankaria Baba, which means "a swami of pebbles." This helped him to remain aloof.

Then the swami started to speak a language which nobody understood. If anybody came to see him, he would say, "Do, do, do, do, do." He did the same thing to me! So I went to him at night when he was all alone, and he explained, "Since people disturb me, I have learned a new language, and no one can converse with me."

This swami taught me to always remain in such a way as not to allow the people of the world to disturb me. A human being has many personalities because the ego has many faces. Some of them we can detect and analyze, but many remain unknown to us. The swami concluded that the world actually worships the ego in the name of God.

When the lower ego is made aware of that self-existent Reality which stands behind it, then it starts turning inwards. Such an ego is called higher ego. Higher ego is helpful, but lower ego makes one miserable.

Temptations on the Path

◆

I went to see a swami, who told me the following story to teach me about temptations on the path to self-realization.

A young man took vows of renunciation and became a swami. His master told him to avoid three things: gold, women, and fame.

One day the swami was crossing a river and noticed that part of the riverbank had been washed away. Then he saw that some big jars full of gold coins had been uncovered. He thought, "I don't need it, because I have renounced the world—but if I build a temple, that will be good." So he went to some builders, showed them what he had found, and asked them to build a temple. They said to one another, "Why should a swami have so much money? Let's throw him in the river and distribute the money amongst ourselves."

He was almost drowned, but by the grace of God he was able to save himself. He thereupon determined with finality: "No matter what happens, no money." He went far into the woods. When anybody came to see him, he said, "Stop there, please. If you have any money, put it aside before you come closer."

A woman came, and he ordered, "Don't come near me." She said, "Sir, I will only leave food here every day and go away." But each day she came slightly closer to him. The swami had confidence that she was a good person. He thought, "She really wants to look after me and wants me to enlighten her."

One day she brought a cat to keep him company. But the cat would not eat the food which had been prepared for the swami. He requested: "I need some milk for the cat each day." She brought a cow. He asked, "Who will look after this cow?" She asked, "May I look after it?" And he agreed.

She looked after the swami more and more. Eventually they began to live together, and the woman bore him a child. One day the swami was taking care of the child when another swami came along and said, "What has happened to you?"

The swami began to weep when he realized how much he had again become entangled with the world. He left, and went even deeper into the forest. He practiced very sincerely, and after some years acquired some *siddhis* [powers].

One day a man from a nearby village sought him out. He bowed and said, "Swamiji, you are so kind and such a great sage. I am very poor; my children do not have enough to eat. Please help me!" Swamiji said, "Take one hair from my beard, put it in your cupboard, and tomorrow your cupboard will be full of money. But don't tell anyone about it."

When he returned to his home that man naturally revealed the secret to his wife, and she to many others. Soon the news had traveled far and wide. Hundreds of people thronged to the swami to pull a hair from his beard. His face was sore and bleeding.

Once again he had to go away and begin his practice anew. But he had learned a valuable lesson. He now knew the consequences of becoming involved with gold, women, and fame.

The swami who told this story to me said, "This is a lesson which you should never forget. Let this story be a lesson to you and relate it to all young swamis whom you meet on the path."

Should I Get Married?

◆

When I was in Uttar Pradesh, a northern state of India, people would come to visit me in the evenings and I would give discourses on the Upanishads. One day a girl who had her master's degree in English literature asked me to grant her an interview. She began by asserting that I had been her spouse in a previous life. She talked for two hours and led me to a state where I agreed that it could have been possible. I had never had such a personal audience with anyone for such a long time before. She tried to persuade me that we should get married in this life as well. Later I talked with her mother, who also supported her imagination. What that girl said was so enticing and I was so naive that I started brooding on what it would be like to live with her. I told her that if my master would permit me to get married, it was all right with me. This was the only time in my life when I considered living with someone, though I was not considering leaving my spiritual path. This girl was from a well-known family. Many of her brothers, cousins, and other relatives held high government positions. They pressed me to marry her.

For one year I was strongly influenced by my emotions. It

was a bad period. I felt frustrated and unfulfilled, but I was very much influenced by the girl and her family and did not know what to do. The experience helped me to see how a student on the path of spirituality, who is committed to the path of renunciation, can be disturbed and distracted. Many obstacles appear on the path, but I am convinced that the grace of the master and the grace of God lead the student to overcome these obstructions.

Finally I went to my master and left the decision with him. He never controlled my life, but would advise me when I needed it. After some resistance and discussion, I always ended up following his advice. My master said, "You have a task and you have not yet completed it. Having examined and compared worldly companionship and spiritual attainments and deciding to follow the path of renunciation, you are now letting yourself be tempted back into the world. If you persist and remain within the influence of your current atmosphere it will take several lifetimes for you to come back to the path." The decision was left to me, but after listening to my master I decided to break this tie and go back to the path of renunciation.

There are two well-known paths: the path of renunciation, and the path of action in the world. My path was the path of renunciation. One should not compare paths and think one superior and the other inferior. I certainly do not condemn the path which involves living and working in the world while having a family. That path furnishes the means of living, but is also time-consuming. In the path of renunciation there is ample time for spiritual practices, but limited means like food, shelter, and clothing. The renunciate must depend on the householder for fulfilling such needs. It is not important which path one follows. What is important is the honesty, sincerity, truthfulness, and faithfulness which one has in either path.

This particular incident brought some humiliation into my life because people put swamis and yogis on high pedestals and look upon them as demigods. In India a swami is expected to live apart from society, without worldly possessions and without any worldly preoccupations. I have met many on the path who live hypocritically because of such expectations. I have heard Western psychologists say that renunciation, and especially celibacy, is ascetic insanity. I leave it to each individual to choose for himself, but it is important to mention here that hypocrisy is a great obstacle. Those who observe celibacy do indeed become abnormal if they do not transform their inner personalities. Those who do not have control over the primitive urges should not follow the path of renunciation.

The drives for food, sex, sleep, and self-preservation are powerful urges. Each has a very strong impact and influence on human life and behavior. Why should there be such a taboo on sex only? In yoga science all the urges are channeled and directed toward spiritual development. Those who cannot control and sublimate these drives should live in the world and experience their fulfillment in a regulated way. They can follow the path of tantra rather than renunciation. They can transform the fulfillment of these drives into spiritual experiences.

There is much confusion created by renunciates who impose rigid discipline on their students. This often makes the students dishonest and hypocritical. Is such discipline necessary? Conflict within and without are the signs and symptoms which clearly indicate that one is not on the path of spirituality.

Swami Rama practicing austerities on a bank of the Narmada River

Spiritual Dignity Is Also Vanity

◆

After I had renewed my resolve to follow the path of renunciation my master thought I was feeling guilty, so he told me to live on a bank of the Narmada River, which flows through central India, and to practice certain austerities there. He instructed me to go to an isolated, dense forest thirty miles south of Kherighat, near Omkareshwar. The river there was full of crocodiles, and in the mornings and evenings several of them would lie on the sand along the river. I lived on the riverbank for six months without anyone disturbing me. I had only a water pot, a blanket, and two loincloths. People from a village six miles distant supplied me with milk and whole-wheat bread once a day. Those six months of intense physical and mental austerities were a high period in my life.

One day a party of big-game hunters came by and saw me sitting in meditation on the sand in the midst of many crocodiles, some of whom were lying just a few yards away from me. The hunters took my photograph without my noticing and sent it to a newspaper. Soon stories about me appeared in many newspapers. At that time the Shankaracharya of Karvirpitham was searching for his successor. [Shankara established four institutions in different sections of India, and a fifth institution at a place where he spent his last days. The heads of these institutions are considered to be the spiritual heads of India and occupy positions analogous to that of the pope in the Christian tradition.] He instructed a few pandits to observe my daily routine from a distance. They stayed in the village at night and watched my activities during the day. They also collected information from others about my life. After observing me for some time and carefully investigating my background, they approached me and tried to persuade me to consider becoming Shankaracharya. At that time the Shankaracharya was Dr. Kurtkoti, a highly intellectual man and a Sanskrit scholar of high repute. He was a close friend of Tilak, an Indian leader and author of *Gita-Rahasya*. I was taken to Dr. Kurtkoti, and he took a liking to me. Then I went to my master and received his permission to accept the position. After a ceremony lasting eighteen days I was installed as a successor of Jagat Guru Shankaracharya. I received thousands of telegrams from well-wishers all over the world, including messages from the pope and other spiritual heads. It was a strange experience for me— such a startling contrast to my six months of solitude and silence. I was less than thirty years old and they gave me such a great responsibility.

Dr. Kurtkoti believed in socio-religious reformation, and handed over his files of valuable correspondence with other spiritual and political leaders. I had numerous meetings with various groups and leaders. I had a busy schedule of traveling and lecturing, and when I wasn't so engaged, people would come to see me from morning to evening and ask for my blessings. It became very difficult for me; I had no freedom. I thought, "I don't get any time to meditate and do my practices; I spend my whole day blessing people. This is not good."

I was not at all happy. My conscience said, "You are not meant for this. Leave!" So after two years I simply ran away,

Swami Rama as Shankaracharya of Karvirpitham, 1949–1951

without any money in my pocket. One day I had a large mansion to live in and many cars for one man to ride in—and the next I had nothing but the clothes I was wearing. Wanting to return to the Himalayas, I boarded the third-class section of a train which was headed where I wanted to go, even though I had no ticket. The people on the train must have wondered whose clothes I had stolen, because I was still wearing the costly garb of Shankaracharya. When the conductor came he forced me to get off at the next station because I had no money and I didn't want to reveal my identity. I had never before committed such a crime as traveling without a ticket. I just bowed my head and got down, saying humbly, "Thank you for not prosecuting me."

The admirers and followers of Shankaracharya did not at all appreciate my resigning the dignity and prestige of the position. They felt that I was forsaking my responsibilities—but I had not been happy, and I never returned to that place again.

When I came to my master he said, "You have seen how worldly temptations follow a swami; how the world wants to absorb a spiritual person. Now nothing will affect you, because you have experienced positions, institutions, and renunciation. People expect a lot from their spiritual leaders. Do what you can to uplift and enlighten the people—but never forget your path."

A Miserable Experiment

◆

A man who knew me used to cut lawns, collect the grass, and sell it for the cows and buffaloes to eat. This is how he earned his living. But he thought, "Swami Rama enjoys life without doing anything. Wherever he goes people bring flowers, spread carpets, and even give him a cottage to live in. People clean and cook for him and take care of all his needs. It must be very good to be a swami."

He said to his wife, "I propose to do an experiment. For six months I will pretend to be a swami." She complained, "But I need money. You have to look after the family." He replied, "Whatever money people give me I will turn over to you."

He saved a little money, bought the proper clothes, and pretended to be a swami. For the first three days nobody asked him if he was hungry. He felt insulted because he saw that many people were coming to me and putting fruit before me, although I was not eating it. (If people bring me anything, I pass it on. In this way, I am free from any obligation. They are expressing their love by giving it to me, and I am expressing my love by giving it to someone else.) After seven days he had lost a great deal of weight and had yet to make any money.

At night he would quietly visit his wife. She said, "What a foolish man you are. You were earning quite a lot of money, and now you are not earning anything. Why don't you at least go to Swamiji and ask him the secret of his success?"

So he came to me in the garb of a swami. I said, "Swamiji, please come forward." He said, "Sir, I want to ask you a question privately." So I asked the others present to please wait outside. He said, "I want to know the secret of your success." I said, "I am not aware that I am successful. In what way do you think I am successful?"

He said, "Without asking for money, you get money. This cottage is at your disposal. Drivers come for you. Many people come and sit with you. Why?" I replied, "You know, when I wanted such things, they never came to me. But the day I determined I didn't want them, I began getting them."

Remember this, as Swami Vivekananda says: "Fortune is like a flirt—she will run away from you when you want her, but if you are not interested in her, she will come chasing you."

Charms of the World

◆

Once there was an educated young man who decided that he would become a swami. He observed how swamis spoke and conducted themselves. On his own, without treading the path or following any disciplines, he set himself up as a swami with the proper attire and external behavior.

One day he came to my ashram at Uttarkashi in the Himalayas and requested if he could stay awhile. Whenever he spoke with me his gaze would always settle on my wristwatch. Someone had given me an Omega chronometer as a gift. I didn't care whether the watch was a simple watch or the expensive item that fascinated this young man. Each time we talked he would bring up the watch in conversation. He would say, "Oh, what a striking watch; how attractive the design; it must keep excellent time."

After three days of this I said, "Young man, I'm leaving for Gangotri for a while. Would you take care of this watch for me?" As I picked up my blanket and sandals and waved goodbye to my guest, I knew that before long my ashram would be empty of this man and my watch. I was not really intending to go to Gangotri; I just wanted to see what would happen. I returned shortly and, sure enough, the young man and the watch had departed. In the days that followed my acquaintances asked about my missing watch. I told them it was being used. I was not concerned.

By chance six months later I ran into this same young man at the Hardwar railway station. He was so embarrassed he wanted to run away. He said, "Sir, what I did was terrible." I replied, "You have done nothing to me; if you think it is wrong, don't do it again."

Then I noticed that he was not wearing the watch, so I asked him where it was and how it was running. He said, "I have sold it. I needed the money."

A short time later the watch was with me again. The buyer was my student, who recognized the watch and returned it to me. So I found the young man again and gave him the watch once more. I said, "If this watch can help you, then you should have it." At first he could not understand and accept the way I related to him, but gradually he came to see that it is possible to have a completely different attitude toward the things of the world than he had known. This incident affected him so much that he later went back to an ashram that I recommended for self-discipline, and today he is a completely transformed person.

Many people are unable to face certain things in themselves. They refuse to confront those conflicts, desires, and habits that they may not like in themselves but can't get rid of. They don't allow others to know their real selves, and continue to put forward defenses and pretenses. With someone, somewhere, in some relationship, we should completely expose ourselves and not keep these embarrassing seeds repressed inside. These hidden secrets only delay our progress. We project onto others the very things we won't face. During meditation one allows all these embarrassing thoughts and desires to come up gently, where one can just observe them without becoming

The temple at Gangotri

involved. In this way meditation serves as an effective tool to recover and live a balanced life.

Those who renounce their homes and duties still carry with them the deep-rooted *samskaras* [latent tendencies which derive from past experiences] sown in earlier lives. It takes a long time to get free of these samskaras. It requires the constant mental ingestion of creative impressions and seeds of spirituality. This cleansing and replacement of mental content is possible if one follows a path of self-discipline. Too many modern teachers profess to teach spirituality and meditation without discipline. They may introduce sound techniques—but without training the students to become disciplined, it is like sowing seeds in the soil that was never tilled. Self-discipline is very important in the path of spirituality. Becoming a swami or a monk is not so important. What is important is to accept a self-disciplined life. There needs to be a bridge between life within and without. Discipline is the foundation of that bridge. People should not be tempted by mere techniques, but learn to cultivate discipline within themselves.

Two Naked Renunciates

◆

On my way to Gangotri I stayed for a month at Uttarkashi, which is deep in the Himalayas. I used to go for my morning walk two or three miles toward Tekhala. Between Tekhala and my residence two completely naked sadhus lived in the two separate rooms of a small wooden house on a bank of the Ganges. They were illiterate widowers in their mid-sixties, and did not have any belongings, not even a pot of water. I knew these two, and they were famous—but not because of their learning and yogic wisdom. They became famous because of their outer appearance of living naked in such a cold climate. In reality they were full of ego, anger, and jealousy. They despised each other.

One sunny day as I was walking toward Tekhala I saw from a distance that they had both spread their straw in the sun to warm it. They did this once in a while to remove the moisture from it. When I approached their house I found that they were wrestling—two naked old sadhus wrestling fiercely. I intervened and said, "What is this?" They stood apart and one of them said, "He stepped on my straw! What he must think of him-self! He thinks that he's the greatest renunciate in the world!"

This experience was a setback in my life, and I started analyzing the path of renunciation. I realized that even after renouncing wealth, home, relatives, wife, and children, one cannot easily renounce the lust for name and fame, nor can one easily purify the ego and direct his emotions toward self-realization. Cultivation of a new mind is a necessary step for enlightenment. Mere renunciation brings unhappiness and frustration. Renunciation without being aware of the purpose of life creates problems for the renunciates and for the people of the world who look for examples from them. The people of the world think that renunciates are the best examples to be followed. But I have met many householders who are far superior to renunciates. The inner condition is more important than the external way of living.

In the World and Yet Above

◆

On the face of it, it may seem that some swamis in India are given whatever they need without doing any labor. But this is not so. Actually there is a public persecution of swamis going on all the time in India. People think that a swami is not a human being. Everyone expects him to live a superhuman life, and disturbs him. People come and say, "You have to speak at such and such a place," "You have to see me," "You have to heal this person," and so on. If a swami does not live according to their expectations, they will say, "What kind of a fake swami is he?" It is a common assumption in India that swamis don't need food or sleep, because they are supposed to have transcended these needs. Because he is a renunciate a swami should not feel hunger, should not have money, and if it is cold, he should not have a blanket. People have this notion, and we have to live according to it at the cost of sleep, food, and everything. Being a swami is not an easy job; there is indeed constant persecution, even if well-intended.

In India, wherever swamis go the people, out of sheer enthusiasm, come with drums and chant continually. Some days I would walk as many as twenty miles on foot and in the evening I would be very tired. It was the only chance I had to rest, and I would have to get up very early for meditation. But the people would come and chant for several hours, and if I asked them to go they would say, "No, sir, we want to chant for you." I needed sleep and they wanted to chant. So I learned to sleep while they chanted, with the drums and everything going on around me. When they closed their eyes in chanting, I closed my eyes in sleep.

You have heard of what is usually called sleepwalking, but there is another kind of sleepwalking of which you have not heard. I learned to sleep with regard to the things which were distracting me, and to walk only on my path. No matter what happened, I went on.

Decide that no matter what happens, you will do what you set out to do. If you are determined, possible distractions will still be there—but you will continue on your path and remain undisturbed. *Sankalpa* (determination) is very important. You cannot change your circumstances, the world, or your society to suit you. But if you have strength and determination you can go through this procession of life very successfully.

To Lose Is to Gain

$\blacklozenge$

There was once a swami who used to go and stay with his disciple. The disciple's whole family loved and revered the swami because he was an example of discipline and a very spiritual man. He always got up before sunrise, bathed, and sat for hours in meditation.

But one day, early in the morning while it was still dark, he shouted, "Hey, get me food!" His disciple said, "Sir, this is your bath time." The swami replied, "Just get me food. I am hungry!" He ate, and then he took a bath. After his bath he went to empty his bowels, and then he went to sleep.

He made everything topsy-turvy, and the whole house was upset. They said, "Something has happened to him; he's gone crazy." The wife said, "Our master is a wonderful man. We should help him." So they called for doctors and told them, "Don't disturb him by saying anything about medicine. Say, 'We want to learn from you.' Be courteous, please."

The doctors came and behaved like disciples because they were paid for that purpose. They said, "Gurudev, how are you?" But he wouldn't respond. They thought he was in a coma, because he was not moving. One looked at his eyes, and there was no movement. Another found that there was little pulse. One said to another, "I don't think he is going to live." A third doctor took out a stethoscope and found the heartbeat decreasing, so he reported, "He has a failing heart." The woman of the house started weeping because she had always looked on him as her spiritual father.

Finally I was asked to come. When I entered he sat up and I asked, "Swamiji, what is the matter?"

He said, "Nothing is the matter. Why do you ask?"

I told him, "Everybody's worried."

He said, "I used to meditate for two things. But today my parents died and I am in sorrow, so I am not meditating." His language was entirely mystical.

I said, "Your parents died? You are a swami. You have nothing to do with parents."

"No, no," he said. "You also have parents. When they die you will understand." He continued: "Attachment was my mother, and anger was my father. They both died, so I have nothing to do. Now I do not need to do anything."

Meditation will become your very nature when you give up attachment, anger, and pride. Then you will not have to pose for meditation, for your whole life will be a sort of meditation.

VII

Experiences on Various Paths

[This section of the book is primarily from Swamiji's diaries.]

KNOWLEDGE OF VARIOUS PATHS LEADS YOU TO form your own conviction. The more you know, the more you decide to learn. When you have sharpened the faculty of discrimination, you firmly tread your path without any doubts.

A Renowned Lady Sage

◆

W e two young aspirants, Nantin Baba and I, lived in the
Laria Kanta forests of Nanital when I was sixteen years
of age. At that time Anandamayi Ma, a well-known spiritual
leader of India, was going on a pilgrimage with her husband.
Although they traveled together they did not have the usual
husband/wife relationship, but had mutually developed an
understanding of the value of abstinence and had decided to
live as celibates. They were both in their forties and were
totally dedicated to the Lord. On this pilgrimage they were
accompanied by a large group of followers and were traveling
from Manasarowar to Kailas, which is near Mount Everest, the
highest of the Himalayan mountains. A pilgrimage to this site
is considered to be the greatest of all, and on the way the
people aspire to have a glance of the sages and to meet the
adepts.

Anandamayi Ma heard about us two young renunciates
and came to visit us on her way to Kailas. When she returned
from Kailas two months later she again passed through
Nanital, and at that time we met her again and attended her
group meetings in the evenings. She was a follower of this path

of love and devotion, and regularly offered discourses on the path to her large following.

There are many paths to enlightenment generally referred to in yoga, but actually there are six main paths, and *bhakti yoga,* the path of devotion, is one of them. This path of love is a path of self-surrender, and music is one of its devotional expressions. Bhakti yoga is based on self-sacrifice, reverence, and compassion. In this path humility, gentleness, purity, simplicity, and sincerity are important virtues. It is the path of the heart. This means that the followers direct the power of emotion toward God. Many on this path start flowing tears when they hear talk of God or when they assemble for chanting. Philosophically, the aspirant on this path does not want to merge his individuality in God, but prefers to have a separate identity and to be always in the service of the Lord. The philosophy of liberation, according to this path, is nearness to God. Liberation means attaining status in the celestial plane where one can constantly remain near to God. Many follow this path, but it is not as easy to follow as most people think. Bhakti yoga is not the path of blind followers.

Jñana yoga is a path of knowledge, and is called the yoga of the intellect. This study involves not merely the cognitive intellect, but rather that intellect which has been sharpened by listening attentively to the sayings of the great sages as they are taught by a competent teacher, and then contemplating on these sayings to finally attain a state of freedom. This path is like the razor's edge, and if one does not tread it with discipline he might become egotistical. Constant company of the sages and contemplation with the help of non-attachment are important requisites in this path.

Karma yoga is a path followed by those who believe in doing duties selflessly. These aspirants understand that all the fruits of one's actions should be surrendered to God, who dwells in everyone's heart. Selfless action performed skillfully liberates one from the bondage created by the fruits therein. Knowledge of karma yoga is essential to attaining liberation. By performing right actions which do not create bondage, and by attaining higher knowledge, one liberates one's self from the rounds of births and deaths.

Kundalini yoga is one of the aspects of yoga which is practiced by those who understand a great deal about the body, the nervous system, and the various channels of energy in the human body. The special disciplines that help the aspirant to control his bodily functions and internal states are essential. The primal force, which remains in the sleeping state at the base of the spinal column, is consciously awakened and led through the *sushumna* to the highest of the chakras, where the Shakti principle unites with the Shiva principle. [*Sushumna* is the most subtle channel on which the primal force travels. Without its application, that kundalini force cannot rise. Chakras are the wheels of life used for the subtle body. Shakti is the Divine Mother who manifests the universe. She is the universal power which can function only through that Mother force.]

Raja yoga is a path of systematic discipline which leads the student upward along the eight-runged ladder to a state called samadhi, or union with the absolute Reality. This is the most comprehensive path and is a highly systematic and evolved science in which karma, bhakti, kundalini, and jñana are combined. The philosophy of raja yoga is based on Sankhya philosophy.

Sri Vidya, in which the microcosm and macrocosm are thoroughly understood, is the highest of all the paths and is practiced by only very few accomplished ones. It is a practical path, but it requires strong philosophical understanding before it is trodden. Practice based on the mere information of books could be time-consuming as well as dangerous. A competent teacher is necessary in this spiritual practice, and the principles

Anandamayi Ma at Almora

of tantra and other philosophies need to be thoroughly under-stood before a student takes such a venture. This extremely rare path is followed only by the highly accomplished sages.

Nantin Baba and I attended a gathering of Anandamayi Ma's students, in which everyone was chanting in Bengali and Hindi. We enjoyed listening to the chants, but felt more like observers than part of the group. We were both more inclined toward meditation and were on the paths of raja yoga and jñana yoga, although we also appreciated the other paths. If a person follows one particular path it does not mean that he hates the other paths. Nonetheless one of Anandamayi Ma's students came up to us and tried to convince us that the path of devotion was the highest one and that we should switch to it.

He asked, "Why are you not participating in the chanting?" I told him, "The horse that pulls the buggy does not enjoy pulling it, but the person who is seated in the buggy enjoys the ride and benefits by witnessing and sitting quietly. The person who is performing the action does not enjoy it as much as the wise man who is witnessing it. Some people chant, and others enjoy chanting silently. We are enjoying more than anybody else. How do you know that we do not follow the path of devotion?"

In his ignorance this student was very adamant that his path was the only one. Our discussion soon led to an argu-ment, and Anandamayi Ma intervened by saying to her fol-lower, "Don't argue with these two young renunciates. One should try to understand one's own inner worth and then follow the path best suited to him. The path of devotion does not mean dumb devotion. Devotion means total dedication, surrender, and love for the Lord. It is the path of the heart, but it does not contradict that intellect or reason which solves many problems of life. Devotion is also part of the other paths. It is not possible for the jñana yogi to attain enlightenment if he does not also have devotion. Everyone wants to follow bhakti, the path of devotion, thinking that it is very easy and simple. But that's not true. The path of devotion means accepting the existence of the Lord instead of worshipping one's own existence. Those who weep, shiver, become emotional, or act in a funny way cannot be called the followers of bhakti yoga. Tranquility of mind should be cultivated; then all the paths can be understood—and not before that. Purification of the mind is necessary, and is achieved by disciplining one's mind, action, and speech. Argumentation is a state of learning and not a state of being."

I remember her remarkable discourse even today. I asked her, "Is it true that your path is superior to other paths and that only what you are doing is authentic? Do you think that others are wasting their time?"

She replied, "My path of devotion suits me, but do not change your paths. Those who do not have guidance become confused and often change their paths. A confused mind is not fit to follow any path. Seekers of truth should learn to search for competence and guidance by seeing certain signs and symptoms in the teacher, such as selflessness, truthfulness, sincerity, and control of mind, action, and speech.

"Students also commit mistakes when they become idealistic without observing their capacity or following any discipline. They see only what they want to see. This prevents them from learning, and then they get attached to the path which they think they are following. They become very fanatical and egotistical and even begin fighting with people. This can happen to any seeker if his inferiority complex goes on developing and creating boundaries, closing all the doors of knowledge and making him self-centered, uncommunicative, and egotistical."

Ma confirmed our ideas and strengthened those principles which we were following. She said, "Learning the scriptures is very good and helpful, but without *satsanga* such learning can also make anyone egotistical. A learned man having satsanga is very humble, communicative, and gentle in his behavior.

"Beginners often argue and boast about the superiority of their way, but one who has trodden the path knows that all paths lead to the same destination. There is no superior or inferior path. It is immaterial which path one follows, but one should carefully watch one's own modifications of mind and learn not to identify with them." As she stared at the eyes of her husband, which were like cups of wine full of devotion, we said goodbye to Anandamayi Ma, and I went to the quiet place where I often used to hide myself.

With My Heart on My Palms
and Tears in My Eyes

◆

In India Hindus, Christians, Muslims, Sikhs, Parsis, and Sufis have lived harmoniously for many centuries. India is a melting pot. Whoever visits India gets into this pot. This has been the history of Indian civilization. In the subcontinent of India people were peaceful, but the aliens who ruled India created hatred among the various religious groups because of their policy of divide and rule.

Sufis from all over the world go to India to pay homage to Indian Sufis. Even today India is the home of Sufism. Sufism is a religion of love and is not followed by Mohammedans exclusively. Among the several Sufi sages I have met, one of the greatest was a woman who lived in the city of Agra, 120 miles away from Delhi. This city is famous because of the Taj Mahal, a symbol of love and one of the wonders of the world.

Once I traveled from the Himalayas to visit this old woman sage, who lived completely naked in a small *dargah* [dwelling and worshipping place of a holy Moslem fakir]. She was ninety-three years of age and never slept at night. I used to call her Bibiji; this word is used for "mother." She would call me "my son" (Bete). During my stay at Agra I regularly visited this

Sufi woman sage between twelve and one in the morning. My visiting Bibiji at nights was misunderstood—so much that people started thinking I had lost my equilibrium. Several high army officials and learned people also used to visit her. Colonel J. S. Khaira was her great devotee. Although she was adored by Hindus and others equally, many people in the city did not understand this great Sufi mystic and her mysterious way of living. Her compassion toward her visitors was immense, but her attitude toward the mundane world was self-explanatory: "The people of the world have learned how to fill up earthen bowls with grains and coins, but no one knows how to fill the bowl of the heart."

One night Bibiji told me that it would be easy for me to meet God. I asked, "What is the way?" She said, "To be one with the Divine, one has simply to detach oneself from this mundane world and be linked with the Beloved. It is so simple. Offer your *rooh* [soul] to the Lord and then there is nothing to be done or realized anymore."

I said, "Bibiji, but how?" She started using a dialogue. I am narrating it exactly as she related it to me.

She said: "As I went to see my Beloved, He asked, 'Who is that standing at the entrance of my shrine?' I said, 'Thy lover, Lord.' The Lord said, 'What proof can you give?' I said, 'Here is my heart on my palms and tears in my eyes.'

"And the Lord said, 'I accept thy offering, for I also love thee. Thou art mine. Go and live in the dargah.' Since then, my son, I live here. I wait for Him day and night, and I will wait for Him till eternity."

I remembered the words of a great man, who said, "This poisonous tree of life has but two fruits: contemplation on immortality, and conversing with the sages."

Many times I would watch a very powerful light emanating from Bibiji's eyes. She impressed me deeply because of her superb divine ecstasy, her complete self-surrender, and her unfathomable love for God. She said, "The pearl of wisdom is already hidden within the shell in the ocean of the heart. Dive deep and one day you will find it."

One day she smilingly cast off her body. A light like that of a star was witnessed by twelve of us who were sitting around her. The light came out of her heart and sped toward the sky like lightning. She remains in my heart always. I remember my Bibiji with great love and reverence.

Karma Is the Maker

◆

I used to hear a lot about a sage called Uria Baba, who was very famous for his learning and spiritual wisdom. He lived in Vrindavan. My master sent me to live with this sage. A devotee of this baba who knew me well took me to Vrindavan. When I arrived there I found hundreds of people waiting to have *darshan* of this great man. The baba was informed by his devotee about my arrival. He very kindly instructed his devotee to take me to his room. This great man was very short in stature and about sixty-five years of age. He was considered to be one of the greatest learned scholars of North India. He had a large following all over the country. He was very kind and generous to me.

In the evenings we used to go on the banks of the Jamuna for evening ablutions. One evening I asked him, "Is renouncing the world superior to living in the world? Which is the right path?" During those days I had been studying the philosophy of karma. I knew that karma means cause and effect; I also knew that it is difficult to get freedom from these twin laws of karma.

The baba, in the course of conversation, told me, "It is not

213

necessary for all human beings to renounce the world, for the path of renunciation is very difficult to tread. Actually it is not necessary to renounce the objects of the world, because a human being does not actually own or possess anything. Therefore it is not necessary to renounce anything—but the sense of possessiveness should be renounced.

"Whether you live in the world or outside, it does not make much difference. Attachment to the objects of the world is the cause of misery. One who practices non-attachment faithfully and sincerely obtains freedom from the bondage of karma. In the path of action, duties are not renounced, but are performed skillfully and selflessly. The renunciate renounces the objects and goes far away from them, but he also performs his essential duties. Those who live in the world as householders also perform their essential duties. Those who become selfish by receiving and using the fruits of their actions create many encumbrances for themselves. It becomes difficult for them to get freedom from this self-created bondage. If all attachments and sense of ownership are not renounced, the path of renunciation becomes miserable. If the householders do not practice non-attachment and continue to strengthen selfishness and possessiveness, it also creates misery for them.

"To attain the purpose of life, it is necessary to do one's duties, whether one lives in the world or outside it. The path of renunciation and the path of action, though two diverse ways, are equally helpful for attaining self-emancipation. One is the path of sacrifice, the other the path of conquest."

Again the baba spoke: "The law of karma is applicable to all equally. Our past *samskaras* are deeply rooted in the unconscious. These latent samskaras, or impressions, create various bubbles of thoughts and express themselves through our speech and actions. It is possible for the aspirant to get freedom from these samskaras. These memories have a stronghold in the bed of our samskaras. Those who can burn these samskaras in the fire of non-attachment or knowledge are free from the bondage created by them. It is like a burnt rope, which loses its binding power though it still looks like a rope. When the latent impressions, though still in the unconscious, are burned by the fire of knowledge and lose the power of germination, they never grow. They are like roasted coffee beans. You can use them to brew a cup of coffee, but they have no power to grow. There are two varieties of diverse qualities of samskaras. One quality of samskara is helpful in the path of spirituality, and the other is an obstacle.

"Non-attachment is like a fire that burns the binding power of past samskaras. The benefits which are derived by the renunciate by renouncing the world are derived by the householder by the practice of non-attachment. The renunciate attains enlightenment outside the world, and the householder in the world.

"Non-attachment does not mean indifference or non-loving. Non-attachment and love are one and the same. Non-attachment gives freedom, but attachment brings bondage. Through non-attachment the householder remains aware of his purpose of life and does his duty selflessly. His actions become means for him. In renunciation, the renunciate remains aware of the purpose of his life constantly and attains enlightenment. Non-attachment and renunciation expand the consciousness. When an individual learns to expand his consciousness or unites with the universal consciousness, then he no longer remains within the bounds of his karma. One remains totally free.

"Such a great man has power to show the path of freedom to others. Whether he is in the world or outside, he can also heal the sickness arising from karmic debts. He can remain untouched and above, without being involved or reaping the fruits arising from others' karmic debts. A true master has control over himself and moves freely in the world. When a potter has completed making his pots, the wheel of the potter still rotates for some time, but is unable to manufacture pots. For a liberated soul the wheel of life remains in motion, but his karma does not create any bondage for him. His actions are called 'actionless actions.' When the student is competent to tread the path of enlightenment it becomes easy for a great man to guide him, and one day he also attains ultimate freedom."

I asked the baba to tell me about the great men and their abilities of healing others. He said, "There are three levels of healing: physical, mental, and spiritual. Man is a citizen of these three levels. One who has spiritual power can heal others on all levels, but if he tries to make healing his profession, his mind and will-force will again start running toward worldly grooves. A dissipated and worldly mind is not fit enough to heal anyone. The moment one becomes selfish, the mind changes its course and starts flowing downward to the lower grooves. Misuse of spiritual power weakens and distracts the very basis of that power, which is called *ichchha shakti*. The great men always say that all the powers belong to the Lord. They are only instruments.

"Every human being has potentials for healing. The healing energy is flowing without any interruption in every human heart. By the right use of the dynamic will, these channels of healing energy can be directed to the suffering part of the body and mind. The healing energy can nourish and strengthen the sufferer. The key to healing is selflessness, love, dynamic will, and undivided devotion to the Lord within."

After fifteen days' stay with the baba I came back with the conclusion that the art of living and being, whether in the world or outside it, lies in awareness toward the purpose of life and non-attachment.

In the Ashram of
Mahatma Gandhi

◆

I n the late 1930s and early '40s I had the opportunity to stay with Mahatma Gandhi in Vardha Ashram, where I met many gentle and loving souls. While I was there I observed Mahatma Gandhi serving a leper. The leper was a learned Sanskrit scholar who was frustrated and angry, but Mahatma Gandhi personally looked after him with great care and love. That was an example to all of us. The way in which he served the sick left a lasting impression on me.

My master told me to observe Mahatma Gandhi particularly when he walked, and when I did so I found that his walk was quite different from the walk of other sages. He walked as though he were separate from his body. He seemed to be pulling his body as the horse pulls the cart. He was a man who constantly prayed for others and who had no hatred for any religion, caste, creed, sex, or color. He had three teachers: Christ, Krishna, and Buddha.

A pioneer in the realm of *ahimsa*-consciousness [non-violence], Gandhi always experimented in expanding man's capacity to love. Such a man finds joy in all the storms and trials of life. Gandhi never protected himself, but rather always

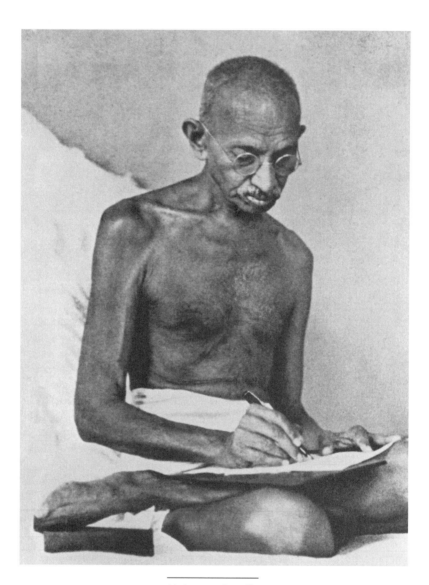

Mahatma Gandhi

protected his one principle of ahimsa, or love. The flame of love burned in him day and night like a fire which nothing could quench. Complete self-reliance and fearlessness were the foundation stones of Gandhi's philosophy. Violence touched the very depths of his being, but valiant in a spirit of ahimsa, he walked on alone. There was not a word of protest, and there was not a flicker of hostility in his life.

While staying with Gandhi, I noted these principles in my diary:

1. Non-violence and cowardice cannot go together, because non-violence is a perfect expression of love that casts out fear. To be brave because one is armed implies an element of fear. The power of ahimsa is an extremely vital and active force which does not come from physical strength.

2. A true follower of ahimsa does not believe in disappointment. He dwells above in perennial happiness and peace. That peace and joy do not come to him who is proud of his intellect or learning; they come to him who is full of faith and has an undivided and single-pointed mind.

3. The intellect can produce many wonders, but non-violence is a matter of the heart. It does not come through intellectual exercises.

4. Hatred is not overcome by hatred, but rather by love. This is an unalterable law.

5. Devotion is not mere worship with the lips. It is self-surrender with mind, action, and speech.

6. Gandhi did not believe in the barriers created by religions, cultures, superstitions, and mistrust. He taught and lived the brotherhood of all religions.

7. Gandhi believed in the art of living without concern for the fruits of one's actions. He practiced not worrying about success or failure, but paid attention to

the work at hand without feeling the slightest anxiety or fatigue.

8. In order to enjoy life one should not be selfishly attached to anything. Non-attachment means to have a pure motive and a correct means without any worry or desired result. He who gives up actions falls, but he who gives up the reward rises and is liberated.

9. Yoga is the complete re-integration of all the states of mind, the intellect, senses, emotions, instincts, and every level of personality. It is a process of becoming whole.

10. One's mantra becomes one's staff of life and carries one through every ordeal. Each repetition has a new meaning and carries one nearer and nearer to God. It is capable of transforming that which is negative in the personality into that which is positive, and it can gradually integrate divided and opposing thoughts at deeper and deeper levels of consciousness.

After meeting many wonderful and striking personalities—like Mahadev Desai, Mira Ben, and Prabhavati Bahen—I became friendly with Ram Dass, son of Mahatma Gandhi, and took him to Kausani, one of the fascinating and beautiful places of the Himalayas.

"Not Sacrifice but Conquest"—
Tagore

◆

When I was a teen-ager I often traveled with my brother disciple Dandi Swami Shivananda of Gangotri, who was about twenty years older than I. Once we went on a journey to Mussoorie, a holiday resort at the foot of the Himalayas. On the way we stopped at a small town called Rajpur. During those days Tagore, a famous poet of the East, was staying in a cottage there. My brother disciple was from Bengal and knew Tagore and his family well, so we went to visit him. We were invited to live in the same cottage with him for two months. Tagore became fond of me and asked my brother disciple to send me to Shantiniketan, the educational institution he had founded.

I strongly felt a desire to visit Shantiniketan and went there in 1940. Rathindranath Tagore, the son of Rabindranath Tagore, received me and arranged for me to stay in one of the cottages next to Sri Malikji, who was a devout and committed admirer of Tagore and his institute. Shantiniketan was then one of the most beautiful and fascinating ashrams of the world. Several hundred students lived and studied there.

Tagore was known as "Gurudeva" by the students of

Swami Rama at Tagore's ashram, Shantiniketan

Shantiniketan and as "Thakur" by the general public. He was a very gifted poet from Bengal, and one of the greatest poets of all times. In the realms of religion, philosophy, literature, music, painting, and education his many-sided, handsome, and towering personality was well-known to the world.

During the period I lived with Tagore I was able to observe his devotion to his work. He was always engaged in his daily practice or was busy writing or painting. He spent very few hours in sleep, and would not recline in the daytime. The infirmities of age did not change his habits. I looked upon him as an earnest *sadhaka* [spiritual seeker]. It is true that one object of all sadhakas of the world is to be somewhat godlike. It was not necessary for a godlike man like Tagore to imitate other god-men of India in order to express himself. His life was not like that of an ascetic's, which is as barren as a desert. Asceticism is the most ancient path of enlightenment, and genuine asceticism is indeed worthy of reverence. Equally worthy is the treading of the more difficult path of remaining in the world while doing one's duties. Tagore believed in living in the world without being of it.

A line from one of his poems, "Liberation by detachment from the world is not mine," is highly expressive of his philosophy. The key point of his life was not sacrifice but conquest.

Humanity has seen three kinds of great men: first, those who were gifted and great by birth; second, those who have attained greatness by sincere and selfless effort; and third, those unfortunate ones on whom greatness is thrust by the press and publicity. Tagore was in the first category—a gifted and highly talented poet and genius. He lived and practiced according to the sayings of the Upanishads: "All—whatsoever that moves in the universe—is indwelt by the Lord. Enjoy thou what hath been allotted by Him. Covet not the wealth of anyone."

I admired Tagore. He was the most universal, encompassing, and complete human being I have known. He was a living embodiment of the whole of humanity, who knew both man the knower and man the maker. He believed in allowing a person to grow by satisfying both the demands of society and the need for solitude. Sometimes I used to call him the Plato of the East.

His views about the East and West were highly admired by the people of both these cultures. Tagore did not want Westerners to become Easterners in their minds and outward behavior. He wanted the West to join hands with the East in the noble contest for the promotion of the highest ideas which are common to the whole world. According to him, the evolution of man is the evolution of the creative personality. Man alone has the courage of standing against the biological laws. Behind all great nations and noble works done in the world there have been noble ideas. An idea is that something which is the very basis of creativity. It is true that life is full of misfortunes, but fortunate is he who knows how to utilize the ideas which can make him creative. Time is the greatest of all filters, and ideas are the best of all wealth. Fortune is that rare opportunity which helps one to express his ideas and abilities at the proper time.

Tagore's philosophies surmounted all the obstacles which at first obscure the truth. According to him death has for ages been a source of fear and misery because people have not pondered over the truth. "O! Who suffer and fear the approach of death should hear and learn the music of Tagore, which teaches how to lose yourself in the infinite and the eternal. Just tune the chords of your being and make them move in harmony with the music of the cosmos. Every woman and man should strive to secure the light of truth, and live simply and wisely for the common good." The rhythm of music supported Tagore's philosophy of life. Music completed his personality, but this is not all. His words and melodies are still going on in the minds of poets and musicians today.

Tagore believed that all existences constitute the one

Rabindranath Tagore

organism of the entire cosmos, emitting love as the highest manifestation of its vital energy and having as its soul the center of the spiritual galaxy. The world so far talks only about the religion of God, but Tagore always talked of the religion of man. It is a religion of feeling through ecstatic experience, which represents opinion in its most intense and living stage, offering a far better solution to the ills of life than philosophy and metaphysics. Love of God is a sympathetic and synthetic response. The finite being is as much a requirement for God as God for the finite being. "The soul of the lotus goes on blossoming for ages in which I am bound, as though without escape. There is no end to the opening of its petals, and the honey in it has such sweetness that thou, like an enchanted being, canst never desert it; and therefore thou art bound, and I am, and salvation is nowhere."

After staying at Shantiniketan, I decided to leave for the Himalayas to assimilate the ideas I had acquired there, and then formulate certain guidelines for my future.

I still remember a few striking lines from Tagore's poems:

I read in the problem of life and the world,
The twist of tears and joy.

I see before myself the busy feet of the wind,
Suggesting humanity and law.
The wind hastens to the shadow whose passion lies;
Shall we go abroad and start anew, O wind,
To build again a better life and song?

Setting History Straight

◆

When I was about twenty years of age I traveled to Simla, one of the holiday resorts in the Punjab Himalayas. I met a swami there whom the people called Punjabi Maharaj. He was a very tall, healthy, handsome, and learned man. I had an umbrella in my hand, and he asked me, "Why do you carry such a burden? Be free!" As we were walking together it started to rain. Since I had the umbrella, I opened it. He said, "What are you doing?" I answered, "I am protecting us from the rain." He said, "Don't do that! This is a link between heaven and earth; why should we be deprived of that? Throw away your umbrella and other belongings if you want to walk with me."

I protested, "Swamiji, I will get wet." He told me, "If you are afraid of getting your clothes wet, either don't wear clothes and walk freely, or get out of the rain." What he said affected me. I left the umbrella right there on the path. Since then, when it rains and I am outside, I really enjoy it.

In the winter this swami would walk about wearing only a thin cotton garb; it was his only possession. He was a man with a very sensitive nature, but he had completely mastered his sensitivity to heat and cold. When the mind contacts the objects of the world through the senses, it experiences sensations of pain and pleasure. If you learn not to contact the objects of the world you will be free from external influences and find greater pleasure within.

This swami was very learned and spoke only English. For hours he would talk about English literature, and we would discuss Swami Rama Tirtha's life and works. He received his master of science degree from Oxford University and his doctorate of science from Lahore University. Though he lectured on the universality of Vedanta philosophy, he detested the alien rule in India. During this time, before India's independence, there was a small sect of modern swamis who did not practice meditation. They were young and learned, and understanding the condition of the country, they participated in the freedom movement. I called them "politician swamis." They would say, "External freedom first, internal freedom later on." This swami was a politician swami. Actually he had become a swami out of frustration, after seeing the condition of the country. He was kind and gentle, but he could be very rebellious. He did not follow the normal disciplines of a renunciate, but rather spent his whole time totally preoccupied with the thought of overthrowing British rule in India. This was his worship and aim of life. Sometimes he was arrested twice a day for insulting Britishers. He would annoy British officers by abruptly telling them to leave the country. He would call them names and say, "You are speaking English and you don't know grammar. You don't know your own language. What a tragedy that the imperial government sends such uneducated people who do not come from good families to India."

Once when we were walking in the hills outside Simla a British officer came galloping on his horse from the opposite direction. He stopped his horse suddenly when he saw us and yelled, "You monkeys, get out of the way!" He jerked the reins and fell off the horse onto the road.

The swami told him, "We have every right to walk on this road. This is my country. Mind your own business. Get up, get on your horse and go away. I'm not your slave." The next day the swami was arrested, but within two hours he was released. The governor of that state knew him from London and also knew that this swami would create more problems if he were in jail.

During this time I had some prejudice against the British rulers of India and thought of helping the freedom movement. The swami said, "Come on, let's use guns and one by one destroy these British administrators." He sincerely wanted me to join him and fight the British. He said that it was not a sin. "If someone comes to your house and tries to destroy your culture, why can't you defend yourself?" He was the most bitter swami I had ever met.

I believed in Mahatma Gandhi's philosophy, psychology, and movement, but I never took an active part in politics. I wanted to influence this swami to leave politics, and he wanted to influence me to enter politics. This went on for four months. He tried to persuade me, but my master said that I should not join any political party. My master said, "You are from the cosmos and a citizen of the world. Why identify with the people of India only? Your concern should be for the whole of humanity. First have inner strength, sharpen your intellect, learn to control your emotions, and then take action. Fanatic devotion to a country, even one as spiritually great as India, does not befit a man of God." My master told me not to become involved in violence, and even predicted the date of independence for India.

Later this Simla swami and I separated. We decided to tread our own paths. The same year he was shot by the British police in the Kulu Valley of the Himalayas.

During my stay in Simla I met a British missionary who was writing a book on Indian culture and philosophy. He allowed me to read the manuscript. I was shocked to read the numerous lies he had written about India, her culture, civilization, and philosophy. He even tried to convert me and tempt me to marry a rich British girl! Conversion to what? Lifestyle and cultural habits? I loved Christianity because of my love for Christ and the Bible, but this man created a repulsion in my mind. After that I avoided the Christian missionaries who roamed around the cities, villages, and mountains. These people were financed and supported by the British government and were politicians in the garb of missionaries. By writing such books they knowingly tried to damage the ancient Vedic civilization. They distorted the Vedic culture and philosophy, which is the mother of several religions, including Hinduism, Jainism, Buddhism, and Sikhism.

The swami in Simla used to oppose such missionaries and say, "You missionaries are not true followers of Christ and have no knowledge of the Bible." For 200 to 300 years these British missionaries tried to destroy the civilization of India. But they could not accomplish this for two main reasons: (1) the architects and custodians of Indian culture and civilization are the women, and (2) seventy-five percent of the people of India live in the villages and remain untouched by the influence of the British rulers and missionaries.

In spite of several hundred years of alien rule in India, they could not change Indian civilization. They were successful, though, in changing the language and dress and in introducing some British customs. The British government launched an extensive campaign by publishing such literature as the book written by the missionary. Indian writers and scholars were suppressed and even arrested and jailed if they refuted these books or wrote against the campaign. Such literature, published by the Britishers, created confusion and misguided Western scholars and travelers, thereby depriving them of studying the vast wealth of Indian literature, philosophy, and science.

Although Paul Deussen, Max Müller, Goethe, and other writers wrote books on yoga and the system of Indian philosophy in the Upanishads, confusion and misunderstanding still remain among the general Western public. Not a single book on yoga was written with honesty and sincerity by Western writers before Annie Besant (the famous theosophist, who became president of the Congress Party of India) and Sir John Woodroffe. He was the foremost of the Western writers on Indian philosophy. Though he could not write on as many scriptures as he desired, he introduced the philosophy of tantra to the Western world. I pity travelers and so-called writers who still persist in writing books on yoga, philosophy, tantra, and various spiritual subjects without studying, knowing, or practicing them.

A distorted history of India was intentionally introduced in the schools. Because of this, Indian students forgot their culture and history. To lose touch with one's tradition is to lose touch with one's self. Education in India was completely changed by the British. All the subjects were taught in the English medium, and every student was forced to pray according to the way of the British missionaries. There was no freedom of thought, so there could be no freedom of speech and action. If someone did not have an education of the kind imparted by the British, he could never get a good job. Through this I learned how power corrupts a nation and destroys its culture and civilization.

The surest way to destroy a country and its culture is by first changing its language. The British were successful because they did this. Even after thirty years of independence, English is still India's official language. Since India did not have one native language, there was and still is a lack of communication among the various states of India. Indian rajas had fought among themselves and could not make a united front. Thus,

India suffered for several hundred years. Unifying the language of India is one of the greatest tasks that the people and the government have yet to complete. A good, sound language produces good literature, which enriches the culture, education, and civilization. In India this is still lacking, and that is why countrymen from various parts of the land cannot communicate even today.

The present system of education and upbringing in India should be carefully adapted to the varied requirements of the Indian civilization. The construction of new types of schools, national literature, and art should be encouraged everywhere. We have still to think about the fundamental reconstruction of the whole order of Indian society through literature, science, art, and education. The passive method of thinking and living needs to be changed into positive and active dynamism. The most characteristic trait of education should be inseparable, connecting the various cultures and their collective civilization. Remember thou the words of the sages, who advised you to acquire and to utilize all that which was valuable in the development of human thought and culture in thy ancient history. Learn thou quickly to realize the necessity of giving truly international education to the rising generation of India.

The swami from Simla made me aware that before British rule India was very rich, not only in culture, civilization, and spirituality but also in jewels and gold. Many miseries were created by invaders like the Moguls (after they crossed the River Sindhu from the West of India) and later by the French, the Portuguese, and finally the British. They destroyed the financial, economic, cultural, and historical India, which was once called the Golden Bird. India's precious jewels, gold, and other riches were looted by these invaders and taken to their own countries. Once, people had abundance and there was much less disparity between the rich and poor. Then the caste system in India was structured according to distribution of labor—but it was completely changed by the Britishers, who created hatred with their policy of divide and rule. When I tell this, I have no hatred; it is the naked truth.

Many travelers even today do not know true Indian history. They repeat the same question again and again: "If India is spiritual, why is there so much poverty?" I am not a politician, but many people ask me why India is so poor. So I say that spirituality and economy could not compromise in any of the histories of the world. They are two entirely different things. Religion and politics always remained separate in India, and spiritual people never became involved in politics. These two diverse forces in India could not unite; therefore power decreased. The poverty in India is not because of spirituality, but because of not practicing spirituality and not knowing the technique of integrating spirituality with external life. Those leading the country now should become aware of this fact. India suffers because the leaders and people of the country today still do not have a unified vision for uplifting the country as a whole. They do not have an answer to the population problem, nor does there seem to be any immediate solution. I think India is surviving only because of her rich spiritual and cultural heritage.

Culture and civilization are two inseparable aspects of the lifestyle of a community, country, or nation. A man may be considered cultured if he dresses nicely and then presents himself before others—but this does not necessarily make him a civilized person. Civilization refers to the way a nation thinks and feels; to its development of ideals such as non-killing, compassion, sincerity, and faithfulness. Culture is an external way of life. Culture is a flower, while civilization is like the fragrance of the flower. A man may be poor and yet be a civilized person. A cultured man, without civilization, who may be successful in the external world is not helpful for society, because he lacks the inner qualities and virtues which enrich the growth of the individual and the nation. Culture is external, civilization is internal. In the modern world the integration of these two is necessary. Indian civilization is very rich, but its culture has become a pseudo-English culture which still creates problems in India today.

Maharshi Raman

◆

Dr. T. N. Dutta, a prominent physician from Gajipur, U.P.,
wrote to me that he was coming to see me at Nasik,
where I was living. After visiting, he told me his reason for
coming. He said he was very anxious to take me with him to
Arunachala in South India to have *darshan* of Maharshi
Raman. In the winter of 1949 we left for Arunachala. My stay
at this ashram was brief, but very pleasant. During those days
Maharshi Raman was observing silence. There were several
foreign students staying in the ashram. Shastriji, one of his
prominent disciples, would give discourses and Maharshi
Raman would sit quietly.

There was one thing that I found in his presence which was
very rare and which I seldom found elsewhere. For those whose
hearts were open to that voice of silence which was perennially
radiating in the ashram, just sitting near him was enough to
answer any question arising from within. It is true that to be in
the presence of a great man is the same as experiencing
savikalpa samadhi ["samadhi with a form"]. Maharshi Raman
did not have a physical guru. "He is the greatest and holiest
man born on the soil of India within a hundred years' period,"

said Dr. Radhakrishnan. A glance of such a great man purifies the way of the soul.

According to Maharshi Raman, contemplating on the single query "Who am I?" can lead the aspirant to the state of self-realization. Though this method of contemplation is the foundation stone of the philosophies of both the East and the West, it was revived again by Maharshi Raman. The entire Vedanta philosophy was brought into practice by the Maharshi. "He put the Iliad in a nutshell": By knowing oneself, one knows the self of all. The very simple, profound method of self-inquiry is accepted by both Easterners and Westerners.

After five days' stay in the spiritually vibrant atmosphere of Arunachala we came back to Nasik. After visiting this great sage I decided to resign the dignity and prestige of Shankaracharya. For a renunciate like myself, leading such a busy life had become burdensome and boring. My visit to Arunachala and the *darshan* of the Maharshi only added fuel to that fire which was already burning within me. "Renounce thee, and you will attain": this echoed in my heart so powerfully that my stay at Nasik became more and more impossible. It was not easy for me to run away, abruptly leaving all the responsibilities—but one day the courage came to me, and I left Nasik for my Himalayan home.

I have a firm conviction that no one can be enlightened by anyone else—but sages inspire and give inner strength, without which self-enlightenment is impossible. In today's world human beings do not have any example to follow. There is no one to inspire them, and that is why enlightenment seems to be so difficult. Great sages are the source of inspiration and enlightenment.

Maharshi Raman

Yogi Sri Aurobindo

Meeting with Sri Aurobindo

◆

I t was unbearable for me to stay in the demanding environment of Nasik, and I thought of visiting Pondicherry and meeting the Mother and Sri Aurobindo. The students of this ashram were very devoted and firm in the conviction that the way of life they led was supreme. The day I arrived at Pondicherry there was a concert given by a famous musician who was a disciple of Sri Aurobindo. The Mother was kind enough to arrange for me to stay in one of the quarters and to hear the devotional songs sung by that great devotee. My stay in Pondicherry for twenty-one days gave me enough time to strengthen the aspirations which I had received at the ashram of Maharshi Raman in Arunachala. During those days of my inner turmoil I was very restless; on one side I was being pulled by renunciation, and on the other side by the call of duty which had been assigned to me. While at Pondicherry I met Sri Aurobindo several times and he was kind enough to talk to me. His personality was very overpowering and inspiring. I started respecting his modern and intellectual approach of Integral Yoga. I want to give you the gist of what I understood this philosophy to be.

Sri Aurobindo's philosophy is described as integral non-dualism. This is an approach which seeks to understand reality in its fundamental oneness. The differences which we observe are looked upon as developments taking place within the framework of the all-inclusive unity of the Absolute. Integral non-dualism erases the distinctions of ethics, religion, logic, and metaphysics. Sri Aurobindo's conviction is that absolute reality in its essence is non-dual, non-conceptual, and logically indefinable. It is only accessible to direct experience through the penetrative insight of pure spiritual intuition. According to non-dualism *(advaita),* reality is beyond materialism, causation, structure, and number. This same conviction is expressed in the philosophy of *Nirguna Brahman* in Vedanta, in the concept of *Shunyata* in Buddhist philosophy, in the concept of *Tao* in Chinese philosophy, and in the philosophy of *Tattvatita* in tantra.

The philosophy of tantra consistently maintains that one can advance spiritually by awakening the latent primal force called the kundalini. When this spiritual potential is systematically channeled along higher levels, living becomes effortless, spontaneous, and attuned to the ultimate goal of existence. Vaishnavism recommends the method of love and devotion through wholehearted self-surrender to God. Christian mysticism and Sufism have a close resemblance to Vaishnavism in this respect: "Let Thy will, not mine, be done" is their secret of spiritual growth. Vedanta, by contrast, lays stress upon the method of contemplation and self-inquiry. It includes discrimination between the self and the not-self and then the renunciation of emotional attachments to the not-self. As soon as false identifications with the not-self are removed, the indwelling light of truth is revealed.

According to Aurobindo's integral philosophy, both the lower nature and the higher nature of man and the universe spring from the same ultimate reality. The lower nature is the physical force in the world and the source of instinctual drives in the unconscious mind. Man's higher nature is composed of pure consciousness and spiritual aspirations. It evolves out of the matrix of the lower nature through the awareness of the ultimate creative force, called Shakti. Aurobindo calls this force Divine Mother. Man has to faithfully be aware of this force in order to attain the realization of the Absolute. This awareness implies a tranquil integration of the material and the spiritual. According to Aurobindo, "The supra-physical can only be really mastered in its fullness when we keep our feet firmly on the physical."

This awareness is developed through two methods. The first is the integration of meditation with action. Through meditation one tears the veil of ignorance; he thus realizes his true self, which is the very self of all. Through selfless and loving actions one relates creatively with others. The second method of awareness of the Divine lies in the knowledge of the ascending and descending forces of consciousness. These powerful movements gradually expand the spiritual outlook and help one to rise to higher levels of consciousness. The descending movement brings down the light and power of higher consciousness into all strata of our material existence. This consists of transforming the physical into effective channels of expression for universal love and all-unifying truth.

Integral non-dualism sees evolution as the progressive self-manifestation of the universal spirit in material conditions. The whole universe is an expression, or play, of the Divine. Man's highest destiny is to be fully aware of the universal spirit and thus advance the cause of evolution. Therefore the essence of Integral Yoga lies in the active and effective awareness of the individual with the superconscious Divine.

Sri Aurobindo synthesizes the ancient philosophy of *advaita* in the belief that it is not necessary for modern man to realize the goal of non-dualistic asceticism through renunciation.

Meditation in action with non-attachment also prepares the *sadhaka* for awakening the primal force: kundalini. By the realization of the union of Shakti and Shiva humanity can be elevated to a higher awareness.

I was fully convinced that Sri Aurobindo's philosophy would have wide recognition by the modern minds of India and especially of the West. But I was accustomed to quiet and solitude and could not adjust to the numerous activities of the ashram like dramas, concerts, and tennis. I returned to Nasik and determined to leave for the Himalayas.

The Wave of Bliss

◆

I once visited Chitrakot, one of the holy places where, according to the epic *Ramayana*, Lord Rama lived during his exile. This place is situated on the Vindhya Range, one of the longest mountain ranges in India. According to ancient tradition *Vairagi* sadhus visit Vrindavan and Chitrakot—Vrindavan for those who love Krishna, and Chitrakot for those who love Rama. In another part of the Vindhya Range, in a holy place called Vindhyachal, there lived many Shakti worshippers. Traveling toward the forests of Rewa State, I went to the Satana forest and there met a swami who was very handsome and highly educated in the Vedantic and yoga tradition. He knew the scriptures and was a very brilliant *sadhaka* [spiritual practitioner]. He was later nominated as Shankaracharya of Jyotirmayapitham, which is in the Himalayas on the way to Badrinath. His name was Brahmananda Sarasvati.

He used to live only on germinated gram seeds mixed with a little bit of salt. He lived on a hillock in a small natural cave near a mountain pool. I was led by the villagers to that place, but I did not find anyone there and became disappointed. The next day I went again, and found a few footprints on the edge

Sri Swami Brahmananda Sarasvati

of the pool made by his wooden sandals. I tried, but I could not track the footprints. Finally on the fifth day of effort, early in the morning before sunrise, I went back to the pool and found him taking a bath. I greeted him saying, "Namo Narayan," which is a commonly used salutation among swamis, meaning "I bow to the divinity in you." He was observing silence, so he motioned for me to follow him to his small cave, and I did so gladly. This was the eighth day of his silence, and after staying the night with him he broke his silence and I gently spoke to him about the purpose of my visit. I wanted to know how he was living and the ways and methods of his spiritual practices.

During our conversation he started talking to me about Sri Vidya, the highest of paths, followed only by accomplished Sanskrit scholars of India. It is a path which joins raja yoga, kundalini yoga, bhakti yoga, and advaita Vedanta. There are two books recommended by the teachers of this path: *The Wave of Bliss* and *The Wave of Beauty;* the compilation of the two books is called *Saundaryalahari* in Sanskrit. There is another part of this literature, called *Prayoga Shastra,* which is in manuscript form and found only in the Mysore and Baroda libraries. No scholar can understand these spiritual yoga poems without the help of a competent teacher who himself practices these teachings.

Later on I found that Sri Vidya and Madhu Vidya are spiritual practices known to a very few—only ten to twelve people in all of India. I became interested in knowing this science, and whatever little I have today is because of it. In this science the body is seen as a temple and the inner dweller, Atman, as God. A human being is like a miniature universe, and by understanding this, one can understand the whole of the universe and ultimately realize the absolute One. Finally, after studying many scriptures and learning various paths, my master helped me in choosing to practice the way of Sri Vidya. In this path the kundalini fire is seen as the Mother Divine, and through yoga practices it is awakened from its primal state and raised to the highest of the chakras. The chakras are wheels of life which form our spiritual body and connect the entire flow of consciousness.

The science of chakra is very terse, but if one knows this science well it serves him on all levels. The chakras operate on the physical, physiological, energetic, mental, and spiritual levels. These energy centers correspond in the physical body to points along the spinal cord. The lowest is located at the coccyx, the second in the sacral area, the third at the navel, the fourth at the heart, the fifth at the base of the throat, the sixth at the point between the eyebrows, and the seventh at the crown of the head. The lowest chakras are the grooves toward which the lower mind rushes. The heart *(anahata)* chakra separates the upper hemisphere from the lower hemisphere and is accepted as the center of divine tranquility. Buddhism, Hinduism, Christianity, and Judaism also recognize this center: that which is called anahata chakra in Hinduism is called the Star of David in Judaism and the Sacred Heart in Christianity. The higher chakras are the centers of upward-traveling energy. There are many levels of consciousness from the heart chakra to the thousand-petaled lotus inside the crown of the head. When one sits erectly for meditation these centers are aligned. Energy can be focused on one chakra or another. Developing the capacity to direct the flow of energy to the higher chakras is one aspect of spiritual development. Knowledge of pranic vehicles is important if one wants to experience all the chakras systematically.

There is a bulk of literature on the chakras in Hinduism and Buddhism, which was later explained and introduced by theosophical writers for Western readers. Western writers have also written many books on the subject of chakras, although most of them (with the exception of those written by Sir John

Woodroffe) are misleading, for they consist merely of second-hand information, without anything to guide one's practice. Such misleading literature on such a highly perfected science is found all over—even in healthfood stores. How ridiculous!

Swami Brahmananda was one of the rare *siddhas* [accomplished ones] who had the knowledge of Sri Vidya. His authoritative knowledge of the Upanishads, and especially of Shankara's commentaries, was superb. He was also a very good speaker. Swami Karpatri, a renowned scholar, was the disciple who requested him to accept the prestige and dignity of Shankaracharya in the North, a seat which had been vacant for 300 years. Whenever he traveled from one city to another, people flocked in the thousands to hear him, and after his nomination as Shankaracharya his followers increased. One thing very attractive about his way of teaching was his combination of the bhakti and advaita systems. During my brief stay with him he also talked about Madhusudana's commentary on the *Bhagavad Gita*.

Swami Brahmananda had a Sri Yantra made out of rubies, and as he showed it to me, he explained the way he worshipped it. It is interesting to note how the great sages direct all their spiritual, mental, and physical resources toward their ultimate goal. Among all the swamis of India I met only a few who radiated such brilliance and yet lived in the public, remaining unaffected by worldly temptations and distractions. I stayed with him for only a week and then left for Uttarkashi.

Three Schools of Tantra

◆

I was asked by my master to go learn from a great tantric teacher who lived in the Malabar Hills of South India. The teacher was 102 years old. He was calm, learned, and healthy. Though he lived a householder's life, he taught many advanced yogis and swamis the philosophy of tantra.

There is a vast amount of literature on the philosophy and science of tantra, but it is not easily understood and is often misused. This highly advanced esoteric science has been practiced by Hindus, Jains, and Buddhists. The Khudabaksha library of Patna, the Baroda library, and the Madras library are filled with manuscripts on the subject, but this literature is beyond the understanding of laymen. Also, competent teachers of tantra are rarely available. However, properly practiced under a competent teacher, this path is the equal of any other spiritual path in self-enlightenment.

According to the science of tantra, male and female are two principles of the universe called Shiva and Shakti. These two principles exist within each individual. There are three main schools of tantra: Kaula, Mishra, and Samaya. The Kaulas, or left-hand tantrists, worship Shakti, and their way of worship involves external rituals, including sexual practices. They meditate on the latent power within (kundalini) and awaken it at the *muladhara* chakra, which is situated at the base of the spinal column. Laymen often misuse this path. In the Mishra (mixed or combined) school, inner worship is combined with external practices. The latent force is awakened and led to the *anahata* chakra (heart center), where it is worshipped. The purest and highest path of tantra is called Samaya or the right-hand path. It is purely yoga; it has nothing to do with any ritual or any form of worship involving sex. Meditation is the key, but this sort of meditation is quite uncommon. In this school meditation is done on the thousand-petaled lotus, the highest of all. This method of worship is called *antaryaga*. The knowledge of Sri Chakra is revealed in this school. Knowledge of the chakras, *nadis* (subtle nerve currents), and *pranas* (vital forces) and a philosophical knowledge of life are required in order to be accepted as a disciple in this school.

I was acquainted with all three schools, but was initiated in the path of Samaya. My favorite books explaining this science are *The Wave of Bliss (Anandalahari)* and *The Wave of Beauty (Saundaryalahari)*. I stayed with this teacher for one month, learning the practical aspects of this science and studying various commentaries on these two scriptures. Then I returned to the mountains.

The mystic philosopher, Professor Ranade

The Seven Systems
of Eastern Philosophy

◆

I often visited Dr. Ranade of Allahabad University, one of the finest exponents of Vedanta philosophy of his time. This matchless teacher and great mystic was popularly known as Gurudeva among his disciples. He took me to his Nembal ashram later on. Among all the university scholars of India I have the most respect for this great man. Whatever I have systematically learned about Indian philosophy was because of him. He taught me that Indian philosophy is divided into seven systems, which attempt to answer the most basic philosophical inquiries. These important questions are:

1. Who am I? From where have I come and why have I come? What is my relationship with the manifold universe and other human beings?

2. What is the essential nature of my being, and what is the essential nature of the manifested world, and its cause?

3. What is the relationship of the center of consciousness and the objects of the world?

4. What is the nature of the forms and names of the objects of the world, and how do they serve the essential nature of man or universal consciousness?

5. What are the guidelines for action as long as we live in the natural body? Do we live after death?

6. What is truth, and how do we arrive at rational conclusions on questions of truth?

The seven systems of Indian philosophy which address themselves to these issues are Vedanta, Yoga, Sankhya, Vaisheshika, Mimamsa, Nyaya, and Buddhism. The dates given for the teachers of the systems below have been determined by Western scholars. Scholars within these systems regard them as many millennia older.

VEDANTA: I am self-existent consciousness and bliss—these are not my attributes but my very being. I do not come from anywhere or go anywhere, but rather I assume many forms having many names. My essential nature is free from all qualifications and limitations. I am like an ocean, and all the creatures are like the waves. The individual soul is essentially Brahman, all-inclusive, all-expansive. The genderless Aum is its name; it is the nucleus—and the universe is its expansion. It is the absolute, transcendent, attributeless Reality, and it also eternally embodies the capacity to bring to measure within itself its own inner shakti. So this power of Brahman, called maya, emanates and gives the appearance of becoming manifold—but in truth there is no manifoldness, and the infinite never becomes finite. There is a superimposition of the finite on the infinite, which is eradicated by unveiling Reality again. Then one realizes himself to be in Brahman as Brahman. He identifies himself with Brahman and becomes one with it. Below are some of the most important statements of the Vedanta philosophy as found in the Upanishads.

1. There is nothing manifold here. From death to death he wanders who sees anything here as though it were manifold.

2. He who is tranquil dwells in Brahman, from whom the universe emanates and into whom it dissolves.

3. All this is Brahman.
4. Brahman is pure gnosis.
5. This self is Brahman.
6. That thou art.
7. I am that.
8. I am Brahman.

The philosophy which was taught by the seers of the Vedas (2000 to 500 B.C.) was passed down through a long line of sages (such as Vyasa, Gaudapada, and Govindapada, the author of many ancient scriptures), who codified these ancient philosophies. Shankaracharya finally systematized the monistic schools in the eighth century A.D., and many *acharyas* after him established various schools of non-dualistic and dualistic philosophies which differed from him.

YOGA: In the Yoga system of philosophy, the individual soul is a seeker, and cosmic consciousness is the ultimate reality it finds within. Yoga accommodates all religions and all systems of philosophy as far as the practical aspects are concerned. While dwelling in the manifold phenomenon of the universe, the soul must take care of the material body, purifying and strengthening its capacity. In this system the individual must practice the highest principle of behavior and the control of the various modifications of mind through the commitments called yama and niyama. By practicing stillness in posture and breath, one then transforms oneself by having control over the senses with concentration and meditation and finally attains samadhi. The final goal of this system is to attain *kaivalya* ["aloneness"]. This yoga system was also known several millennia before Patanjali, who codified it in the first century A.D. by compiling 196 aphorisms, called the *Yoga Sutras*. The Yoga and Sankhya systems of philosophy are alike.

SANKHYA: The Sankhya system is dualistic and believes the conscious *Purusha* and the unconscious *Prakriti* to be separate, co-existent and interdependent realities. In Sankhya the conscious principle is again twofold: it consists of the individual soul *(jiva)* and the universal soul or God *(Ishvara)*. (In other systems of Sankhya philosophy, the existence of God is irrelevant.) All the schools of the Sankhya system believe in removing the pains and miseries which arise from Purusha's involvement with Prakriti, forgetting its ever-pure, ever-wise, and ever-free nature.

Like a rope with three strands, Prakriti has three attributes, called *sattva, rajas,* and *tamas* [tranquility, activity, and sloth]. All phenomena of the universe, including mental operations, are nothing but interactions among these three *gunas* (qualities) of Prakriti. These bring to manifestation various aspects which remain in unmanifested form in the cause. When the three gunas are in balance, Prakriti is in a state of equilibrium. The mental and physical universe is created and passes through twenty-four, thirty-six, or sixty states that include all phenomena and experiences.

All the schools of Indian philosophy have included something from Sankhya philosophy in their systems. This system is the very basis of Indian psychology. It gave birth to the positive science of mathematics and then to the medical system of India, for to understand the body is to understand all human nature. The founder of the Sankhya school was Asuri, and Kapila, one of the most ancient seers, is called the *acharya* of this science. Then followed Ishvara Krishna, who systematized the philosophy into the *Sankhya Karika* around the third century A.D.

VAISHESHIKA: This philosophy deals with the physics and chemistry of the body and the universe. Discussing the particular elements, their atoms, and their mutual interactions, Kanada, perhaps 300 B.C., states the subject of his philosophy to be dharma, the code of conduct which leads human beings to prosperity in this life and the highest good in the next. This philosophy discusses nine subjects—earth, water, fire, air, space, time, dimension, mind, and soul—and their mutual relationships. This philosophy was developed by Prashas-tapada in the fourth century A.D.

MIMAMSA: The Mimamsa system was founded by Jaimini. In this system the Vedas are accepted as self-evident scriptures revealing internal knowledge. This system believes in salvation through action. It established a detailed philosophy of the efficacy of ritual, worship, and ethical conduct, which developed into the philosophy of karma. This school challenges the predominance of grammarians and logicians who maintain linguistics and rhetoric. It is a school of philosophy in action. Jaimini's date was perhaps c. 400 B.C.

NYAYA: Nyaya is the school of logicians founded by Gautama, one of the ancient sages. It regards doubt as a prerequisite for philosophical inquiry, and elaborates rules for debate. All the schools of Indian philosophy to this day follow the Nyaya system of logic, which was further developed in the sixteenth century and which is now called neologic, a complex system similar to the mathematical logic of the West today.

BUDDHISM: Gautama the Buddha was born 2,600 years ago in Kapilavastu at the site of the ancient ashram of the sage Kapila, who is one of the founders of the Sankhya philosophy. Gautama studied this philosophy in depth under a teacher named Adara Kalama, and he later discovered the four noble truths:

1. There exists sorrow.
2. There is a cause of sorrow.
3. The sorrow can be eradicated.
4. There are means for the eradication of sorrow.

These four noble truths are already found in the *Yoga Sutras* of Patanjali, but the difference lies in Buddha's doctrine of *anatta*, or non-self. The word *neti* ("not this") was fully understood by the ancient *rishis* (Vedic seers). The Buddha refused to participate in metaphysical speculation. He would not discuss the existence of God, and he would not answer the question of whether the Buddhas exist after nirvana. He said that such questions were not worthy of consideration. The Enlightened One, a highly practical teacher, wanted his disciples to practice the eightfold right path of action that would lead them to *bodhi,* the finest level of consciousness. He accepted Pali as a language for communication.

After Buddha's *para-nirvana,* various groups of monks started following their own way. There then formed two major schools: Theravada, the doctrine of the elders, and Mahayana, the formal philosophical school of Buddhism which disappeared in India. Great volumes have been written on the major historical and doctrinal differences between the two paths. Theravadins considered the teachings of Buddha to be completely separate from the rest of the Indian philosophical developments. They retained Pali as their medium to study the scriptures, although not a great deal of philosophical speculation developed in Pali. The Buddha remains their enlightened teacher, and great temples having beautiful statues were built to honor him, where ancient Hindu-style *puja* (worship) is still offered. This doctrine does not accept Buddha as a savior, however. Each person finds his own light, is then enlightened, and finally reaches anatta or non-self.

The Mahayana debated with other schools of Indian philosophy and was forced to adopt the sophistication of the Sanskrit language. One of the greatest scholars, Nagarjuna, describes *shunya* and calls it the void. The storehouse of consciousness, *alaya-vijñana,* of the *vijñana-vadin* school is cosmic consciousness. Hindus had begun to accept the Buddha as the ninth incarnation of God, but the Buddhists were at a loss to fulfill the spiritual call and the human need for devotion to a higher being. So there developed the thought of a higher reality that incarnates. Here the Buddha has three bodies or levels of existence:

1. *Dharma-kaya*—the absolute being (like *Shukla Brahman* of the Upanishads).
2. *Sambhoga-kaya*—the universe as the emanation (like *Shabala Brahman* of the Upanishads and *Ishvara* or personal God).
3. *Nirmana-kaya*—the historical body of the Buddha, an avatar or incarnation.

The Mahayana school still uses kundalini and knowledge of chakra in their teachings. Visualizations of symbolic figures and elaborate ritualistic preparations are used exactly as Hindus do. Faith and the surrender to a higher compassionate being are practiced exactly as they were taught in Hindu scriptures. The Buddha's own path was *majjhima patipada,* the middle way. The Buddha's teachings were primarily for the monks, but like other ancient teachings Buddhism became a way of life for a large section of people in the world. By following this middle path one can eradicate *avidya* (ignorance), which leads to *tanha* (craving). Only then can one gain freedom from sorrow, pain, and misery.

These seven systems deal with various aspects of reality and truth. They hold a higher transcendental goal as sacred and agree on some basic essentials. For this reason the syncretic literature of India such as the *Puranas* and epics like the *Mahabharata* and *Ramayana* regard all these systems as authentic.

Soma

◆

I read a book written by a mountain scholar who did research on soma, the famous herb used by the Himalayan medicine men in their worship and rituals. A portion of the Vedas talks about this herb, how it is used, the way it is prepared, and where it grows. That book created a curiosity in my mind, and I contacted the writer. The writer introduced me to Vaidya Bhairavdutt, a famous herbologist of the Himalayan mountains, who was considered to be the only living authority on soma. He is no longer living, but his center and laboratory continue to supply herbs to various parts of the country. He was well-versed in the scriptures too. This herbalist promised to bring the herb and also tell me how to use it. He said that it is a creeper which grows above 11,000 feet. There are only two or three places where it grows at that altitude. I gave him one thousand rupees for his traveling expenses, and after the winter was over he brought me somewhat less than a pound of that creeper.

He then prepared the soma, and we experimented with it on those sadhus who use marijuana and hashish. The use of this herb created a fearlessness in them. The descriptions of their experiences were somewhat similar to those of Westerners who had ingested psychedelic mushrooms. The herbologist explained to me that there are several varieties of mushrooms which have similar effects. However, he said that the soma creeper was definitely not from the mushroom family, but that it was from the succulent family. In an ancient Ayurvedic text varieties of mushrooms are described, with details of their color, size, and the way they are used. The text indicates that the ancients also used these for psychic experiences, although the books on cacti and succulents do not use the name "soma" for this creeper. Other succulents do not produce the same effect. There are a few herbs—such as Agaricus, Hyoscyamus, and Stramonium—which are poisonous, but in small doses have hallucinogenic properties. It is important to know the proper quantity in using these herbs.

The ancients wrote so much about soma and mercury preparations that some scriptures describe hundreds of ways of preparing such intoxicants for human usage. Such external stimuli, however, are not permitted to be used in any of the schools of yoga. There are inferior sects of sadhus who use some of these herbs without knowing their proper usage. These sadhus are often found dumb, sitting here and there. The ancient medicine men knew how and when to use such herbs. Homeopaths recommend a single dose of Arsenicum 10M to a dying patient for fearlessness, and hemlock poison was used by Egyptians and Greeks on the deathbed so that the dying person would feel no pain and could accept death pleasantly. Similarly, the use of soma was especially recommended by the mountain herbalists of India to turn the mind inwards, and they included this herb in rituals which became part of the religious cere-monies of the ancient Aryans.

Patanjali, the codifier of yoga science, says in the first *sutra* of the fourth chapter of the *Yoga Sutras* that *ausadhi*— medicine prepared from herbs—can help one in having psychic experiences. These psychic experiences have some validity and are higher than the experiences we receive through the senses, but they are definitely of no use as far as spirituality is concerned. The *soma-rasa* [soma juice] mentioned in the ancient literature was used to help inferior students who were not capable of sitting in one position for a long time and who did not have the ability to concentrate their minds. This herb affects the locomotor system and makes one insensitive to external stimuli, so that thoughts start running in one direction. The body becomes still and free of pain. Some of those who did not practice steady posture through systematic discipline used soma along with ritual worship before meditation. This was not as common as psychedelics are today. The use of this herb was restricted and controlled by a particular tradition of herbologists, who spent their whole lives researching and experimenting on the use of various herbs.

According to Vaidya Bhairavdutt, administering these intoxicants with the use of mantra was a common practice. Mantras were used in solitude with fasting and other austerities under the guidance of an expert. A sect of sadhus was custodian of this knowledge.

For those who have not practiced austerities and trained their minds, psychedelics are harmful. They might damage the nervous system and especially disturb the finer channels of energy *(nadis)*. Hallucinations occur, and one may become psychotic. I have examined the effects of drugs on people who have used them and have not found any spiritual symptoms in their behavior. They might have an unusual experience, but what good is that experience which has an adverse effect and a harmful reaction later on? A prolonged subtle depression is a common symptom of these drugs if the mind is not prepared and dietary habits are not carefully observed. A healthy diet, calm atmosphere, mantra, and guidance were important factors when soma-rasa was used.

I heard from this herbologist that he himself used what he called soma-rasa (actually I had no way of verifying whether it was indeed the soma used by the ancients or something else). He said that it had a very pleasant and elevating effect, but if he used it regularly it brought on a depression as a reactionary effect. He also came to the conclusion that the repeated use of such herbs can also lead to a psychological addiction. But he persuaded me to try it once, saying, "It's wonderful. You've never had an experience like it before."

One morning he prepared the juice of *ashtha varga* [a mixture of eight herbs] and mixed soma creeper juice in it. We both drank this mixture. Its taste was a little bit bitter and sour. After a while he started chanting and swinging, and ultimately threw off all his clothes and started dancing. But I had a severe headache. I felt as though my head were going to blow up. I held my head in both my hands. The man who used to attend me could not understand why we were acting so peculiarly. He shook his head in puzzlement and said, "Lord! One is dancing outside, and the other is sitting in the corner of the room holding his head." I became so restless I felt like jumping into the Ganges, crossing it, and running away into the forest. It was a chaotic experience.

As he danced, the herbologist began shouting that he was Shiva, the Lord of the universe, and cried, "Where is my Parvati? [Shiva's wife.] I want to make love to her." This disturbed all the students who came to visit me in the morning. They tried to restrain him, but he became so strong that five people could not hold him down. Though he was a slightly built man he threw them off, one after another. I saw what was happening from a window, but I did not come out of my room because of my heavy head. Another swami brought three quarts of warm water and told me to do an upper wash. [This yogic technique for cleansing the stomach involves drinking a large quantity of water and then vomiting it up.] This relieved me a bit. This experience, which occurred during my stay at Ujaili Ashram in Uttarkashi, disturbed the whole routine of the ashram, and I did not know how to explain it to my students.

After a careful study of the use of psychedelic preparations over a number of years I have concluded that the harm they can do far outweighs any positive benefits they might have. Those who are not psychologically prepared will have negative experiences either when they ingest the intoxicant or later. Those who are prepared don't need such drugs.

VIII

Beyond the Great Religions

◆

ALL THE GREAT RELIGIONS OF THE WORLD HAVE come out of one Truth. If we follow religion without practicing the Truth, it is like the blind leading the blind. Those who belong to God love all. Love is the religion of the universe. A compassionate one transcends the boundaries of religion and realizes the undivided, absolute Reality.

A Christian Sage
of the Himalayas

◆

There once lived a sage in our monastery who was very knowledgeable about Christ. His name was Sadhu Sundar Singh. When he visited Madras tens of thousands of people would come to hear him speak on the beach. In fact people used to fly all the way from Europe just to hear him. He was born in Amritsar, Punjab, and was a Sikh by birth.

When he was still young he had a vision, which returned night after night. He did not understand whether it was a dream, something guiding him, or something harmful. He saw someone who was asking him to get up and go toward the Himalayas. He tried to avoid going to sleep, but eventually he would become tired and close his eyes. Then he would see the vision and would hear a voice saying, "Are you prepared to listen to me? I am your savior. There is no other way for you."

He did not know who it was that was coming to him, so he asked some people for advice. One person said it was Christ, another said it was Krishna, and a third said it was Buddha. But when he saw a picture of Christ he said, "Here is the master who appears to me in my dream and awakens me." Again and again Christ would appear in his dreams and say,

"My son, why are you delaying?" Finally one day he left his home without informing anyone and went to the Himalayas, where he remained for a long time. He lived in our cave monastery several years.

He was the person who introduced the Christian Bible to me. He also taught me the comparative study of the *Bhagavad Gita* and the Bible. He said, "The message that was given in the morning was the message of Krishna; the message that was given in the afternoon was the message of Buddha; and the message that was given in the evening was the message of Christ. There is no difference. Christ the compassionate, Buddha the enlightened, and Krishna the perfect gave their messages according to their times and the need of the masses who were prepared to follow them. These great ones were representatives of one absolute Reality Who assumes various forms and descends to guide humanity whenever He is needed. The sages have a tradition of reverence for all the great religions of the world."

Sadhu Sundar Singh was a very loving, kind, and highly evolved soul. I used to revere him and call him one of my teachers. Once he gave a beautiful comparison of Buddhism and Christianity. He said, "Christianity is a child of Judaism exactly like Buddhism is a child of Hinduism. These two great religions of the world varied, evolved, and assumed innumerable forms throughout the many centuries of their gradual growth. There are a few important characteristics which are commonly seen in these two great and noble religions.

"They both rejected the sense of the flesh which springs from the lower levels of human hearts and minds. Both these religions believe that this sense is the root of evil. The doctrine of sin and selfishness leads one toward pessimism. They place a positive emphasis upon suffering and compassion for the whole of humanity. Both these religions fundamentally embrace the ideal of love to the extreme of accepting death in the service of others and loving others as themselves. They both consider selfless love essential in man and seek to cultivate it in their followers. The love of Buddhism has a wider extension than that of Christianity: Christianity limits this interest to humanity, while Buddhism extends its tenderness to every form of sentient animal life. Christianity analyzes life with the help of theology and stops at the barrier of faith, while Buddhism rationalizes life and stops at nirvana. Buddhist asceticism teaches peace, and Christian asceticism teaches joy—but the understanding of both religions comes to the point of peace and joy which the world can neither give nor take away. Buddhism, like Christianity, emphasizes the will, but in the cultivation of moral life, they both lay stress upon discipline, training, and habit formation. In their broader aspects of teaching these two religions are not much divided.

"A follower of Buddha is very intently aware of his thought, word, and action. History reveals that those who lived with Jesus were also totally dedicated to a larger self rather than to their petty selves. Both Christianity and Buddhism believe in teaching individuals to seek their own moral perfection. Buddhism believes in the four noble truths, which recognize that the great source of sorrow is rooted in desire. Christianity has something of the typical Western willingness to take chance and make use of it. Buddhists choose as their supreme symbol and ideal the figure of a sage seated in deep meditation and contemplation—perfect calm. Christianity uses the symbol of a young man being crucified on a cross, which demonstrates supreme suffering being overcome by love. The characteristics of both Buddha and Christ are similar yet diverse. Jesus was the intense lover of truth; Buddha, the calm and compassionate sage. In the metaphysical attitudes of both religions there is a contrast on the question of ethics. Christianity is theistic, while Buddhism is apparently agnostic. This contrast clarifies that followers of both religions are mistaken when they assert that their own religion contains all the values of both, forgetting the truth that both have a particular genius and have made contributions in building humanity.

"Christians, like Vaishnavites, believe in dualism. Buddhists believe in nirvana exactly as the Vedas also say. Nirvana is a Sanskrit word already mentioned in the Vedas. Emancipation or nirvana is the modified word of liberation which the sages believe in. The path of the sages is most ancient; it includes the teachings of both Christianity and Buddhism. We are not discussing Hinduism or the Hindu religion here, for the Hindu religion believes in the path of avatars or the Incarnate Ones. But the path of the sages is supreme. They are the founders of the most ancient religion of the Vedas. Is there any religion in the world which the Vedas do not contain in all their moral ethics, philosophy, and man's relationship with the universe? The Vedas, which are the most ancient records in the library of man today, encompass all the principles of Buddhism and Christianity.

"The latter part of the Vedas are called the Upanishads. These Upanishads truly deliver the message of the sages, and have various interpretations. These teachings are timeless, universal, and meant for all. No one particular person founded the Vedas; many sages in their highest state of contemplation and meditation realized these profound truths. From this source of knowledge there arose seven different fountains, which gradually grew and became streams. These streams of external knowledge are universal.

"The custodians of the knowledge of the Vedas were the Aryans. But the question is: Who follows the Vedas? In the Vedas, numerous paths have been explained. Those who are not able to follow the path of renunciation should try to understand that it is karma that binds the doer and that there is no way to escape from the law of karma. Karma has twin laws of cause and effect. They are inseparable. Without profound devotion and love, karma cannot become a means for liberation. Karma creates bondage for human beings by creating obstacles in the path of self-realization. The philosophy of reincarnation is inseparable from the philosophy of karma. They are one and the same.

"The path of the sages is a meditative and contemplative path. It is ascetic and yet fulfills the need of man in the world. It provides practical lessons for leading a spiritual life, and firmly maintains the conviction that by doing one's own duty skillfully and selflessly one can realize the ultimate Reality here and now. As Christianity talks about the kingdom of God within and Buddhism speaks of nirvana, the path of the sages refers to the state of self-realization. In the path of the sages one realizes the absolute, undivided Reality through knowledge of the self alone. Unlike Christianity and Buddhism, the path of the sages does not have any particular symbol as an ideal of worship. From mere self to the real self and then to the self of all is the path of the sages, which includes all and excludes none."

Sadhu Sundar Singh's powerful speech had a profound effect on the hearts of others. He used to walk in Christ-consciousness all the time.

One day I asked him, "Have you seen God?" He said, "You insult me by asking this. I see God all the time. Do you think I have seen God only once, twice, or thrice? No, I am with my Lord all the time. When I cannot be with Him, then He is with me."

I said, "Kindly explain." He explained it beautifully. He said, "As long as you remain conscious, be with God consciously by remembering Him. When your conscious mind starts fading as you fall asleep, surrender yourself. The last thought before you go to bed should be, 'O Lord, be with me. I am Thine and Thou art mine.' The whole night the Lord will remain with you. You can always remain together."

One day this great sage vanished in the high Himalayas. Nobody knew where he went. I tried many times to trace him, but always failed. He helped me to realize that it is possible to live in God-consciousness constantly. There still exist such unknown sages. Blessed are those who live in Christ-consciousness all the time.

My Meeting with a Jesuit Sadhu

When I was Shankaracharya, I happened to meet a Jesuit sadhu (a sadhu is he who is in the service of the Lord). Sometimes sadhus and swamis wear white robes or gunnysacks, but the saffron garb is given to them when they are initiated in the path of renunciation. This saffron garb stands for the color of fire. Only one who has burnt all worldly desires into the fire of knowledge is permitted to wear it. Some of the advanced monks ignore wearing such garb and do not observe these formalities. They wear white gowns, wrap blankets around themselves, or use gunnysacks. For them, the use of a particular garb is immaterial.

There are ten orders of swamis and several of sadhus. Out of the ten orders of swamis, four of them are exclusively for brahmins, because the brahmins practice and learn spiritual books from their early childhood. The environment in which they are brought up is spiritual. They study the scriptures of wisdom and thus can impart the knowledge properly, but the other six orders are given to other classes.

This Jesuit sadhu was wearing saffron garb and a cross around his neck. This made me curious. He was only the third

Christian sadhu that I had met, and we started discussing the practical aspect of Christianity. This Jesuit was an educated monk who knew Sanskrit, English, and most of the South Indian languages. He lived exactly like the Hindu swamis live. There seems to be a difference in Indian and Western Christianity. Indian Christians practice meditation and give philosophical expositions of the Bible exactly as swamis explain the Upanishads and their various commentaries. He said that Christianity could be revived by teaching its practicality. In the West practicality in Christianity is not understood. He firmly believed that Christ had lived in the Himalayas, although it did not matter to me whether he had lived there or not.

This Jesuit swami was a very humble man and talked to me about walking with the Christ. I asked him, "How can you walk with someone who lived two thousand years ago?"

He laughed and said, "What ignorance. Christ is a state of perfection, a state of oneness, and a state of truth. Truth is everlasting reality and is not subject to death. I live with Christ-consciousness. Follow his footprints."

I said, "Where are those footprints?" And he again laughed and said, "Anywhere I go toward any direction I move, I find Him guiding me. They are everywhere—but you will have to see with the eye of your faith. Do you have that?"

I admired his love for Christ-consciousness and bade good-bye to him.

Jesus in the Himalayas

◆

After renouncing the seat of Shankaracharya I went to my master and stayed with him for a few days. From there I decided to go on a pilgrimage to Amarnath, the highest shrine of Kashmir. Amarnath is a cave which is covered by snow all year-round. The dripping water icicle looks like a Shiva-linga—a symbol adored by Hindus, exactly as the cross is by Christians or the Star of David is by Jews. The story of a pair of white pigeons is very famous in this area. It is said that a pair of white pigeons come on the day of pilgrimage.

A Kashmiri pandit who was a learned man was my guide on this journey. He started telling me a story about Jesus Christ, claiming that Jesus had lived in Kashmir practicing meditation. The pandit referred to a manuscript written in the Tibetan language that is preserved in a monastery situated at the height of 14,000 feet in the Himalayas. It was later translated by a Russian writer and then into English and published as *The Unknown Life of Jesus Christ*. In this part of the Himalayas many people believe this story, and you dare not disagree with it. There is a nearby mount which is famous because Jesus lived practicing meditation there. My guide gave

Amarnath, the cave shrine in Kashmir

me three reasons to support this statement: first, the garb which Jesus wore was a traditional Kashmiri garb; second, his hairstyle was also Kashmiri; and third, the miracles that he performed are well-known yogic miracles. The pandit claimed that Jesus Christ left Asia Minor for the unknown period of his life when he was thirteen years of age, and that he lived in the valleys of Kashmir until he was thirty. I did not know whether to believe him, but I certainly didn't want to dismiss this idea. His love for Jesus Christ was immense. I did not want to argue with him.

On our way to Amarnath he took me to an ashram which was seven miles away in the forests of Gulmarg. Gulmarg is one of the places of interest often visited by foreigners. A swami lived there who was a scholar of Kashmir Shaivism and who practiced meditation most of the time.

Kashmir Shaivism has many scriptures still untranslated and unexplained. So much is left unsaid in these great scriptures that they are only understood by those fortunate ones who are on the path and have already understood something of it. These scriptures can never be understood without a highly competent and accomplished teacher. This philosophy views the spirit, mind, body, and all levels of reality in the entire universe as a manifestation of the principle termed *spanda,* spontaneous vibration. The subject matter of these scriptures is *shaktipata* and awakening the latent force buried in human beings.

This swami informed me of a roving adept who visited Amarnath cave shrine every summer, but no one knew where that adept lived permanently. People coming from Ladakh often saw him treading the mountain paths all alone. My interest was not only to visit the cave shrine but to meet this roving adept of the Himalayas. Of all those I have met in my life, three were very impressive and left deep imprints in the bed of my memory. That adept was one of them. I stayed with him for seven days, just fifty yards away from the shrine. He visited this cave shrine practically every year.

He was about twenty years of age, was very handsome, and the luster of his cheeks was like that of cherries. He was a *brahmachari* who wore only a loincloth and possessed nothing. He was so acclimated to high altitudes that, with the help of yoga practices, he could travel barefoot and live at elevations of 10,000 to 12,000 feet. He was insensitive to cold. Living with him was an enlightening experience to me. He was perfect and full of yoga wisdom and serenity. People called this young adept Bal Bhagawan (Child-God Incarnate), but he always kept himself above such praises and constantly traveled in the Himalayan mountains. He already knew my master and had lived in our cave monastery. He asked about several students who were then practicing meditation with my master. He spoke briefly in gentle sentences, but I could feel that he was not pleased when my guide started bowing, touching his feet, and running around in emotional devotion. This great adept became an example for me.

I had never before seen a man who could sit still without blinking his eyelids for eight to ten hours, but this adept was very unusual. He levitated two and a half feet during his meditations. We measured this with a string which was later measured by a foot rule. I would like to make it clear, though, as I have already told you, that I don't consider levitation to be a spiritual practice. It is an advanced practice of pranayama with application of *bandhas* (locks). One who knows about the relationship between mass and weight understands that it is possible to levitate, but only after long practice. But this was not what I was seeking. I directly wanted to have an experience with this adept.

I asked him a question about the highest state of enlightenment, and muttering a mantra from the Upanishads, he answered, "When the senses are well-controlled and withdrawn from contact with the objects of the world, then sense perceptions no longer create images in the mind. The mind is then trained in one-pointedness. When the mind no longer recalls thought-patterns from the unconscious, a balanced state of mind leads to a higher state of consciousness. A perfect state of serenity established in *sattva* is the highest state of enlightenment. The practice of meditation and non-attachment are the two keynotes. A very firm conviction is essential for establishing a definite philosophy of life. Intellect intervenes and blind emotion misguides. Though both are great powers, they should be known first, analyzed, and then directed toward the source of intuition. Intuition is the only source of true knowledge. All this—whatever you see in the world—is unreal because of its constantly changing nature. Reality is hidden beneath all these changes." He instructed me to march fearlessly on the path that I was treading. After seven days of *satsanga* the guide and I left this great sage. I returned to Shrinagar and then went on to my abode in the Himalayas to enjoy the autumn.

Shrine in Kashmir where Jesus is said to have lived

A Vision of Christ

◆

In 1947, after the declaration of independence in India, while on my way back from Tibet I stayed a few days in Sikkim visiting a few prominent Buddhist yogis. Then I went to Shillong in Assam. It is one of the strongholds of Christianity in India. There I met a Garhwali sadhu, a well-known Christian mystic. This lovable old man was far beyond the influence of the material world. He taught me the Sermon on the Mount and the Book of Revelation, comparing them to the yoga system of Patanjali. He spoke many languages and took me to the Naga and Gairo hills, where both Protestant and Catholic tribes lived in forest dwellings. This sadhu served as a harmonizing link between the two groups and always taught practical Christianity rather than theorizing and delivering sermons. He would say, "I love Christianity but not 'Churchianity.'" I'm sure this offended at least some followers of the churches.

He believed that the kingdom of God is within every human being and that Jesus, after being anointed, became Christ. He held that Christ is universal consciousness and that no one can reach the ultimate Reality without reaching

Christ-consciousness. This is rarely understood by Christians in general, although the mystics of Christianity understood it well. This sadhu removed many of my doubts regarding Christian theology. I had long before developed a love for Christ and His teachings, but I had never understood the dogma that through Christ alone can one achieve salvation. My problem was resolved when it was explained in terms of the Father and the Son and the perfection that can be attained by all human beings.

Two days after meeting this great Christian sadhu I again had some problems with the authorities. There were several political parties spreading propaganda in preparation for municipal elections in the city. My opinion was sought, and I told questioners that they should not vote for the ruling party if they thought it dishonest. I was a stranger in the city, and the police arrested me. They charged me with not being a supporter of the new Indian government, though as a matter of fact I had no political motivations whatsoever. At that time democracy in India was still very new, and the people and the authorities still had much to learn about what living in and administering a democracy really means.

Once again I wondered, "After I have spent so much of my time trying to avoid hurting anyone, why do I have to suffer in this way?" I prayed to the Lord for help. That night when I was asleep I had a clear vision of Jesus Christ. He grasped my arm comfortingly and blessed me, saying, "Do not worry; nothing bad will happen to you."

The next day the case went to court, and I was brought before a Christian judge. Because of my short beard, wooden sandles, long staff, and garb, people often thought that I was Christian. The judge looked at me and asked, "Are you Christian?" I replied, "No, not by birth." Of course I loved and respected Christianity as I did the other great and profound religions.

He asked, "Why were you arrested?" I replied, "I expressed my opinion. People asked me who they should vote for and I advised, 'Who you vote for depends on you.'" The police had fabricated a case against me, and when the judge learned the facts he agreed that I had been arrested unjustly. He acquitted me.

I stayed in Shillong for four months, studying with that Christian mystic. I have never met another sadhu who could so clearly compare the philosophy of the *Gita* and the teachings of the Bible, with the end result of a much clearer understanding of both. He regularly meditated and was calm, serene, and fearless. After studying with him I spent much time contemplating the Sermon on the Mount and the Book of Revelation, which for a long time remained my favorite scriptures. I have a firm conviction that the Bible contains much wisdom, though sometimes preachers who would interpret it cloud it and confuse it.

This sage told me, "After having made a comparative study of all the great religions of the world I found out that the fundamental truths of all great religions are one and the same. If this is true, then why all this hatred, jealousy, and dogma? That led me to realize that even the most ancient Vedic religion, which is in fact universal, was lost, and the priestly wisdom of India was not able to convey the message of the Vedic sages. Yet these priests call themselves the knowers of the Vedas. Shankara, in his commentary on the *Bhagavad Gita,* clearly explains that the Gita is a modified version of the Vedas and that Lord Krishna is only a narrator. Truth always existed. The founders and great messengers of the religions of the world were only narrators, but actually the sages, and not the reincarnations of God, are the founders of the noble truths. This itself is proof that great reincarnations of God only modified the message given by the sages. The reincarnations of God are the messengers of the sages. They only change the baskets, and the eggs are the same." When this Christian sadhu explained this to me, my eyes were opened to another dimension.

He continued: "Religions play their important part in binding society as a whole. The spiritual leaders and founders of religions are accepted as authorities—but according to my analysis, the wisdom given by the sages is eternal and perfect. The great messengers and leaders of various religions are only channels of the ancient sages. Worshipping the leaders and founders of religions is just like creating a dogma and cult without any solid philosophy behind it. There is no hero worship in following the path of the sages, for their teachings are universal and for all times. When religious teachers could not impart practical knowledge to their students, this corrupted the religions of the world. They said, 'You should have faith in God,' and then dismissed the genuine quest of the soul. The doctrine of faith in the East and West is being exploited by all the preachers of the world. Modern man is confused more by the preachers than by his own problems. Social problems and religious problems create serious conflicts and prejudices, which become difficult for one to dispel. What is the worth of that religion which creates bondage and misery for man? Freedom is one of the prime messages given by the sages, but it has been obstructed so much that today's religious man lives like a slave, terrified and obsessed by evil and devils. He is more concerned about sin and Satan than self-realization and God.

"The philosophy of the New Age demands complete modification of such religious concepts—but, alas, there hasn't been a revolution in any of the religions so far. Without going through a socio-religious revolutionary process the flower of true religion cannot bloom. Reformation and revolution are the signs and symptoms of the evolution of man. This revolution is made possible by changing the heart and practicing *ahimsa* in daily life. Love alone has the power to change. Such a revolution and change will prepare modern man for the next dimension of awareness, which will then unite the whole of humanity."

That great Christian sage really opened my inner eye, and I started looking forward to that day to come when all of humanity will follow the religion of man by worshipping one truth and practicing love. Then there will be no place for hatred, jealousy, and other prejudices of life. My four months' stay with this great man helped me in understanding Christianity in a better way. The vision of Christ deepened my love for His teachings, and He stays in the calmest chamber of my heart as my guide and protector.

Judaism in Yoga

O nce I was invited by the followers of Baha'ism to preside
at a three-day conference at Poona, where I met two
Jewish rabbis of Indian origin. They discussed the kabbalah,
and I better understood the practices of Judaism after talking
to them. There is a small group of Jews in India. Jews have
been persecuted almost everywhere—except in India. Parsis,
worshippers of the divine fire, and Jews, meditators on the Star
of David, enjoy Indian citizenship exactly as others do. Yoga
practices and the practices of the kabbalah are similar. After
studying the literature I have concluded that the spiritual practices are identical in all the great religions of the world.

The ancient philosophy of Sankhya, which is the basis of
yoga, and the philosophy of kabbalah seem to have the same
source. According to the kabbalistic system, life is associated
with numbers. This is an ancient Sankhya concept. Many of the
teachings of the *Gita* are similar to Judaism. These two great
religions, Hinduism and Judaism, are similar, and are the most
ancient religions in the world. The Baha'i temple and religion
accepts and emphasizes this fact in its monogram and its literature. The concept of Sri Yantra, a highly and scientifically

evolved ancient yoga process for enlightenment, centers on the Star of David, also known as the *anahata chakra* in yoga literature and as the Sacred Heart in Christian practices. Sri Yantra was most probably known to the ancients of the Temple of Solomon. According to the spiritual literature of the ancients it is a very sacred yoga process. It helps one to establish his relationship with other beings, the universe, and its Creator.

I believe that yoga is a complete science of life which is equally applicable and helpful for men, women, and children. Religions are social sciences which help to maintain culture and tradition and support the lawful structure of human society. Yoga is a universal science for self-improvement and enlightenment. All the methods of self-growth which are found in any religion are already in yoga literature.

During this conference I found out that it is necessary for the religious and spiritual leaders of various groups from different parts of the world to meet, discuss, and share their philosophies and ideas. I am very firm in my opinion that all great religions are one and the same, though their ways seem to be different. Diverse are the ways of enlightenment, but the goal is one and the same. If the spiritual leaders meet, discuss, and understand other paths, they can help their communities and thus lead them to communicate with different groups and religions of the world. Anyone who says that his religion is the only true religion is ignorant and misguides the followers of that religion. Prejudice is like a poison that kills human growth. Love is inclusive and is the foundation of all great religions.

I Belong to None but God

◆───────────────────────

I once went to see a sage who was living by a river. At the time I had the foolish notion that genuine sages are found only in the Himalayas. I thought, "It cannot be possible for a genuine sage to live on the banks of this small river situated so close to a city." But I wanted to directly experience his way of living.

When I was still four miles from him he sent food to me, but I was not impressed with this. I thought, "This is nothing. If someone is coming to see me, I also may sense that he is on the way and prepare food for him. This is not true wisdom."

When I met him, he said, "You are late. I am casting off my body tomorrow morning." I asked, "Why do you not wait for another twelve hours and teach me something?" He said, "No, I have no time."

He had many followers of various faiths. Hindus knew him as a swami, Muslims considered him a follower of Islam, and Christians believed that he was a Christian. The Christians intended after his death to take him to their cemetery; the Muslims were adamant they planned to take him to their graveyard; and the Hindus thought of burying him and building a memorial.

The next day he left his body. A doctor came and declared him dead. For the next several hours there was great confusion. The people of all religions and their leaders started fighting for his body. The prestige of each group was at stake. The district magistrate came to me and said, "You were staying with him. Perhaps you know what he really was. You can help me in resolving this dispute."

I replied, "I don't know anything about him." Then I thought, "What type of sage is he? He died and created a problem for me and others and did not teach me anything." I said in my mind, "If he was a great sage, he should not have created such a confusion."

This was the fourth hour after his death—but suddenly he got up and said, "Look, I have decided not to die because you are fighting!" The magistrate and all the people looked at him with awe. The sage said, "Get out of my sight, you Hindus, you Christians and Muslims; you are all foolish people. I belong to God and no one else." Then he looked at me and said, "My son, don't worry. Now I will stay with you and teach you for three days, and on the fourth day I will cast off my body quietly."

I lived with him for three days. My stay with him was very enlightening. It was one of the best times of my life. He taught me many things. Many times each day he repeated the same phrase: "Be that which you really are; don't pretend to be what you are not." He repeated this again and again.

After three days he said, "I want to get into the waters." Then he walked into the river and disappeared. When people came to look for him I told them that he had got into the river and had never come out. They searched for his body and made all possible efforts to recover it, but it was never found.

The great sages do not identify themselves with any particular religion or creed. They are above all such distinctions. They belong to the whole of humanity.

IX

Divine Protection

◆

SELF-SURRENDER IS THE HIGHEST AND EASIEST method for enlightenment. One who has surrendered himself is always protected by the divine power. One who possesses nothing and has no one to protect him belongs to God and is constantly under the protection of the Divine.

Protecting Arms

I know many calm and quiet places in the lap of the Himalayas where one can live and meditate without being disturbed. Whenever I get tired I think of recharging myself by going to the Himalayas for a short period. One of my favorite places for such a retreat is in the district of Garhwal, twelve miles north of Landsdowne, where at the height of 6,500 feet there is a small Shiva temple surrounded by thick fir trees.

In that region nobody eats corn without offering it to the deity of that temple. According to the local folklore, if anyone does this by mistake, their house starts shaking and the people act in a funny way. When I first heard this, at the age of four-teen, I had a desire to visit that temple. I thought that people create such myths out of their imagination, and that the myths then travel far and wide and are believed by everyone, though they have no basis in reality. I decided to visit that place to see for myself. I was approaching there at seven o'clock in the evening. It had already become dark. I was traveling along the edge of a cliff. I did not have a light with me, and in those days I used to wear wooden sandals which were very slippery. I slipped, and was at the verge of falling down the cliff, which

The Shiva temple at Tarkeshwar

was very steep, when suddenly a tall, old man dressed in white caught me in his arms and brought me back to the footpath. He said, "This is a holy place and you are fully protected. I will take you to your destination." He led me along the path for about ten minutes, until we neared a thatched cottage which had a torch burning outside. When we came to the stone wall surrounding the cottage, I thought he was walking just behind me—but when I turned to thank him, I could not find him anywhere. I shouted after him, and the sadhu who lived in the cottage heard me and came out. He was pleased to have a guest and told me to follow him to his small room, where a fire was burning. I told the sadhu about the old man who had shown me the path in the dark. I described his appearance, and explained how he had saved me from falling off the cliff.

This sadhu started weeping and said, "You were fortunate to encounter that great man. Do you know why I am here? Seven years ago I also lost my way at exactly the same place. It was eleven o'clock at night. The same old man took hold of my arm and brought me to this thatched hut where I now live. I have never seen him again. I call him Siddha Baba. His loving arms have also saved me."

The next morning I searched the whole area, but did not find any such man. I went to the cliff and saw the marks where I had slipped. I often remember those loving arms that protected me from falling from the cliff. It was a very dangerous place, and had I fallen, there would have been no chance for my survival. Later I talked to the villagers about my experience and they all knew about this *siddha*. They believe that he protects their women and children in the forest—but none of the villagers have seen him. During that time I was strictly following the austerities and instructions given to me by my master, and I did not possess or carry anything with me. My experience has often confirmed the belief that those who have nothing are taken care of by the Divine.

The thatched cottage in which the sadhu lived was just a hundred yards from the small Shiva temple. The temple was in a little clearing in the woods and was surrounded by tall fir trees. That place was highly charged with spiritual vibrations. I learned that a great *siddha* had lived there six hundred years ago. He instructed and guided those who lived in that area, although he remained in silence. After his death the people built a six-foot-square temple where he lived. Inside there was a Shiva-linga [an oval-shaped stone which is a symbol of Shiva]. The villagers even today visit the temple once in three months before the new season begins to keep their memories of that great man alive. Some say it was he who saved me from falling off the cliff. I stayed in a small room near the temple for several months, remaining alone and practicing silence and certain austerities.

A few years after my first visit to that temple some brahmins decided to build a larger, more solid, and more majestic temple in place of the small, old temple which was no longer in good repair. When the laborers began digging around the foundation to remove the old temple they found that the earth was full of small snakes of various colors. So they started picking up the snakes along with the dirt, and throwing both aside. But the deeper they dug, the more the snakes would appear. An old woman from a nearby village would come to the temple each morning and evening. In the evening she would walk three miles to the temple in order to light the lamp inside, and in the morning she would come and extinguish it. She had done this regularly for several years. She didn't want the temple to be modified and warned the builders not to disturb it, but the engineer who was in charge of the project didn't pay her any heed. After digging for six days, they found there was no end to the snakes. The more they removed, the more there seemed to be left. They dug around the Shiva-linga in order to move it, but found that it was buried deep in the ground. They dug down eight feet, but could not remove it. On the eighth night the engineer had a dream in which the old yogi who had rescued me appeared with his white beard and long gown. He told the engineer that the Shiva-linga was sacred and should not be moved and that the temple should not be enlarged. So the old temple was rebuilt to the exact dimensions in which it had stood for six centuries.

I visited this place again in the spring of 1973 with Swami Ajaya and a small group of students. We stayed there for six days in a small two-storied earthen and stone house which had been built a few hundred feet from the temple. Another old sadhu lives and serves as a sort of priest to the temple there now. He is very hospitable and serves anyone who comes there. That place is very serene and beautiful. At the top of the tall hills that surround the valley one can see the long ranges of the Himalayas as though all the snowy peaks are tightly clinging to one another and are determined to stand firmly from eternity to eternity.

Swami Rama on his way to Mount Kailas

Lost in the Land of Devas

◆——————————————

I had heard and read so much about a village called Jñanganj
that my desire for visiting this place became intense. Many
pilgrims have heard about that place, but it is rare that
someone perseveres enough to reach there. This small community of spiritual people is situated deep within the lap of the
Himalayas, surrounded by snowy peaks. For eight months of
the year one cannot enter or come out of that place. A small
community of yogis lives there all the time. These yogis observe
silence and spend most of their time in meditation. Small log
houses provide shelter, and their main food is potatoes and
barley, which they store for the whole year. This particular
community is made up of Indian, Tibetan, and Nepalese
sadhus. This small group of adepts resides on the Himalayan
border between Tibet and Pithora Garh. There is no other
place but this which can be called Jñanganj.

I decided to go to Mount Kailas along with another four
renunciates in order to visit this village. We went from Almora
to Dorhchola to Garbiank, and after several days when we
reached Rakshastal we lost our way. It was in the month of July
when the snow melts in the Himalayan mountains. During this

season of the year the glaciers move and sometimes an entire glacier crashes down and blocks the path. For several days there may be no way to go.

As we were walking we found glaciers collapsing, blocking the way behind and in front of us. I was accustomed to such sudden calamities, but the other swamis were new to these adventures. The swamis were very much frightened. They held me responsible for this and started putting the blame on me because I was from the Himalayas. They said, "You should have known better. You are from the mountains. You misguided us. We have no food, the path is blocked, it is very cold. We are dying here."

We were stranded there by the side of an enormous lake, called Rakshastal, which means "Lake of the Devil." Because of the melting snow and avalanches, the water started rising. By the second day everyone was in panic. I said, "We are not ordinary worldly people. We are renunciates. We should die happily. Remember God. Panic is not going to help us."

Everyone started remembering his mantra and praying, but nothing seemed to help. Here their faith was tested—but none of them had any. They were afraid of being buried in the snow. I started joking and said, "Suppose you all die: what will be the fate of your institutions, wealth, and followers?" They said, "We may be dying, but first we will see that you die." My jokes and my taking this situation lightly made them more angry.

Very few people know how to enjoy humor. Most people become very serious in such adverse situations. Humor is an important quality that makes one cheerful in all walks of life. To cultivate this quality is very important. When the poison was given to Socrates, he was very humorous and made a few jokes. When the cup of hemlock was given to him he said, "Can I share a bit of it with the gods?" Then he smiled and said, "Poison has no power to kill a sage, for a sage lives in reality, and reality is eternal." He smiled and took the poison.

I said to these renunciates, "If we have to live and if we are on the right path, the Lord will protect us. Why should we worry?" It started becoming dark and again snow started falling. Suddenly a man with a long beard wearing a white robe and carrying a lantern appeared before us. He asked, "Have you lost your way?"

"For almost two days we have had nothing to eat, and we do not know how to get out of this place," we replied. He told us to follow him. There had seemed to be no way through that avalanche—but when we followed him we eventually found ourselves on the other side. He showed us the way to a village which was a few miles away and instructed us to pass the night there. He then suddenly disappeared. We all wondered who he was. The villagers say that such experiences are not uncommon in this land of *devas*. These bright beings guide innocent travelers when they lose their way. We stayed in this village that night. The next day the other four renunciates refused to travel with me. They all turned back. They did not want to go further into the mountains because they feared more dangers. After being given directions by the villagers I went all alone toward Jñanganj. One of the sadhus there was kind enough to give me shelter, and I stayed for one and a half months. This place is surrounded by high snowy peaks and is one of the most beautiful places that I have ever seen.

Returning from Jñanganj, I came back by the way that leads to Manasarowar at the foot of Mount Kailas. I met many advanced Indian and Tibetan yogis. For a week I lived in a camp of lamas at the foot of Mount Kailas. I still treasure this experience. I traveled to Garviyauk with a herd of sheep. The shepherds with whom I traveled talked about the beings who guide travelers in the Himalayas. They narrated many such experiences to me. These beings are called *devas*, or bright beings. It is said that the *devas* are the beings who can travel between both the known and unknown side of life. They can penetrate through physical existence to guide aspirants, and yet they live in the non-physical plane. The *devas* too have their plane of existence. Esoteric science and occultism talk much about such beings, but modern scientists dismiss this theory, saying that such beings are either fantasies or hallucinations. I have heard young scientists saying that old men who believe in the existence of such beings must be hallucinating. Old age is another childhood which is full of follies and can give hallucinations. But spiritual people become more wise in old age. They have no chance to hallucinate, for they purify their minds first and then experience the higher levels of consciousness.

Scientists have not studied many dimensions of life as yet. They are still studying the brain and its various zones. The aspect of psychology which is termed transpersonal or transcendental psychology is beyond the grasp of modern scientists. The perennial psychology of the ancients which has been cultivated for several centuries in the past is an exact science. It is based on the finest knowledge, which is called intuition. The physical sciences have limitations, and their investigations are only on the gross levels of matter, body, and brain.

The Land of Hamsas

$\blacklozenge$

Of all the places I have visited in my life I have found none more fascinating than Gangotri. It is a land of the *Hamsas,* where the mountain peaks are perennially blanketed with snow. When I was young between thirty and fifty yogis lived there in small caves along both sides of the Ganges. Most of them did not wear any clothes, and some did not even use fire. For three full winters I lived there by myself in a small cave some five hundred yards away from the cave where my brother disciple was staying. I rarely communicated with anyone. Those of us who lived there would see one another from a distance, but no one disturbed anyone else; no one was interested in socializing. That was one of the most fulfilling periods of my life. I spent most of my time doing yoga practices and living on a mixture of wheat and gram. I would soak the wheat and gram, and when it germinated after two days, add in a little salt. This was the only food I took.

In a nearby cave lived a sage who was widely respected throughout India. His name was Krishnashram. One night at about twelve o'clock I was overwhelmed by a deafening sound as if many bombs were exploding. It was an avalanche, very

Swami Rama as a young brahmachari in Gangotri

close by. I emerged from my cave to view what had happened. It was a moonlit night and I could see the other bank of the frozen Ganges, where Krishnashram lived. When I saw where the avalanche occurred I concluded that Sri Krishnashram had been buried beneath it. I quickly put on my long Tibetan coat, took a torch, and rushed to his cave. The Ganges there is just a narrow stream, so I crossed it easily—and found that his small cave was quite safe and untouched. He was sitting there smiling.

He was not speaking at that time, so he pointed upward and said, "Hm, hm, hm, hm." Then he wrote on a slate: "Nothing can harm me. I have to live for a long time. These noises and avalanches do not frighten me. My cave is protected." Seeing that he was unharmed and in good spirits, I returned to my cave. In the morning when I could see more clearly I found that the avalanche had come down on both sides of his cave. The tall fir trees were completely buried. Only his cave remained undamaged.

I often visited Krishnashram from two to five in the afternoon. I would ask him questions, and he would answer on the slate. His eyes glowed like two bowls of fire, and his skin was as thick as an elephant's. He was almost eighty years of age and very healthy. I wondered how he was able to live without any woolens, fire, or protection from the cold. He had no possessions at all. A swami who lived half a mile up toward Gomukh regularly brought him some food. Once a day he ate some roasted potatoes and a piece of whole-wheat bread.

Everyone there drank green tea mixed with an herb called *gangatulsi (Artemisia cina)*. The yogis and swamis whom I met there taught me many things about herbs and their uses, and also discussed the scriptures with me. Those yogis did not like to come down to the plains of India. Every summer a few hundred pilgrims would visit this shrine, which is one of the highest in the Himalayas. In those days they had to walk ninety-six miles in the mountains to reach there. If anyone wants to see firsthand the power of spirit over mind and body, he can find a few rare yogis there even today.

An Atheistic Swami

◆

There was a swami who was learned and highly intellectual. He did not believe in the existence of God. Whatever someone else believed in he would try to undermine with cleverly formulated arguments. Many scholars avoided him, but he and I were good friends. I was attracted to him for his learning and logic. His entire mind and energy were focused on only one thing: how to argue. He was learned—and obstinate.

He would say, "I don't know why people don't come to learn from me." And I would tell him, "You destroy their beliefs and their faith, so why should they come? They are afraid of you."

He was a well-known man. He had written a book in which he attempted to refute all the classical philosophies. It's a good book, a wonderful book for mental gymnastics. It is called *Khat-Dharshana* or *Six Systems of Indian Philosophy*. The Tibetan and Chinese scholars admired him as a logician and invited him to China. They apparently decided that if there were any learned man anywhere in India, it must be this man.

He did not believe in God, yet he was a monk. He used to say that he became a monk to refute and eliminate the order of monks. "They are all fake," he would say. "They are a burden on society. I have found out that there is nothing genuine in it, and I am going to tell the world." He vowed that if anybody could convince him that there was a God, he would become that person's disciple.

Once he asked me, "Do you know my vow?"

I replied, "He would be the greatest fool who would make you a disciple."

He asked, "What do you mean?"

I said, "What can anyone do with your silly mind? You have sharpened your mind in one way, but you have not known any other dimension."

He retorted, "You are the silly one. You also talk of unknown dimensions. This is all rubbish, fantasy."

I prayed to God and said, "No matter what happens, if I have to lay down my life, I will make this man aware of some deeper truths."

One day I asked, "Have you seen the Himalayas?"

He replied, "No, I never have."

I told him, "In the summer it is pleasant to travel in the mountains. They are beautiful." I was hoping that if he came with me I would find an opportunity to set him right.

He said, "That's one thing I would love. With such beautiful mountains, why do we need God?"

I thought, "I will force him into a situation where he has to believe." I planned to take him to one of the high mountains. With a small tent and some biscuits and dried fruits we left for Kailas. It was in the month of September, when the snow starts. I firmly believed in God, and I prayed to the Lord to create a situation in which this swami would be helpless and then cry for God's help. I was young and reckless, so I took him on an arduous path. I myself did not know where we were going, so we soon were lost.

I was born in the Himalayas so I have developed a

resistance to cold. There is a special posture and a breathing technique which helped to protect me from the cold. But the poor swami shivered painfully because he was unaccustomed to the mountain cold. Out of compassion and to show that I loved him, I gave him my blanket.

I took him up to a height of 14,000 feet. After 14,000 feet he complained, "I can't breathe properly."

I told him, "I don't have any difficulty."

He said, "You are a young man, so it doesn't affect you."

I said, "Don't accept defeat."

Every day he would teach me philosophy and I would charm him by talking about the mountains. I would say, "What a beautiful thing, to be so close to nature."

After we had been walking in the mountains four days, it started snowing. We camped at a height of 15,000 feet. We had only a small tent—four feet by five. When it had snowed up to two feet, I said, "Do you know that it will snow seven to eight feet and our tent will be buried, and we will be buried inside the tent?"

"Don't say that!" he exclaimed.

I said, "It is true."

"Can we go back?"

"There is no way, Swamiji."

"What shall we do?"

I replied, "I will pray to God."

He said, "I believe in facts; I do not believe in the silly things you are talking of."

I said, "By the grace of my God, the snow will stop. If you want to use your philosophy and intelligence to stop it, you are welcome. Just try."

He said, "How will I know if your prayers work? Suppose you pray and the snow stops. Even then I won't believe in God, because the snow might have stopped anyway."

The snow was soon four feet deep on all sides of the small

tent, and he started to feel suffocated. I would make a hole in the snow so we could breathe, but it would soon close again. I knew that something was sure to happen. Either we would die, or he would believe in God.

Finally it happened. He said, "Do something! Your master is a great man, and I have insulted him many times. Perhaps that is why I am now being put through this torture and danger." He started to become frightened.

I said, "If you pray to God, in five minutes the snow will stop and there will be sunshine. If you don't, you will die and you will kill me too. God has whispered this to me."

He asked, "Really? How are you hearing this?"

I said, "He is speaking to me."

He began to believe me. He said, "If there is no sunshine, I am going to kill you, because I am breaking my vow. I have only one basic unconditional vow, and that is not to believe in God."

Under pressure of the fear of death, such a man reverses himself and quickly acquires great devotion. He started praying with tears in his eyes. And I thought, "If the snow doesn't stop in five minutes then he will harden his heart even more." So I also prayed.

By the grace of God, in exactly five minutes the snow stopped and the sun started to shine. He was surprised—and so was I!

He asked, "Will we live?"

I said, "Yes, God wants us to live."

He said, "Now I realize that there really must be something which I did not understand."

After that, he vowed to live in silence for the rest of his life. He lived twenty-one years more and never spoke to anyone. And if anyone would talk about God, he would weep tears of ecstasy. After that he did write more books, one a commentary on *Mahimnastotra—Hymns of the Lord*.

After we have gone through intellectual gymnastics, we find something beyond the intellect. A stage comes when intellect cannot guide us, and only intuition can show us the way. Intellect examines, calculates, decides, accepts, and rejects all that is happening within the spheres of mind, but intuition is an uninterrupted flow which dawns spontaneously from its source, down deep within. It dawns only when the mind attains a state of tranquility, equilibrium, and equanimity. That pure intuition expands the human consciousness in a way that one starts seeing things clearly. Life as a whole is comprehended, and ignorance is dispelled. After a series of experiences, direct experience becomes a guide and one starts receiving intuition spontaneously.

Suddenly a thought flashed into my mind, and then I remembered the saying of a great sage called Tulsidasa: "Without being God-fearing, love for God is not possible, and without love for God, realization is impossible." The fear of God makes one aware of God-consciousness, and fear of the world creates fear and thus danger. This atheistic swami became God-fearing when he experienced God-consciousness. Intellectual gymnastics is a mere exercise which creates fears, but love of God liberates one from all fears.

An Appointment with Death

◆

The first part of this story took place when I was seven years old, and its conclusion when I was twenty-eight.

When I was seven, several learned pandits and astrologers of Banaras were invited by one of my relatives to consider my future. [Our country is famous for this science. You will find many charlatans, and you'll also find genuine astrological practitioners. If you decide to consult one, before you arrive he may write a description of your whole life, and on the front will be your name. It will be waiting for you when you arrive, even if you have not told anyone you are going to see him. Such an ability is rare. You will find it at only two or three places, but it is quite genuine.]

I was standing just outside the door, overhearing what they said. They all said, "This boy is going to die at the age of twenty-eight." They even gave the exact day.

I was so upset that I started sobbing. Then I thought, "I have such a short span of time. I will die without accomplishing anything. How am I possibly going to complete the mission of my life?"

My master came up to me and inquired, "Why are you weeping?"

"I am going to die," I told him.

He asked, "And who told you that?"

I said, "All these people," and pointed to the astrologers gathered inside.

He took hold of my hand and said, "Come." He took me into the room and confronted the astrologers. "Do you really mean to say that this lad is going to die at the age of twenty-eight?" he asked.

The unanimous response was "Yes."

"Are you sure?"

"Yes, he is going to die at that time, and nobody has the power to prevent it."

My master turned to me and said, "Do you know, these astrologers will all die before you do, and you will live for a long time, because I will give you my own years." [Today none of them is alive. They all died before I was twenty-eight years old.]

They said, "How is such a thing possible?"

My master replied, "Your prediction is wrong. There is something beyond astrology." Then he said to me, "Don't worry—but you will have to experience death face-to-face on that fateful day." During the intervening years I forgot all about what had been predicted.

When I was twenty-eight I was asked by my guru to go to a mountain peak some 11,000 feet high and some sixty miles from Rishikesh, where for nine days I performed a ritual *Durga-puja* [worship of the Divine Mother]. I wore wooden sandals, a loincloth, and a shawl. I carried a pot of water with me, and nothing else. I used to go about freely in the mountains, chanting and reciting the hymns of the Mother Goddess. The mountains were my home. I had once climbed to a height of 20,000 feet, and I was confident that I could climb any mountain without special equipment.

One day I was singing as I walked all alone beside a steep

cliff, feeling like the Lord himself in that solitude. I was on my way to the top of the mountain, where there was a small temple, to worship the Divine Mother. There were pine trees all around. Suddenly I slipped on the pine needles and began to roll down the mountain. I thought that my life was finished— but as I plummeted downward, after about 500 feet I was caught by a small thorny bush. A sharp branch pierced me in the abdomen, and that held me. There was a precipitous drop below—and the bush started swinging with my weight: first I would see the mountains, and then the Ganges far below. I closed my eyes. When I opened them again, I saw blood flowing where the branch pierced my abdomen—but that was nothing compared to the stark imminence of death. I paid no attention to the pain because of the larger concern, the antici-pation of death.

I repeated all the mantras I knew. I even repeated Christian and Buddhist mantras. I had been to many monasteries and had learned mantras from all faiths—but no mantra worked. I remembered many deities: I said, "O Bright Being such-and-such, please help me." But no help was forthcoming. There was only one thing which I had not tested: my courage! When I started testing my courage I suddenly remembered: "I am not going to die, for there is no death for my soul. And death for this body is inevitable but unimportant. I am eternal. Why am I afraid? I have been identifying myself with my body—what a poor fool I have been."

I remained suspended on that bush for something like twenty minutes. Then I remembered something my master had told me. He said, "Do not form this habit—but whenever you really need me and remember me, I will be there, in one way or another." I thought, "I have tested my courage; now I think I should also test my master." (This is natural for a disciple. All the time he wants to test his master. He avoids facing his own weaknesses by looking for faults in his master.) Because of the

310

excessive bleeding I began to feel dizzy. Everything became hazy, and I began to lose consciousness. Then I heard some women on the path just above me. They had come to the mountains to collect grass and a few roots for their animals. One of them looked down and saw me. She cried, "Look, a dead man!"

I thought, "If they think that I am dead, they will leave me like this." How could I communicate to them? My head was down and my feet were upward. They were a few hundred feet away. I couldn't speak, so I started waving my legs.

They said, "No, no, he's not dead—his legs are still moving: he must be still alive." They were brave women and came down, tied a rope around my waist, and lifted me up. The stem was still inside me. I thought, "This is surely a time for courage." I pressed my stomach in and I pulled the stem out of my abdomen. They pulled me up and took me to a small mountain path. They asked me if I could walk, and I said, "Yes." At first I didn't realize the severity of my condition, for the injury caused by the stem was mostly internal. They thought that since I was a swami I could take care of myself without their help. They told me to follow the path until I came to a village; then they went on their way. I tried to walk, but after a few minutes I fainted and fell. I thought of my master and said to him, "My life is over. You brought me up and did everything for me. But now I am dying without realization."

Suddenly my master appeared. I thought my mind was playing tricks on me. I said, "Are you really here? I thought you had left me!" He said, "Why do you worry? Nothing is going to happen to you. Don't you remember that this is the time and date predicted for your death? You need face death no more today. You are all right now."

I gradually came to my senses. He brought some leaves, crushed them, and put them on the wound. He took me to a nearby cave and asked some people there to care for me. He said, "Even death can be prevented." Then he went away. In two weeks' time the wound was healed, but the scar is still on my body.

In that experience I found out how a genuine and selfless master helps his disciple even if he is far away. I realized that the relationship between master and disciple is the highest and purest of all. It is indescribable.

X

Powers of the Mind

THE MIND IS A RESERVOIR FOR NUMEROUS POWERS.
By utilizing the resources which are hidden within
it, one can attain any height of success in the
world. If the mind is trained, made one-pointed
and inward, it also has power to penetrate into
the deeper levels of our being. It is the finest
instrument that a human being can ever have.

Lessons on the Sands

◆

I f you look at someone with full attention by focusing your
conscious mind, it can immediately influence him. A swami
taught me this when I was young. His name was Chakravarti.
He was one of the most eminent mathematicians of India and
the author of the book *Chakravarti's Mathematics*. Later he
renounced the world to become a swami. He was a student of
my master. He contended that gaze *(trataka)* is a very powerful
tool for influencing anything external and strengthening concentration.

When the mind is focused externally on some object, it is
called gaze; when it is focused internally, it is called concentration. The power of a focused mind is immense. There are various methods of gazing, each of which gives a different power
to the human mind. One may gaze at the space between the
two eyebrows, the bridge between the two nostrils, a candle
light in a dark room, the early morning sun, or the moon. But
certain precautions must be observed or one can injure himself
both physically and mentally.

Thought-power is known all over the world. A one-pointed
mind can do wonders, but when we direct it toward worldly

gains we are caught in the whirlpool of selfish desires. Many on the path become victims of the temptations of acquiring *siddhis* [powers], forgetting their real goal of attaining serenity, tranquility, and self-realization.

One day the swami said to me, "Today I am going to show you something. Go to the court and find a person who is being persecuted unjustly."

So I asked one of the lawyers, "Can you tell me of anyone who is being tried unjustly in this court?" He said, "Yes, I have such a case."

I went back, and Swamiji said: "Okay, this man will be acquitted, and I will now tell you word for word the judgment that will be handed down." He dictated the judgment to me, although he was not a lawyer. He said, "I have made three mistakes purposefully. The judgment will be exactly like my dictation, and it will also have these three mistakes." I typed up his dictation.

When the judgment was later handed down every word, comma, and period was exactly the same as what had been dictated to me. He said, "Compare my dictation with the judgment and you will find that the same two commas and one period are missing." The dictation perfectly matched the judgment.

I said, "Swamiji, you can change the course of the world." He said, "I don't claim to do that; that is not my purpose. I am demonstrating this so that you can understand how a man can influence the mind of another from any part of the world if it is for a good reason. Helping others is possible from a distance."

I asked him to give me the secret of this power. He said, "I will give you the secret, but you won't want to practice it." I did practice the method for some time and it helped me, but later I discontinued it because it was distracting and time-consuming.

The swami was very kind and also taught me philosophy

through mathematics. Every digit was explained with verses from the Upanishads. From zero to one hundred, he explained the philosophical meaning of the science of mathematics.

Mathematics has the digit 1. All other digits are multiples of the same 1. Similarly, there is only one absolute Reality and all the names and forms of the universe are multiple manifestations of that One. Drawing lines on the sand of the Ganges with his staff, he made a triangle and taught me how life should be an equilateral triangle. The angle of the body, the angle of internal states, and the angle of the external world make up the equilateral triangle of life. As all numbers are the outcome of a point which cannot be measured, similarly this whole universe has come out of an unmeasurable void. Life is like a wheel, which he compared with a circle or zero. This circle is an expansion of the point. He used another analogy: "There are two points, called death and birth, and life here is a line between the two. The unknown part of life is an infinite line."

My repulsion toward the study of mathematics was dispelled. After that I began studying mathematics with considerable interest. I learned that mathematics is a positive science which is the very basis of all sciences, but it is itself based on the exact science of Sankhya philosophy. Sankhya philosophy is the most ancient philosophy for knowing the body, its components, and various functions of the mind. Yoga is a practical science which leads one to the superconscious state. Through understanding Sankhya all philosophical questions arising in my mind were solved easily and then I understood the scriptures properly.

The last day of his teaching was enchanting. He said, "Now make a zero first, then put one afterwards: 01. Every zero has value if the one is put first, but zero has no value if the one is not put first. All the things of the world are like zeros, and without being conscious of the one Reality they have no value at all. When we remember the one Reality, then life becomes worthwhile. Otherwise it is burdensome."

This swami left for the deep Himalayas and I never met him again. I am grateful to those teachers who spent their valuable time in teaching me.

Transmutation of Matter

◆

In 1942 I started on a journey to Badrinath, the famous Himalayan shrine. On the way there is a place called Shrinagar, which is situated on a bank of the Ganges. Five miles from Shrinagar there is a small Shakti temple, and just two miles below that was the cave of an *aghori baba*. *Aghor* is a very mysterious study which is rarely mentioned in books and hardly understood even by the yogis and swamis of India. It is an esoteric path involving solar science and is used for healing. This science is devoted to understanding and mastering the finer forces of life—finer than prana. It creates a bridge between life here and hereafter. There are very few yogis who practice the aghori science, and those who do are shunned by most people because of their strange ways.

The villagers in the area around Shrinagar were very much afraid of the aghori baba. They never went near him, because whenever anyone had approached him in the past he called them names and threw pebbles at them. He was about six feet five inches tall and very strongly built. He was about seventy-five years of age. He had long hair and a beard and wore a loin-cloth made of jute. He had nothing in his cave except a few pieces of gunnysack.

I went to see him, thinking that I would pass the night there and learn something from him. I asked a local pandit to show me the way. The pandit said, "This aghori is no sage; he is dirty. You don't want to see him." But the pandit knew much about my master and me, and I persuaded him to take me to the baba's cave.

We arrived in the evening just before dark. We found the aghori sitting on a rock between the Ganges and his cave. He asked us to sit beside him. Then he confronted the pandit, saying, "Behind my back you call me names and yet you greet me with folded hands." The pandit wanted to leave, but the aghori said, "No! Go to the river and fetch me a pot of water." When the frightened pandit came back with the water, the aghori handed him a cleaver and said, "There is a dead body which is floating in the river. Pull it ashore, chop off the thigh and calf muscles, and bring a few pounds of the flesh to me." The aghori's demand shook the pandit. He became very nervous—and so did I. He was extremely frightened and did not want to carry out the aghori's wishes. But the aghori became fierce and shouted at him, saying, "Either you will bring the flesh from that dead body or I will chop you and take *your* flesh. Which do you prefer?"

The poor pandit, out of deep anxiety and fear, went to the dead body and started cutting it up. He was so upset that he also accidentally cut the first and second fingers of his left hand, and they started bleeding profusely. He brought the flesh to the baba. Neither the pandit nor I were then in our normal senses. When the pandit came near, the aghori touched the cuts on his fingers—and they were healed instantly. There was not even a scar.

The aghori ordered him to put the pieces of flesh into an earthen pot, to put the pot on the fire, and to cover the lid with a stone. He said, "Don't you know this young swami is hungry, and you also have to eat?"

We both said, "Sir, we are vegetarians."

The baba was irritated by this and said to me, "Do you think I eat meat? Do you agree with the people here that I am dirty? I too am a pure vegetarian."

After ten minutes had passed he told the pandit to bring him the earthen pot. He gathered a few large leaves and said, "Spread these on the ground to serve the food on." The pandit, with trembling hands, did so. Then the aghori went inside the cave to fetch three earthen bowls. While he was gone the pandit whispered to me, "I don't think I will live through this. This is against everything that I have learned and practiced all my life. I should commit suicide. What have you done to me? Why did you bring me here?" I said, "Be quiet. We cannot escape, so let us at least see what happens."

The aghori ordered the pandit to serve the food. When the pandit took the lid off the pot and began filling my bowl we were astonished to find a sweet called *rasgula,* which is made from cheese and sugar. This was my favorite dish, and I had been thinking of it as I was walking to the baba's cave. I thought it was all very strange. The aghori said, "This sweet has no meat in it."

I ate the sweet, and the pandit had to eat it too. It was very delicious. What was left over was given to the pandit to distribute among the villagers. This was done to prove that we had not been fooled by means of a hypnotic technique. All alone in the darkness the pandit left for his village, which was three miles away from the cave. I preferred to stay with the aghori to solve the mystery of how the food was transformed and to understand his bewildering way of living. "Why was the flesh of a dead body cooked, and how could it turn into sweets? Why does he live here all alone?" I wondered. I had heard about such people, but this was my first chance to meet one in person.

After I meditated for two hours we began talking about the

scriptures. He was extraordinarily intelligent and well-read. His Sanskrit, however, was so terse and tough that each time he spoke it took a few minutes to decipher what he was saying before I could answer him. He was, no doubt, a very learned man, but his way was different from any other sadhu that I had ever met.

Aghor is a path which has been described in the *Atharva Veda,* but in none of the scriptures have I ever read that human flesh should be eaten. I asked him, "Why do you live like this, eating the flesh of dead bodies?"

He replied, "Why do you call it a 'dead body'? It's no longer human. It's just matter that is not being used. You're associating it with human beings. No one else will use that body, so I will. I'm a scientist doing experiments, trying to discover the underlying principles of matter and energy. I'm changing one form of matter to another form of matter. My teacher is Mother Nature; she makes many forms, and I am only following her law to change the forms around. I did this for that pandit so that he would warn others to stay away. This is my thirteenth year at this cave, and no one has visited me. People are afraid of me because of my appearance. They think I am dirty and that I live on flesh and dead bodies. I throw pebbles, but I never hit anybody."

His external behavior was very crude, but he told me that he was behaving that way knowingly so that no one would disturb him as he studied and so that he would not become dependent on the villagers for food and other necessities. He was not imbalanced, but to avoid people he behaved as though he were. His way of living was totally self-dependent, and although he continued to live in that cave for twenty-one years, no villager ever visited him.

We stayed up through the night and he instructed me, talking the entire time about his aghor path. This path was not for me, but I was curious to know why he lived such a lifestyle and did all that he was doing. He had the power to transform matter into different forms, like changing a rock into a sugar cube. One after another the next morning he did many such things. He told me to touch the sand—and the grains of sand turned into almonds and cashews. I had heard of this science before and knew its basic principles, but I had hardly believed such stories. I did not explore this field, but I am fully acquainted with the governing laws of the science.

At noon the aghori insisted that I eat something before leaving. This time he took out a different sweet from the same earthen jar. He was very gentle with me, all the time discussing the tantra scriptures. He said, "This science is dying. Learned people do not want to practice it, so there will be a time when this knowledge will be forgotten."

I asked, "What is the use of doing all this?" He said, "What do you mean by 'use'? This is a science, and a scientist of this knowledge should use it for healing purposes, and should tell other scientists that matter can be changed into energy and energy into matter. The law that governs matter and energy is one and the same. Beneath all names and forms there lies one unifying principle, which is still not known in its entirety by modern scientists. Vedanta and the ancient sciences described this underlying principle of life. There is only one life-force, and all the forms and names in this universe are but varieties of that One. It is not difficult to understand the relationship between two forms of matter, because the source is one and the same. When water becomes solid, it is called ice; when it starts evaporating, it is called vapor. Young children do not know that these three are forms of the same matter, and that essentially there is no difference in their composition. The difference is only in the form it takes. The scientists today are like children. They do not realize the unity behind all matter, nor the principles for changing it from one form to another."

Intellectually I agreed with him, and yet I did not approve

of his way of living. I said goodbye and promised to visit him again, but I never have. I was curious about the fate of the pandit who had gone to his village the previous night in a state of fear, so I went to see him. To my surprise he was completely changed, and was thinking of following the aghori and becoming his disciple.

Where Is My Donkey?

◆

When I stayed in Mau, a small city in Uttar Pradesh, I lived in a small hut which was built for wandering swamis and sadhus. Most of the time I stayed in my room, doing my exercises and sitting in meditation. I came out just for a short while in the morning and evening.

A laundry man used to wash clothes nearby. He had no wife and children—only a donkey. One day he lost his donkey. He was so worried that he became stunned and went into a trance. People thought he was in samadhi.

In India people will do anything in the name of samadhi. They will even sell their homes and offer money to that person who has apparently attained that state. They believe that giving gifts is the way to express their love and devotion for a holy man. The laundry man sat in one position for two days—and people started placing money, flowers, and fruit all around him. Two people declared themselves his disciples and began collecting the money. But that laundry man did not stir. His followers began encouraging others to come. They wanted everyone to know that they were the disciples of this great guru. Through word of mouth he soon became famous.

I received information through one of his disciples that there was a great man in samadhi near the place where I was staying. I went to see him. There was indeed someone sitting very still with his eyes closed. Many people were sitting around him, chanting, "O Lord, bring him back. *Hari Rama, Hari Rama, Hari Krishna, Hari Krishna.*"

I asked them, "What are you doing?" They said, "He is our guru and is in samadhi." I became curious and thought, "Let me see what happens when he comes out of this state."

After two days he opened his eyes. Everyone looked on expectantly to hear what profound sermon he would deliver—but when he came out of the trance he only said, "Where is my donkey?"

The desire with which one goes into meditation is a prime factor. When a fool goes into sleep, he comes out as a fool. But if one does meditation with a single desire for enlightenment, he comes out as a sage.

There is a fine distinction between the person who becomes preoccupied and pensive, and the aspirant who really meditates. Intense worry can drive the mind toward one-pointedness, but in a negative way. Through meditation the mind becomes positive, one-pointed, and inward. The outer signs and symptoms are similar. Worry makes the body inert and tense, while meditation makes it relaxed, steady, and still. For meditation purification of the mind is essential; for worry it is not needed. When intense worry controls the mind, the mind becomes inert and insensitive. But if a great man contemplates on the miseries of the world it is not a worry at all, but a loving and selfless concern for humanity. In this case the individual mind expands and unites itself with the cosmic One. When the mind is engrossed in individual interests one-pointedly, it is called worry. When the mind is made aware of the misery of others, it starts contemplating positively. In both cases mind can become one-pointed, but in the latter case consciousness is expanded.

When John was put in the isolated cell on the island of Patmos, he worried because he thought that the message of his master would not reach the masses. But actually this sort of worry was not for the fulfillment of his own desires; it was a universal issue on which he contemplated and meditated. Meditation is expansion, and worry is contraction.

The same power that can flow toward negative grooves can also voluntarily be directed toward positive grooves. Therefore it is important for a student to purify the mind first, and then to meditate: without a disciplined and purified mind meditation cannot become helpful in the path of enlightenment. Preparation is important. The preliminary steps—control of actions, speech, dietary habits, and other appetites—are essential requisites in preparation. Those who discipline themselves and then meditate receive valid experiences. They come in touch with their positive and powerful potentials. These experiences become guides in fathoming the deeper levels of consciousness. The untrained and impure mind cannot create anything worthwhile, but the meditative and contemplative mind is always creative. Both worry and meditation leave their deeper imprint on the unconscious mind. Worry creates several psychosomatic diseases, while meditation makes one aware of other dimensions of consciousness. If the aspirant knows how to meditate he will naturally be free from his worrying habits. Hatred and worry are two negative powers which control the mind. Meditation and contemplation expand the mind.

I concluded that the poor laundry man, though sitting still, was deeply engrossed in misery. He was in deep sorrow, and his mind lost its balance. In that state he became still without knowing where he was. In samadhi the mind is consciously led to higher dimensions of awareness. The aspirants who try to attain samadhi without purification of mind are disappointed, because such an impure mind creates obstacles in attaining this state. Samadhi is the result of a conscious and controlled effort. It is a state of transcendent consciousness. Worry contracts the mind, while meditation expands it. Expansion of individual consciousness and union with the transcendent consciousness is called samadhi.

Who Was That
Other Gopinath?

◆

I was staying on the other side of the Ganges, six miles from the city of Kanpur. I lived in a garden by a bank of the river. During those days I didn't care for anything of the world. I never went to the city, but many people wanted to see me. They would come with fruit and sit before me. In order to avoid that I used to keep some *malas,* and when anyone came I would say, "First sit down and repeat this mantra two thousand times and then we will talk." Most of my visitors would leave the *malas* and quietly depart.

There was a man called Gopinath, who was treasurer of the Reserve Bank of India at Kanpur. He came with four people one afternoon. They sat down and started chanting. They became so engrossed in chanting that the time slipped by unnoticed. At nine o'clock in the evening he suddenly opened his eyes and said, "Something very terrible has happened!"

Everyone asked, "What is it?"

He said, "My niece was to get married at seven o'clock tonight. All the ornaments for the marriage ceremony are locked in my safe, and I have the only key with me here. Swamiji, what have you done to me?"

I replied, "I haven't done anything. The atmosphere here does that to you. It happens to everyone who comes here. You relax and forget the world's problems; you experience and enjoy divinity. Why are you so worried?"

"But the ornaments and jewelry which I have to give them are in my safe."

I said, "Look, did you really forget yourself in chanting today?"

He said, "That's why I am still here."

"Then don't worry. God will take care of the situation. If something bad can happen because of chanting the Lord's name, let it happen; something worse would happen without it."

They got into their horse cart and quickly returned to the city. When he arrived he anxiously asked what had happened. The people there were confused by his concern. They said, "What is the matter with you? The ceremony is over. Everything is fine."

He said, "I was on the other side of the Ganges and had my keys with me. What about the ornaments?"

They said, "You gave the ornaments. Have you lost your memory?"

His wife came and said, "You presented the ornaments ten minutes before the ceremony; now the marriage party is over and everyone is taking his food."

But the four people who were with him confirmed that he was with me, chanting. They said, "Either you are fools, or we are fools." They were quite disturbed because they could not reconcile the reports with their own memories. Gopinath completely lost his mental equilibrium. He said, "I am Gopinath—but who was that Gopinath who came here?" When he went to the office the next day he wouldn't talk to anyone, except to ask one question. He would say, "I am only one Gopinath. Can you tell me who that was?" For three years he was obsessed.

He had to resign from his job because of it.

His wife came to see me but I could not help. I asked, "Does he speak with you?" She said, "Yes, but all the time he asks, 'Tell me, honey, who was that other Gopinath? Did he look exactly like me?'"

After this incident many people came running to me, saying, "You are a sage of great miracles." I said, "You are praising me for nothing." Neither I nor they knew what had happened. And really, I did not know how it had happened.

Later I asked my master, "What was it?" My master said that he was fully aware of this fact and that it was possible that one of the sages from our tradition helped Gopinath because he was fully absorbed in chanting God's name.

Throughout my life it has been my personal experience that sages are kind and generous in guiding and protecting the devotees of God. As far as my experiences go, a sage can live in the Himalayas, yet can travel and project himself in any part of the world.

An Experience with a Psychic

On our way to Rishikesh in 1973 we stayed in one of the hotels at New Delhi. There I met Dr. Rudolph Ballentine, a psychiatrist and former professor of a medical school in the United States. He had recently come from touring the countries of the Middle East via Pakistan. Dr. Ballentine started telling me about an experience he had had at Connaught Place, which is a famous shopping center in New Delhi. A stranger had called him by name and then abruptly told him the name of his girlfriend in England.

The doctor asked, "How did you know these things?" He said, "You were born on such and such date and your grandfather's name is such and such." Then the man told him something very personal which no one except Dr. Ballentine knew. The doctor thought, "This is the person for whom I have come to India." The man said, "Sir, give me five dollars," and the doctor obliged. The man was looking here and there because he was afraid the police might see him. If the police had known what he was about, they would have arrested him. He said, "Stay here. I will come right back." The doctor waited there for half an hour, but the man did not return.

Dr. Ballentine told me, "Swamiji, he was a great man." I asked, "What did he do?" He answered, "He told me all those personal things about myself although I was a complete stranger." I replied, "Didn't you already know those things?" "Yes."

"Then what big thing did he do? If somebody knows what you are thinking, then you obviously already know it too. This knowledge doesn't improve you in any way. This ability may amaze you for some time, but it cannot help anyone in self-growth."

Fakes like the one Dr. Ballentine encountered are often found disguised as sadhus at Connaught Place, telling about someone's past and predicting the future. They learn such tricks just to make their living. Naive tourists mistake them for great sages. Such tourists never reach the places where the real sages are. These pretenders give a bad name to spirituality and to spiritual people.

Dr. Ballentine then started traveling with us. When we left India he stayed at Rishikesh and in other parts of India for several months, visiting the schools of Indian medicine. He returned to the United States to join us, and he is now conducting and directing the Institute's Combined Therapy Program.

XI

Healing Power

◆

THE POWER OF SELF-HEALING IS BURIED IN THE TOMB of every human life. By uncovering the potentials of that power one can heal oneself. A completely selfless man of God can heal anyone. The highest of all healings is to attain freedom from all miseries.

My First Exposure to
the Power of Healing

◆

When I was twelve years of age I was traveling by foot with my master through the plains of India. We stopped at a railway station in Etah, where my master went to the stationmaster and said, "My child is with me and he is hungry. Please give us some food." The stationmaster went to his home for food, but when he arrived his wife cried, "You know that our only son is suffering from smallpox. How can you be concerned about giving food to these wandering sadhus? My son is dying! Get out of this house! I am in distress."

He returned with a long face and apologized: "What can I do? My wife says, 'If he is a real swami, why doesn't he realize our situation and cure our child? Doesn't he have any sense? Our only child is on his deathbed, and he's worried about a food offering.'"

My master smiled and told me to follow him. We went to the stationmaster's home. It was a challenge, and he always enjoyed being challenged. But I complained, "I am hungry. When are we going to eat?" He said, "You will have to wait."

This was a frequent complaint of mine. Often I used to cry, "You don't give me food in time." I would run away weeping.

But he was teaching me to have patience.

He said, "You are disturbed right now. Wait for five minutes and you won't be disturbed at all. In this situation it is right to wait." But I continued to complain and the woman wanted to chase me from her house. It was the first time I had seen someone suffering from smallpox. The boy had big abscesses all over his body, even on his face, and pus was issuing from them. My master said to the parents, "Don't worry— in two minutes your son will be completely well." He took a glass of water and walked around the cot on which the boy was lying. He did this three times, and then drank the water. Then he looked at the woman and said, "He's getting well—don't you see?" To our amazement the abscesses began to disappear from the boy—but to my dismay, at the same time they began to appear on my master's face. I was terrified and I started to cry. He calmly said, "Don't worry, nothing will happen to me." Within two minutes the child's face was perfectly clear, and we left the house. I followed my master until he came to a banyan tree. He sat under the tree—and soon the abscesses began to disappear from him and then to appear on the tree. After ten minutes they also disappeared from the tree. When I saw that my master was all right, I hugged him and wept.

"Don't do that again!" I pleaded. "You didn't look nice, and it frightened me." Then many people started searching for us. I asked, "Have we done anything bad?"

He said, "No; come with me." He held my hand and we started walking again on a bank of the Jamuna River. Finally we stopped at another house and were given some food. We then went to an enclosed courtyard where no one would find us, took our meal, and rested.

The sages find pleasure in suffering to help others. This is beyond the conception of the ordinary mind. Human history has provided many instances of spiritual leaders who suffered for others. Such sages become examples, and many people even today follow in the footsteps of such great people. When individual consciousness expands itself to cosmic consciousness it becomes easy to feel delight in suffering for the sake of others. For them it is not suffering, though the ordinary people think that they are suffering. When one's consciousness remains limited to the individual boundaries only, then the individual suffers. A great man does not suffer when something happens to his own self, but feels more pain in the suffering of others.

Pain and pleasure are a pair of opposites experienced when the senses contact objects of the world. Those whose consciousness has expanded beyond the sensory level get freedom from this pair of opposites. There are techniques for voluntarily withdrawing the mind from the senses and focusing inwards to reveal the center of consciousness. In such a state of mind one is not affected by sensory pleasure or pain. Such a one-pointed mind also creates a dynamic will which can be used for healing others. All such healing powers flow through the human being from the one source of consciousness. The moment the healer becomes conscious of his individuality, that spontaneous flow of healing power stops. Healing is a natural power in man. The healing of others is possible through that willpower which is not interrupted by the lower mind.

My Master Sends Me
to Heal Someone

◆

One fine morning my master and I were sitting outside our cave when suddenly he said, "You have to catch a bus. The bus route is seven miles from here, so hurry up." He often told me to get up and go somewhere on the spur of the moment. Sometimes I wouldn't know why, but I would find out when I reached there. I rose and picked up the pot of water I always carried. He said, "Take the bus to the Hardwar railroad station. You'll get a ticket and from there go to Kanpur. Dr. Mitra is bedridden and is constantly remembering me. He is having a brain hemorrhage and is bleeding out of his right nostril, but his wife will not allow him to go to the hospital. His brother-in-law, Dr. Basu, knows that it is a hemorrhage, but there are no facilities there to perform brain surgery."

I asked, "What shall I do?"

"Just give him a love pat on the cheek. Don't consider yourself a healer. Think that you are an instrument and go there, for I have promised him and his wife that we will always help them. Go as quickly as you can."

I said, "I'm surprised to find that you make promises on my behalf without my knowledge." I was reluctant to go on such a long journey, but I could not disobey. I went to the bus route, which was seven miles away from the cave, and stood by the side of the road until the bus for Rishikesh/Hardwar picked me up. The drivers would always give a swami a ride when they saw one on the roadside. I got off the bus at the railway station at Hardwar with no money, and I had only half an hour until the train was to leave for Kanpur. I looked at my watch and thought I might be able to sell it to buy a ticket. Approaching a gentleman at the railway station, I asked if I could exchange my watch with him for the money to buy a ticket. Surprisingly he said, "My son could not come with me, so I have an extra ticket. Please take it. I don't need your watch."

I got into the train and met a lady who was also going to Kanpur and who was a close relative of Dr. Mitra. She had heard about me and my master from Dr. Mitra and his wife, and she gave me something to eat. We traveled all night and in the morning the train arrived at Kanpur. There was so much rush at the railway station that it took me ten minutes to get through the gate. Outside the station I suddenly met a man who knew me well. He had his car parked nearby and had been waiting for someone, but that person never turned up—he had missed his train at Delhi. This man wanted to drive me to his house, but I insisted that we go to Dr. Mitra's instead.

When we reached there I knocked on the door and entered to find three doctors examining Dr. Mitra. Mrs. Mitra was delighted to see me and said, "Now that you have come, I hand over my husband to you." This is called Indian blind faith in sadhus.

I said, "I am not a healer. I have just come to see him." I went over to Dr. Mitra's bed, but he was not allowed to sit up because of the bleeding from his nostril.

When he saw me he asked, "How is my master?" I gave him the gentle pat on his right cheek. After a few minutes there was no more bleeding. One of the doctors explained that the slap which I had given him on the cheek closed the opening in the blood vessel and that it was now sealed.

I did not know what I had done, but I followed my master's instructions. Dr. Mitra's sudden recovery quickly became the talk of the town, and hundreds of patients started searching for me, so I left the city later that day and reached Hardwar the next morning. From there I went to the place where my master was staying. I told my master teasingly, "I know the secret and can stop a hemorrhage in anyone."

He laughed at me and said, "The doctor who gave you that explanation is quite ignorant. There are various modes and levels of suffering, but ignorance is the mother of all."

On several occasions I had to leave suddenly according to my master's instructions without having any knowledge of my purpose and destination. I had many experiences like this. I came to the conclusion that the ways of the sages are mysterious and beyond the ability of ordinary minds to understand. I would just do and then experience. Experience would give me knowledge. One who is free from the conditionings of the mind knows past, present, and future alike. These conditionings are called time, space, and causation. The ordinary mind cannot fathom these conditionings, but the great men do. It becomes difficult for ordinary men to understand this science, but it does not take extraordinary ability for those who are on the path.

I once asked my master, "Is it possible for a man in the world to get freedom from all conditionings of the mind, or does he have to live in the Himalayas his whole life to develop powers such as yours?" He said, "If a human being remains constantly aware of the purpose of his life and directs all his actions toward the fulfillment of that purpose, there remains nothing impossible for him. Those who are not aware of the purpose of life are easily caught by the whirlpool of miseries."

It is a law that one cannot live without doing his duties, but it is also true that duties make the doer a slave. If the duties are performed skillfully and selflessly, then the duties do not bind the doer. All actions and duties performed with love become means in the path of liberation. Performing one's duty is very important, but more important is love, without which duty creates bondage. Fortunate is he who serves others selflessly and learns to cross this mire of delusion.

A human being is fully equipped with all necessary healing powers, but does not know their usage. The moment he comes in touch with the healing potentials within, he can heal himself. All the powers belong to only one God. A human being is only an instrument.

Swami Rama after coming to the West

Unorthodox Ways of Healing

◆

The belief in possession is as old as the oldest cultures. We still hear that such and such a person is possessed by a demon or ghost or spirit. From 1960 to the present, in my extensive travels all over the world I have found that not only ignorant people but also educated priests believe in the reality of possession. But this possession is just a mental imbalance. It is possible to treat such cases with religious rituals and ceremonies. In most communities of the world such rituals are still practiced, though sometimes clandestinely. In most of the cases which I had an opportunity to examine the problem was hysteria, usually created by the repression of sexual urges. There are other causes, such as pathological fear of losing something or of not being able to obtain something that is desperately desired.

There are certain places in India where patients are brought to be freed from a "possession." The "therapists" use crude methods, including whipping the patient before an idol. During the treatment one of the therapists, called a *vakya*, comes forward as though he were also possessed, but by a *deva* (good spirit). Sometimes, while in a highly concentrated state of emotion, the *vakya* jumps into the flames of a fire to prove how mighty his powers are. Then, chanting hymns, he tries to aid the patient out of his condition. There are many such practitioners scattered throughout the Himalayan mountains.

A few years ago Dr. Elmer Green, Alyce Green, and some of their colleagues from the Menninger Foundation came to India with sensitive physiological instruments to examine yogis. They visited my ashram, situated on a bank of the Ganges at Rishikesh. They arrived a year later than originally planned, however, and could not contact the yogis who had agreed to come to the ashram for the experiments. I had appointed a man named Hari Singh to serve as a watchman, and he offered himself as a subject for one of the experiments. There were forty American observers, including doctors and psychologists who were staying in my ashram at that time.

A movie-maker from the United States who had accompanied Dr. Green's party started his camera as Hari Singh put a steel blade in a fire. When it became red-hot Hari Singh pulled it from the fire and licked it with his tongue. There was a hissing sound and vapor arose—but nothing happened to his tongue! It was not burned or scarred in any way. Such phenomena are often performed by non-yogis, and people then consider them to be yogis. Out of curiosity Westerners frequently go to India and to the Himalayan foothills to find such people. The phenomena are common enough and genuine, but they are not part of yoga and are not taught in the yoga schools.

Once in 1945 a neurologist from Australia came to see me at my mountain home and stayed with me for ten days. There were few hospitals or dispensaries in the mountains thirty years ago, although the Indian government is now trying to build treatment centers here and there to treat minor health complications. I had hoped that this man could help the villagers by prescribing a few medicines. His reason for coming to the

Himalayas to see me was to find a way to get rid of his severe chronic headaches, which prevented him from leading a normal life. Although he was a doctor himself and had been examined by many other doctors, he could not find the cause of the headaches, and no one had been able to successfully treat him.

An old woman who used to bring milk to my cabin smiled when she saw him and said, "Is he a doctor?" She laughed and said to me, "If I am permitted, I can remove his headache in two minutes' time." I said, "Please try." She brought one of the herbs that is well-known and widely used in the mountains for making fire. A spark made by friction between two rocks ignites the herb. She crushed the herb and put a bit of it on the doctor's right temple and said, "Believe me, you will be free from headaches forever. Lie down." When he did so, she placed an iron hook in the fire and heated the point until it was red. Then she put the red-hot point on the herb which had been placed on his temple. The doctor screamed and jumped up. I also was shocked. The woman calmly returned to her village—and the doctor's headaches were gone.

Such treatments are often used by the villagers. The doctor said, "Which science is this? I want to learn more about it." I did not encourage him, for although I believe that occasionally such treatments may help, they are not systematic, and it is very difficult to evaluate which ones are truly effective and which are only a matter of superstition. The doctor persisted, though, and left for the Garhwal mountains, where he studied under a mountain medicine man, Vaidya Bhairavdutt, who knew more than 3,000 varieties of herbs. When the doctor met me again six months later he reported, "I know the explanation of that treatment which I received from the old lady. It is based on the principles which were used by travelers who went across the Tibetan border to China and which have been systematized as acupuncture. Charaka, the ancient Indian master of medicine, mentions it as *suchi vedha, sui* in modern Hindi, the needle-pricking treatment."

I concluded that he had been relieved of one kind of headache, but was now creating a new headache for himself by investigating these cures. There are many things known to the villagers which work, but we would be wise not to adopt them until we understand their underlying principles. We must keep an open mind.

Herbs and medicine prepared from metals are not in common use in the West today. Although we have many modern means to prepare drugs, which do help patients, drugs cannot be the remedy for all diseases. Ayurvedic treatment uses herbs and many other methods of treatment. Water therapy, clay therapy, steam therapy, color therapy, sun baths, and the use of juices of various fruits, flowers, and vegetables are essential components of Ayurvedic therapy. The Ayurvedic method of treating disease is divided into two sections: *Nidana* and *Pathya*. Therapists prescribe changes in eating, sleeping, and even climate, instead of putting patients in the terrifying conditions that we often find in crowded modern hospitals.

I have often wondered how it is possible for the people of the Himalayas to remain so healthy and have such longevity though they enjoy very few of the benefits of modern medicine. There are many diseases for which modern medical science has not discovered a remedy, but these mountaineers do not even suffer from these. Perhaps fresh food, fresh air, and, above all, free thinking with no anxiety is responsible for their health. Millions of patients all over the world who suffer from psychosomatic diseases can be helped through right diet, juices, relaxation, breathing, and meditation. Preventive and alternative medicine should not be ignored.

Healing in a Himalayan Shrine

A party of businessmen and a few doctors decided to visit the shrine of Badrinath in the Himalayas. Mr. Jaipuria, a prominent businessman from Kanpur, organized this pilgrimage, and Dr. Sharma went along to serve as health custodian to the forty people in the party. They persisted that I go with them to teach the group. With the exception of the organizer, who was carried in a palanquin, we went on foot from Karnaprayag, and after several days' journey reached Badrinath. By that time, since they were not used to walking on foot in the mountains, all the members of the party were worn and tired and were suffering from aches and pains, especially from swollen knee joints. Upon reaching Badrinath everyone rushed for a bath in the hot springs. The sun was about to go to bed, and my room was in a quiet side of a very big building where there lived many travelers who had come to visit this shrine.

I was in the habit of remaining awake at night and taking my rest from one o'clock to three-thirty in the afternoon. This habit has become a part of my life. At two-thirty in the morning somebody knocked at my door and said, "Swamiji,

The town of Badrinath

please come out! My brother is suffering from a severe heart attack and the doctors cannot handle it. Please help now!" It was Mr. Jaipuria, who loves me very much—but I strictly maintain that early period of the morning for meditation, and this distraction was a disturbance to my willpower. I also knew that there were several doctors there with oxygen and medical kits, so rather than open the door, I said from inside, "We yogis and swamis aspire to die in a place like this, and it never happens. How can it be possible for your brother to have chosen such an auspicious place to die? It is not possible; he is not dying. Go away and don't disturb me." I found Jaipuria's brother quite normal in the morning. This retort of mine became a joke among the businessmen: "If the holy men are not fortunate enough to die in a shrine like Badrinath, how is it possible for businessmen to have such a peaceful death? It's not possible!"

The next morning everyone went to the shrine and met many swamis who lived in nearby caves. At five o'clock in the evening I was informed by Dr. Sharma, the head physician of the party, that Mrs. Jaipuria was suffering from bloody diarrhea. She was a fine little old lady who always looked after my comforts. I used to call her Mother. I felt sad and rushed to see her. Her face was very pale, and she was so completely exhausted that she could move only her lips. Her two sons, who were sitting next to her, did not believe that the old lady was going to live. The doctor gave her medications, but nothing happened. Her breath was very shallow, and the doctors declared her case hopeless. I put my hand over her head in sympathy. I did not know what to do. Suddenly I turned my head and found a tall young swami calling my name, and my attention was diverted toward him. This swami said, "Where is the doctor?" and the doctor came forward. The swami said, "That's all your medical science can do? You people are really killing people and drugging them. What poor knowledge!"

The doctor was annoyed and told him, "How is it that you two swamis cannot heal her? I accept that I have failed and that the other doctors have also failed."

Mr. Jaipuria loved his wife immensely and was sobbing in a corner of the room. His sons and in-laws were also crying. I looked at the young swami, and he smiled and asked if there were a flower he could have. Here people carry flowers to offer at the shrine, and someone came forward with the red petals of roses. The swami told Mrs. Jaipuria to get up. He roughly pulled her arm, forcibly made her sit, and poured a glass of water containing the petals into her mouth while muttering something that nobody knew. He then laid her on the bed, covered her with the blanket, and told all the people to get out of the room, saying, "She will be going into deep sleep now."

Everyone thought that "deep sleep" meant dying, and they started screaming and crying. We were both smiling at them. This was not at all appreciated by them, and the old lady's son said, "You irresponsible people have nothing to lose, but I have

Swami Rama with the grandson of Mrs. Jaipuria

lost my mother and now you are making fun of us!" The young swami and I stood outside that house and waited for the woman to wake up. Her family members were preparing for her cremation. After half an hour the young swami asked Mr. Jaipuria to go inside and be with his wife. He found her sitting up and in perfectly good health.

I am not against medicines and remedies which help in curing diseases, but I love to make others aware of preventive medicines. There is another, higher, way of helping people through the use of willpower. Willpower here means that dynamic will which is created by a one-pointed mind, meditation, and spiritual discipline. In today's medicine this cultivation of willpower is totally missing.

The young swami accepted the doctor's challenge and became aware of his potential to heal the suffering old lady. My experience with many medical professionals has convinced me that in treating diseases the doctor's behavior and use of willpower is more important than mere medication. The more the medical profession understands this fact the more they will agree with me that they can help humanity not only by using medicine but also by teaching certain methods of prevention. In this way more patients can be made aware of their inner capacities to heal themselves.

No one can believe how much the whole party then adored us and how everybody wanted to give us money, build us houses, and present us with cars. We both smiled and laughed at them. I found out that rich people want to pay for everything with coins and that they even try to bribe renunciates—but for those who are truly on the path of renunciation, riches cannot tempt them. Those who are already treading the path like to be poor materially but very rich spiritually. When they compare these higher riches to mere worldly riches they will not be held back by the charms, temptations, and attractions which can obstruct the way of a renunciate. Beginners who aspire to lead an austere life and to follow the path of renunciation often become the victims of such temptations. Some suffer a setback or may even become mentally deranged. The pleasures of the world are no doubt powerful; attachment to these pleasures is considered to be the mother of all ignorance. A one-pointed mind, a strong will, and, above all, the grace of God help a fortunate few to remain above temptation, unaffected by these worldly fetters.

I bade goodbye to the members of the party with whom I had visited the shrine of Badrinath. I stayed back with my friend to listen to the music played by a great sage called Parvatikar Maharaja. We stayed another six days in the cave of Phalahari Baba (who was known by this name because he lived only on fruits and milk) and came down to the shrine to listen to this sage every evening. His instrument was the *bichitra veena,* which has several strings. There was a crowd of five hundred people sitting in the corridor of this shrine. Before he started tuning his instrument he broke the silence and said, "Blessed ones, I am tuning my instrument, and you can tune yours. The chords of life should be tuned properly. It is an art to tune the chords first, and then to hold the instrument in a comfortable and steady way. Let you be instruments now. Let Him play through you. Just surrender yourself. Offer this tuned instrument of yours to the Musician."

Some people understood him, others not. I and my other friend were quietly sitting in a corner, and we became attentive after listening to his words. He held his *veena* in his arms, closed his eyes, and started playing on it. If the sitar and guitar, along with all string instruments, were played together harmoniously, they could not create such a beautiful melody. The audience did not know the music, yet everybody was swaying. He played his instrument for two and a half hours. He was one musician who really helped me believe that music could also be a means for peace and joy. I call it meditation in music.

Among all the fine arts, the finest is music. Music is not composed of songs, melodies, or words only, but of the most subtle sound—*nada*—the vibration that spontaneously inspires all the cells and makes them dance. There could be no dance without the vibrations of *nada*. Because of this *nada* the stream of life sings with a particular rhythm and flows through various curves of life, giving its environment a new experience every time.

The most ancient traveler of this universe is this stream of life that sings and dances in its joy from eternity to eternity. In the ecstasy of meeting the Beloved, it finally unites with the ocean of bliss. From beginning to end there is a perennial sound, but on various pitches which make seven key notes. In music all over the world there are seven key notes, which personify seven levels of consciousness. These sounds make one aware of the various levels of consciousness and finally lead one to the fountain of consciousness, from where arises the stream of life which vibrates in all directions. In one direction it is called music, in another dance, in a third painting, and in a fourth poetry.

There is one more form of this sound, which is called soundless sound. Insiders alone become aware of that sound which is called *anahata nada* (inner sound). This flows through the vocal cords and is called music. Kabir says, "O sadhu, lift the veil of ignorance and you'll be one with the Beloved. Light the lamp of love in the inner chamber of your being and you will meet the Beloved. There you hear the finest of all music—*anahata nada*."

In the path of devotion yogis learn to hear this soundless sound, the voice of the silence, the perennial music going on in every human heart. But how many of us hear that music? Genuine musicians, overwhelmed by this *para-bhava* [ecstasy], chant the words and sing the praises of the Beloved. This devotional music has a profound influence in directing the emotional life of an aspirant toward ecstasy and enables him to enjoy the highest moment. This is called meditation in music. No self-effort is necessary—but that which does seem to be necessary in this path is to kindle a flame of love for the Beloved. The path of devotion is the simplest, and leads one to the height of spiritual ecstasy. Love expressed through music is meditation in music. Gradually the mind becomes one-pointed, and the day comes when the aspirant starts listening to *anahata nada*. There are numerous and inspiring sounds. With their help the aspirant attains the highest state of joy. In the path of devotion, music becomes a means for self-realization.

After playing the *veena*, Parvatikar Maharaja went to the silence again.

At the Feet of the Masters

I went to Kasardevi in Almora, and there I met a well-known painter from the West, and a Buddhist monk. These people lived in a small hermitage, enjoying the Himalayan peaks in solitude. They talked to the mountains constantly, and held that the Himalayan mountains, unlike the Alps and other mountains, are not only beautiful but alive as well.

They said, "We talk to the mountains and the mountains answer."

I asked, "In what sense? How can mountains talk?"

They replied, "You were born and brought up in these mountains, and, as always, familiarity breeds contempt. Remember that these mountains are holy and create a spiritual atmosphere for the seeker. Their beauty is there for all who will but behold it. You have forgotten how to appreciate these gods." They went on praising the beauty of the snow-blanketed Himalayan peaks.

My stay with them was brief. I soon left for Shyamadevi, which was thirty miles beyond Kasardevi, where there lived a swami all alone in a small Shakti temple. I wanted to be with him for a while. Soon after I arrived Nantin Baba, a very well-known sadhu from that part of the Himalayas, joined us. I had previously lived with him in various caves at Bageswar and Ramgarh. The swami who lived at the Shakti temple claimed that he was a direct disciple of Sombari Baba, a well-known sage who lived forty years earlier. During those days Sombari Baba and Hariakhan Baba often were seen together. My master and Hariakhan Baba were disciples of the same guru, who had been born in India but lived mostly in Tibet. Both Hariakhan Baba and my master were called Babaji. This title of respect simply means "grandfather," and is often used for very old sages. Even today, especially in Nepal, Nanital, Kashipur, and Almora, everyone has some story to tell about these sages and talks about their amazing spiritual miracles and healing powers. There is no end to the stories they tell. During our stay there our host talked about his gurudeva uninterruptedly for hours on end.

This host was a *siddha*. He was widely known for his healing powers. Whenever anyone started traveling to the Shakti temple at which he stayed, he knew it. Without being introduced to strangers he would straight away call them by their names. He did not want to be disturbed, and sometimes he would feign anger in order to keep people away, but within he was very soft. Villagers gave him the name Durbasa, which means "foul tongue." He used to perform a primitive austerity called *Panchagni Siddhi,* which means having control over five fires. He did both external and internal worship. He said that God is fire, and would expound on this theme at the slightest opportunity.

This accomplished man gave me several lessons on solar science, which I still remember, though I did not practice what he taught me, for it is not possible to practice all of these different sciences in one short lifetime. This science is helpful in healing the sick. After collecting scattered material on this subject and learning its principles I wanted to set up a clinic to help

Sombari Baba

the suffering masses, but my master stopped me, for he felt this would distract me from an even greater purpose. Whenever I used to sing, compose a poem, or paint he objected. He advised me to avoid such diversions and to practice silence. He would say, "The voice of silence is supreme. It is beyond all levels of consciousness and all methods of communication. Learn to listen to the voice of silence. Rather than discussing scriptures and arguing with sages, just enjoy their presence. You are on a journey; don't stop for long at one place and get attached to anything. Silence will give you what the world can never give you."

When I left Shyamadevi I returned to my mountain abode. The villagers of Boodha Kedar built a small stone dwelling for me, where I used to go and remain in silence. It is still there today, at a height of 6,000 feet. From that dwelling I had a panoramic view of the Himalayan ranges. Occasionally the silence would suddenly be broken by a wandering yogi who would knock on my door. Only a few seekers go deep into the Himalayas. Most travelers remain on the mountain roads and trails and visit the well-known shrines and places of interest, but the more serious seekers avoid these routes and visit the isolated hermitages, caves, and mountain abodes of sages. The Himalayan mountains stretch for 1,500 miles from China to Pakistan. They are the highest mountains in the world. Though there are other mountain ranges that have great beauty, the Himalayas offer one thing that is unique: the spiritual atmosphere and the opportunity to meet and learn from the highly evolved sages who make the Himalayas their home.

XII

Grace of the Master

♦

PERFECTION IS THE GOAL OF HUMAN LIFE, BUT human efforts are very limited. Happiness does not come merely through human endeavor, but comes through grace. Blessed are those who have the grace of both God and master.

Guru Is a Stream and
a Channel of Knowledge

◆

The word *guru* is so misused that I feel hurt sometimes. It is
such a noble word, such a wonderful word. After your
mother has given birth to you, and your parents have raised
you, then the role of the guru begins, and he helps you fulfill
the purpose of your life. Even if I'm a very bad man and somebody calls me guru, I have to become the best for the sake of
the person who expects it of me. A guru is different from a
teacher. *Guru* is a compound of two words, *gu* and *ru*. *Gu*
means "darkness"; *ru* means "light": that which dispels the
darkness of ignorance is called guru. In the West the word *guru*
is often misused. In India this word is used with reverence and
is always associated with holiness and the highest wisdom. It is
a very sacred word. It is seldom used by itself, but always with
its suffix, *deva*. *Deva* means "bright being." An enlightened
master or guru is called gurudeva.

There is a vast difference between an ordinary teacher and a
spiritual master. All followers of a guru, whatever their age, even
if they are eighty years old, are like children to him. He will feed
them, give them shelter, and then teach them, without expecting
anything in return. I asked my master, "Why does he do this?"

He said, "He has no other desires but teaching those aspirants who are prepared. If he doesn't do this, what shall he do?"

When a student goes to a guru he takes a bundle of dry sticks. With reverence and love he bows and says, "Here, I offer this." That indicates that he is surrendering himself with all his mind, action, and speech with a single desire to attain the highest wisdom. The guru burns those sticks and says, "Now I will guide you and protect you in the future." Then he initiates the student on various levels and gives him the disciplines to practice. It is such a pure relationship that I don't think any other relationship is even comparable. Everything the guru has, even his body, mind, and soul, belongs to his student. But if he has any odd habits at all, they belong only to himself.

The guru imparts a word and says, "This will be an eternal friend to you. Remember this word. It will help you." That is called mantra initiation. Then he explains how to use the mantra. He removes obstacles. Since the student has desires and many problems, he does not know how to make decisions properly. So the guru will teach him how to decide and how to remain peaceful and tranquil. He will say, "Sometimes you have noble thoughts, but you do not bring them into action. Come on, make your mind one-pointed. You are powerful, and my blessings are with you."

You try your best to do something for him, but you cannot, because he doesn't need anything. Such a compassionate one spontaneously attracts your attention, for you are bewildered. You wonder, "Why is he doing so much for me? What does he want from me?" He wants nothing, for what he is doing is his duty, the purpose of his life. If he guides you, he is not obliging you, he is doing his work. He cannot live without doing his duty.

Such people are called gurus. They guide humanity. As the sun shines and lives far above, the guru gives his spiritual love and remains unattached. Guru is not a physical being. Those who think of the guru as a body or as a man do not understand this pious word. If a guru comes to think that his power is his own, then he is a guide no more. The guru is tradition; he is a stream of knowledge. That stream of knowledge goes through many channels. Christ also said this when he healed people and they called him Lord. He said, "This is because of my Father; I am only a channel."

No human being can ever become a guru. But when a human being allows himself to be used as a channel for receiving and transmitting by the Power of Powers, then it happens. And for that, a human being should learn to be selfless. Usually love is mingled with selfishness. I need something, so I say, "I love you." You need something, so you love me. This is what we call love in the world. But when you do actions selflessly in a spontaneous way, then that is really love. You don't expect any reward. Genuine gurus cannot live without selflessness, for selfless love is the very basis of their enlightenment. They radiate life and light from the unknown corners of the world. The world does not know them, and they do not want recognition.

Don't ever believe anyone who comes to you and demands, "Worship me." Even Christ and Buddha did not ask that. Never forget that guru is not the goal. Guru is like a boat for crossing the river. It is very important to have a good boat, and it is very dangerous to have a boat that is leaking. But after you have crossed the river you don't need to hang on to your boat, and you certainly don't worship the boat.

Many fanatics think they should worship a guru. A guru should receive your love and respect—that is different from worship. If my guru and the Lord both come together, I will go to my guru first and say, "Thank you very much. You have introduced me to the Lord." I will not go to the Lord and say, "Thank you very much, Lord. You have given me my guru."

A Weeping Statue

$\blacklozenge$

I often visited Uttarvrindavan, an ashram in the Himalayas, and did *satsanga* with Krishna Prem (Professor Nixon) and Anand Bikkhu (Dr. Alexander). These two Europeans, one of whom had been a professor of English and the other a professor of medicine, were disciples of Yashoda Ma, a female mystic from Bengal. They lived quietly, avoiding visitors. During those days Krishna Prem was writing two books: one was *The Yoga of the Bhagavad Gita,* and the other *The Yoga of the Kathopanishad.* They were later published in London. They had sufficient funds to meet their daily expenses, so they were not dependent on others. Their way of living was very simple, neat, and clean. They were very particular in cooking their meals, not allowing anyone to come into their kitchen.

By then Yashoda Ma had left her body and they had built a memorial to her, called "Samadhi." At the top of the monument a beautiful marble statue of Krishna had been installed. On one of my visits shortly after the statue was installed I noticed that Krishna Prem was wearing something on his arm. I asked him about it and he said, "You won't believe me." I said, "Please explain it to me."

He replied, "You intellectualize everything and I'm afraid you might think I have gone crazy, but I will tell you. Fifteen days ago the statue of Krishna which was installed on the memorial started flowing tears. The tears dripped from the statue continuously. We dismantled the base of the statue to see if there was some source of the seeping water, but found nothing. There was no way that water could come up through the statue and flow from its eyes. When we put the statue back in place the tears began to flow once more. This made me very sad. I decided that I must be committing some mistake in my *sadhana* and that Ma was not happy with me. To keep myself ever reminded of this I took some cotton, soaked it in the tears, and put it in the locket which I am now wearing on my arm. What I am telling you is true, and I know why this is happening. Don't tell anyone about this. They will think that I have gone insane."

I said, "I don't doubt your integrity. Please explain to me why it occurs."

He said, "The guru guides from the other side in many ways. This is an instruction to me. I have become lazy. Instead of doing my evening *sadhana* I have been retiring early. It was her habit to remind us whenever we fell into the grip of sloth and missed our practice. This has to be the right explanation." He became very serious and then started to sob. His love for his guru was immense, and this inspired me. Love for guru is the first rung on the ladder to the Divine. But this love is not love for the human form.

People in India, except for the brahmins, greatly admired these two European swamis—Krishna Prem and his brother disciple, Anand Bikkhu. The brahmins did not treat them well, though they were more pure and spiritually advanced than many of the temple priests. Whenever they visited any temple they were considered to be untouchables. I condemned those brahmins and often would tell my two friends that out of ignorance many people become fanatic, and fanaticism is not part of any religion. India has suffered from the caste system, just as the West has suffered from the race and class systems. Both are injurious for human society.

My Master's Photograph

I committed a breach of trust with my master when I met in September 1939 two photographers from France who had traveled to the Himalayas to take pictures. I wanted them to take a picture of my master. I had a few rupees in my pocket which I gave to the photographers, and I borrowed 150 more to get the amount they wanted. Then I led them over a narrow wooden bridge across the Ganges to a small hut where my master and I had been staying for fifteen days.

When my master saw the photographers he looked at me and said, "You are a bad boy. Why must you be so obstinate? They will have nothing!" I didn't understand. Sometimes I stubbornly thought my master was my property. The photographers each took a roll of pictures with their separate cameras. Inserting two new rolls, they asked me to sit next to my master so they could take some pictures of the two of us together. This time my master sealed his lips and closed his eyes. In all, four rolls of pictures were taken with two separate cameras from three o'clock to five-thirty in the afternoon. After taking a few more pictures of the mountains, the photographers left for Delhi. When my pictures were developed and returned, I could not believe the results. Everything around where my master had been sitting appeared in the pictures, but my master's image did not appear at all!

On three or four other occasions I attempted to get a picture of my master, but he always said, "A picture of the mortal body might obstruct your vision of the light within me. You should not be attached to my mortal body; be aware of our divine link."

Later, before I started traveling abroad in Europe and then in Japan, he told me, "I don't want you to sell me in the Western market." I have respected his feelings and have never made any attempt to make a reprint of the only photograph of my master in existence. My brother disciple got this one photograph from a cameraman of Shrinagar, who had taken it with a box camera. It is possible for a yogi to put a veil between himself and the camera so that he does not appear in the photograph, but for some reason on that one occasion my master did not do so.

Who Can Kill the Eternal?

◆

Once in the mountains a landslide started rumbling toward us. I cried, "We are going to die!"

My master said, "Who can kill the eternal?"

I said, "The mountain is coming down and you say, 'Who can kill the eternal?' Look at the mountain!"

He shouted, "Stop! Let us cross!"—and the landslide stopped! Then we passed that place and he said, "Now you can fall down," and the landslide continued.

On another occasion some people were following him when he was going toward a mountain. It started snowing, and it snowed constantly for three hours. The people did not have enough clothing, so they said, "Sir, you are considered to be eternal. It is said that you have miraculous powers. Why do you not stop this snow?" He said, "It's easy." Then he said in a loud voice, "Stop, and let the sun shine!" And it happened.

The power of will-force is very little known among modern men. There are three channels of power: one is called *kriya shakti,* another is called *ichchha shakti,* and the third is called *jñana shakti. Shakti* is that force which manifests itself through these three channels. This power may be either latent or active.

With the help of *kriya shakti* we *do* our actions; with *ichchha shakti* we *will* to act; and with *jñana shakti* we *decide* to act. One can cultivate one or another aspect of this force. Some yogis learn to perform their actions skillfully and become successful in the world. Others develop their willpower and then direct their speech and actions in accord with their will. Some sharpen *buddhi,* the faculty of discrimination, and attain a state of *prajña*—a unified state of tranquility. The discipline undertaken differs according to the aspect of *shakti* which is being developed, though discipline is necessary in each case. Developing *ichchha shakti* strengthens willpower, and with the help of willpower one can have command over the phenomenal world exactly as one has command over his limbs. It was through this power that my master was able to control the forces of nature.

Half "Here," Half "There"

O nce I was staying with my master in a shrine on a bank of the Ganges River. We were at Karnaprayag. My master wears almost no clothing because he is hardly aware of his physical self. He is always in inner joy. Suddenly at night he said, "Let's go now."

It was dark and it had been raining outside for some time. I thought, "If I say no, he will start walking anyway. He will just go like a lord with nothing on." So I put a blanket over him, hooked it with a thorn, and started to walk with him. It was bitterly cold. After going barefoot for half a mile my whole body was freezing. I was wearing very little, only one woolen blanket. I wondered, "What shall I do?"

After we had walked for two miles, we came to a crossroads and I asked, "Do you know which way to go here?" He said, "This way." But I turned him around and said, "No, no. This is the way." So we reversed directions and returned to the very place from where we had set out.

It was dark, and he did not know where he was. I said, "Now we have to stay here." He said, "Okay." I took off my blanket, laid it out, and he sat down near the fire.

In the morning he opened his eyes and started giggling. He said, "We walked all night and are still in the same place! How is it possible?" I said, "I tricked you." "Why?" I said, "It was freezing and you were not aware of it."

He used to enjoy such experiences. In that high state of ecstasy he was often oblivious to the mundane things of the world—but when he became aware of them he would enjoy them like a joyous child.

At another time I had a very strange experience with my master. It was a sunny June day in the forest near Varanasi, where the temperature goes up to 114 degrees. Since the day was very warm I asked my master, "Will you take a bath?" He said, "Okay."

Often you will come across wells in India when you travel from one city to another. If you want to take a bath you find someone nearby who has a bucket and a rope. Then you draw water from the well, take a bath, and go on. We came upon such a well, so I said, "Please sit down and wait. I'll go and get a bucket and a rope."

When I returned, he was not there. I shouted for him, and heard someone answering from the bottom of the well, which was about sixty feet deep. He had jumped in and was playing in the water. Normally if someone jumped from sixty feet he would be injured, but in a high state of ecstasy one is a child of nature and is protected. It became a problem for me because he wouldn't come out! I could not coax him out, so I asked some people from the village to help. Three people came, and we threw down a basket with a rope tied to it. I shouted, "Sit in the basket and we will pull you up!" He answered, "Leave me alone. Let me take my bath." He was enjoying himself.

Then they tied me with the rope and lowered me down into the well. I said, "Come on!" But he said, "Let me take my bath!" He was still playing there.

I told him, "It's been almost one hour now. You have had

Swami Rama at Karnaprayag

enough bath!" "Have I?" "Yes!" Finally after a long time I convinced him to come out. Every day he would take a bath, but his mind would be somewhere else. I would say, "Now you have taken your bath. Come out."

He lived most of the time "there," in a constant state of bliss, and very little of the time "here," conscious of the mundane world.

How a Young Widow
Was Rescued

O nce in a desert village of Rajasthan fifty miles west of
Pilani there lived a landlord who had only one son. Just
after his wedding ceremony this boy died of a high fever. His
poor young widow, who was very beautiful and hardly seventeen years of age, was not able to enjoy her honeymoon. In
certain communities the law is "once married, married forever," and widows cannot remarry. This system was changed
by a movement called Arya Samaj. The founder of this movement was Swami Dayananda, who was a great leader of socio-
religious reform.

This young girl preferred to lead a holy life and lived in a
room which was on the second story of her father-in-law's
brick building. In her room were two pictures. Besides these the
girl had only one blanket which she used as a mattress, and
another to protect herself from the cold. There was a window
in the back of that room and a door made of strong, thick
wood in the front.

One night three fully armed men came to rob that house.
Their intention was to rape and kidnap this young widow.
They locked all the members of her family in one room and

wanted to break into her room. When she discovered this she started praying, "Gurudeva, I am pure. Save me, protect me. Where are your protective arms? What has happened to you?"

Suddenly an old, white-haired man with a beard appeared on camel's back at her rear window. He said, "Come with me, my child, otherwise you are in danger. You'll be raped by them and you'll be disgraced and finally commit suicide." The robbers were very disappointed when they found, after breaking down the door, that there was no one inside. The girl and her rescuer traveled all night on the camel, and before sunrise arrived safely at her father's house, which was sixty-five miles away.

I visited this village in 1951 and heard this story from that very woman, who was known for her purity and spirituality. After narrating her story she asked me many questions about my master. Her father was known to us; he had a divine link with our tradition. Through our conversation I discovered that the two pictures the girl had in her room were of Mira Bai and of my master. Her whole family worshipped his picture, which my brother disciple had given to her father after he had completed a journey from the Himalayas. The face of her rescuer was the same as the one in her photograph. It was my master. I wanted to see my master's picture, and I liked it so much that I took it from her with the promise that I would send her a copy of it, but for many reasons, I could not do so. This is the only picture of my master in existence. There is no doubt in my mind and heart as to the truth of this experience. How it happened, however, I have no way to explain.

By telling this story I do not want to build a guru cult, but want to make you aware that the ways of the masters are very mysterious and that they help their students from any corner of the world, even from the other side of the world. Physical presence is not always necessary for the teacher to help, guide, and protect his student.

My Master Saves
a Drowning Man

◆

A learned man from Rajasthan once came to my ashram at Uttarkashi. He was a well-known pandit. He was on a pilgrimage to Gangotri in the Himalayas. He was then about seventy years of age. One day he wanted to take a dip in the holy Ganges River, but did not know how to swim. The river was just a short distance from my ashram. He saw that monkeys on the other bank of the river were jumping into the water, diving, and coming up. So he thought, "If monkeys can dive in and swim, why can't I, an educated man, do it?" Thereupon he jumped into the water and started drowning.

One of my companions saw him drowning and began shouting. I rushed out and asked, "What happened?" He replied, "That man is drowning!" I rushed to the river. I was worried. I thought, "Is someone going to be killed in front of my ashram?"

When I got there the old man was sitting on the bank gasping for air. After he caught his breath, I asked him what had happened. He said, "I was taken by the currents." "Then how did you get out?" I asked. He said, "A swami pulled me out."

I asked him who it was, and he gave an exact description of my master. I had only one picture of my master and never

The village of Gangotri

showed it to anyone. But in this case I wanted to verify whether it was indeed my master who had pulled him out, so I showed that picture to him.

He said, "Yes, that's the man. After I had gone under three times I went down to the bottom and started inhaling water. I thought, 'If this is a holy place, somebody will help me'—and then suddenly someone pulled me out of the water. And *he* is the very one."

I told him, "You were hallucinating." He said, "No! I have so much faith now that I must find this man and stay with him. I shall never go back home."

I asked, "What will your family say?" He said, "My children are grown up. I'm going to the Himalayas." And he left.

My gurudeva sent word to him on the way not to come until he was better prepared. Now he lives some twelve miles away from our monastery, where he spends his time in meditation. When I left for the West he was still waiting to see my master. He says, "The day I am prepared, I'll go and see him."

Shaktipata—Bestowing Bliss

◆

I was preoccupied with the desire to experience samadhi. My master had told me, "Unless you sit completely still for four hours, you will never realize samadhi." So I practiced sitting from childhood on. More than anything else, my time was spent sitting to experience samadhi—but I failed to attain it.

After studying many books I became a teacher, but I felt that it was not good to impart secondhand or indirect knowledge. It would be better to teach philosophy in the university and elsewhere than to teach monks in the monastery in this way. I thought, "This is not right; I am not realized. I only teach what I have studied through books and what I have learned from teachers rather than what I have experienced." So one day I said to my master, "Today I am going to give you an ultimatum."

He said, "What is that?"

"Either you give me samadhi or I will commit suicide!" I was really determined.

He asked, "Are you sure?"

"Yes!"

Then he calmly said, "My dear boy, go right ahead."

I never expected him to say that. I had expected him to say, "Wait for ten or fifteen days." He had never been rude to me, but that day he was very rude. He said, "Going to sleep at night does not solve your problems—you will have to face them the next day. In the same way, committing suicide will not solve your real problems either. You will have to face them in your next life. You have studied the ancient scriptures and you understand these things. Yet you are talking about committing suicide. But if you really want to, go ahead."

I always used to hear about *shaktipata. Shakti* means "energy"; *pata* means "bestowing." *Shaktipata* means "bestowing the energy, lighting the lamp." I said, "You have not done shaktipata for me, so it means either you don't have shakti or you don't intend to do it. For so long now I have been closing my eyes in meditation, and I end up with nothing but a headache. My time has been a waste, and I find little joy in life." He didn't say anything, so I continued. "I worked hard and sincerely. You said it would take fourteen years; this is my seventeenth year of practice, and whatever you have asked me to do I have done."

He said, "Are you sure? Are you really following the practices I have taught you? Is this the fruit of my teaching, that you are committing suicide?" Then he asked, "When do you want to commit suicide?"

I said, "Right now! I am talking to you before I commit suicide. You are no longer my master now. I gave up everything. I am of no use to the world; I am of no use to you." I got up to go to the Ganges to drown myself. The river was quite near.

He said, "You know how to swim, so when you jump in the Ganges, naturally you will start swimming. You'd better find some way so that you will start drowning and not come up. Perhaps you should tie some weight to yourself."

He was teasing me. I said, "What has happened to you? You used to love me so much." Then I said, "Now I am going, thank you." I went to the Ganges with a rope and tied some big rocks to myself. Finally when he noticed that I was indeed serious and was ready to jump, he called and said, "Wait! Sit down there and in one minute I will give you samadhi."

I did not know if he really meant it, but I thought, "I can at least wait for a minute to see." I sat down in my meditation posture and he came and touched me on the forehead. I remained in that position for nine hours, and did not have a single worldly thought. The experience was indescribable. When I returned to normal consciousness I thought it was still nine o'clock in the morning, for samadhi annihilates time. I begged, "Sir, please forgive me."

The first thing that I lost with that touch was fear, and I also found that I was no longer selfish. My life was transformed. After that I started understanding life properly.

Later I questioned my master. I asked, "Was it my effort, or your effort?" He replied, "Grace."

What does grace mean? People think that by the grace of God alone they will be enlightened. That is not the case. My master said, "A human being should make all possible sincere efforts. When he has become exhausted, and then cries out in despair in the highest state of devotional emotion, he will attain ecstasy. That is the grace of God. Grace is the fruit that you receive from your faithful and sincere efforts."

I now realize that shaktipata is only possible with a disciple who has gone through a long period of discipline, austerity, and spiritual practices. Shaktipata on a mass scale seems suspicious to me. It is true that when the disciple is ready the master appears and gives the appropriate initiation. When a student has done his *sadhana* with all faithfulness, truthfulness, and sincerity, then the subtlest obstacle is removed by the master. The experience of enlightenment comes from the sincere effort of both master and disciple. Let us put it in different words. When you have done your duty skillfully and wholeheartedly, you reap the fruits gracefully. Grace dawns when action ends. Shaktipata is the grace of God through the master.

I eagerly anticipate the times when I can be alone at night and can sit in meditation and experience that state. Nothing else even approaches being so enjoyable.

My Grandmaster
in Sacred Tibet

◆

In 1939 I wanted to go to Tibet. The border was only nine miles from where I lived with my master, but I was not allowed to cross through Mana Pass and go to Tibet. Seven years later I made another attempt. Early in 1946 I started a journey to Lhasa, the capital of Tibet, via Darjeeling, Kalingpong, Sikkim, Pedong, Gyansee, and Shigatse. My main purpose in going to Tibet was to see my grandmaster (my master's master) and to learn certain advanced practices under his guidance.

I stayed a few days in Darjeeling and gave some public lectures. The British officers thought that I was a rebel who wanted to go to Lhasa to disturb the British government in India. They knew about my plans for the journey, but did not know my motives. After ten days I left for Kalingpong and stayed in the monastery where I had learned kung fu and other similar arts when I was young. After staying with my old teacher of kung fu I went to Sikkim and stayed with a close relative of the Dalai Lama of Tibet. In Sikkim the political officer, Mr. Hopkinson, was afraid that I would prejudice the minds of the administrators in Tibet against the British. I had several

Swami Rama before leaving for Tibet

meetings with him, but he wouldn't permit me to go to Tibet.

He suspected me of being a spy for the Indian Congress Party, which was then fighting the British government. There were two groups in India at that time: one was Mahatma Gandhi's group, which practiced non-violence and used the methods of passive resistance and non-cooperation; the other was the Terrorist Party of India. I was not a member of either, but the political officer found two letters in my possession, one written by Pandit Nehru, and another from Mahatma Gandhi. These letters were non-political, but they caused the political officer to be even more suspicious, and I was put under house arrest and forced to stay in an inspection bungalow [a government house usually used for traveling inspectors or officials]. I had every comfort, but for two months I could not leave the house, write to anyone, nor have visitors. The political officer said, "I can't prove you have done anything, but I suspect you of being a political spy. Until I get reports about you, you are not to leave." There was a guard outside the bungalow day and night. At least the time which I spent there gave me the opportunity to study the Tibetan language so I would be better able to converse with the Tibetans if and when I was able to get into their country.

In spite of my continuing requests to various officials the political officer did not receive any orders to release me—so after two months I decided that I would go secretly. I bought a long coat from one of the guards (it was very old and dirty) and tried to disguise my face. At eleven o'clock on a cold night, when the guard on duty was drunk and fast asleep, I left for Pedong, wearing my long Tibetan coat. It was July 15 when I left. Before I left I placed a note on the table in my room saying that I was leaving for Delhi. This did not bother my conscience, because I felt that the administrators were not justified in preventing my going to Tibet. It took me three days to get to the last checkpoint, where Gurkha soldiers were posted by the

Sikkim government. They wanted to know about me and asked for identification. I spoke to them in Nepalese, which I knew fluently, so they thought I was from Nepal and allowed me to cross the border into Tibet.

I was to face many more hardships in Tibet. I was a vegetarian, but could get little to eat except meat. I did not meet a single vegetarian in Tibet, because of the climate and high altitude. Everyone lived on meat and fish. Even I started eating eggs. I was also able to find a few seasonal vegetables, but I could not imagine eating meat and fish. Because of the change in my diet I suffered from diarrhea and my health deteriorated. But I was determined to visit certain monasteries and caves to fulfill the purpose of my journey, which was to stay with my master's master.

Wherever I camped at night people would check my belongings, apparently with the intention of robbing me; but I had nothing in my possession except a few pounds of biscuits, some gram, and a bottle of water which was given to me by one of the soldiers who was posted at the border. I had 2,000 rupees, which was not much for such a journey, and I tied them inside my stockings. I would never take my shoes off before anyone.

I would travel ten or fifteen miles per day, sometimes on foot and sometimes on a mule. I would talk to the people I met about astrology and fortune-telling, although it bothered my conscience. But the Tibetans loved to hear about such things. When they discovered I knew something about these subjects they became friendly and would gladly help me by providing mules to go from one mountain camp to another. Several times I came face-to-face with wild snow bears and huge *Bhotiya* dogs. (These dogs are used for guarding the Tibetan villages.)

In spite of being tired and fatigued as a result of all the problems I was encountering, I felt that there was a power calling me onward to learn more about the hidden teachings of the Himalayan sages. I never expected to return to India again, because the British government in India was sure to imprison me.

I took courage and completed this tedious journey of crossing the mountain streams, glaciers, and passes without any pre-planning, resources, or guides. I surrendered myself to providence and left my fate in the hands of my master and grandmaster, having complete faith that they would protect me and help me if I lost my way. During those days I was fearless. I was not afraid of death. My burning desire to see my grand-master was strong. I thought it was my prime duty to live with him for some time. He was in Tibet because of the solitude he wanted and also to teach a few advanced yogis who were pre-pared and wanted him there. I was very anxious to meet him. I came to know from my master that Hariakhan Baba and other sages of the Himalayas adored him and studied with him for many years. Hariakhan Baba, who was very famous in the Kumayun hills, and who is considered by some to be the eternal Babaji of the Himalayas, was taught by my grand-master. This constantly strengthened my desire, which finally led me to this adventure.

I reached Lhasa after two months of strenuous travel. I met a Catholic priest who lived there. He took me to his small house, which also served as his church, and which he shared with two other missionaries. These three were the only Catholic missionaries in Lhasa, and their activities were closely monitored by the Tibetan government. I lived with them for ten days, resting and regaining my strength. By that time the politi-cal officer in Sikkim and the police in India knew that I was in Tibet. My case was given over to the CID [Central Intelligence Division].

I met one of the lamas and convinced him that I was a spir-itual man and did not have any political motives. I lived with this lama for fifteen days, and he finally became convinced that

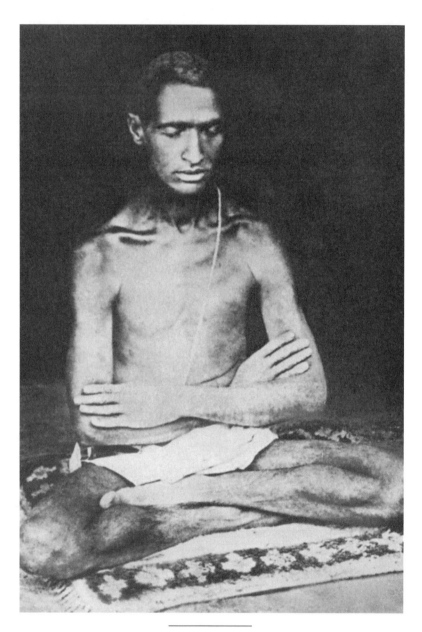

Hariakhan Baba

I had nothing to do with any political movement in India. He assured me that I would not be deported from Tibet, and introduced me to some high government officials. Though I could not express myself well in their language I succeeded in convincing them of my sincerity. The lama with whom I had stayed in Lhasa was a close friend of another lama, whose monastery was close to my destination. It was seventy-five miles northeast of Lhasa, far from civilization. My host provided some guides who took me to the monastery. From there I would be able to make my way to the final goal of my journey.

In that monastery there were more than three hundred lamas. There are many monasteries in Tibet, having thousands of lamas from various traditions. Lamaism seemed to me to be an individualistic religion mingled with Buddhism. Every lama had his own way of performing rituals and ceremonies, chanting, rotating the prayer wheel, and using mantras. These mantras were usually distorted versions of Sanskrit mantras. I had previously studied at Nalanda University in Behar, an ancient Buddhist university in India, so I knew about many of the Buddhist beliefs and practices. I had studied Buddhism as it originated in India, and as it exists in Tibet, China, Japan, and Southeast Asia.

A thousand years ago a Tibetan scholar came to India, studied, and then took the scriptures back to Tibet. Many scholars from India then started going to Tibet to teach the Buddhist literature of India. I was fully aware of the various sects of Buddhism in Tibet, including those who believe in the existence of many gods and demons and accept Buddha as one of the gods.

Tibetan Buddhism is inseparably mingled with tantrism. Before going to see my grandmaster I visited another small monastery, where I met a lama who was supposed to be a great Tibetan yogi. What is called Tibetan yoga is actually a distorted form of tantra—the part of tantra which is called *vama marga* (the left-hand path). Those who follow this path believe in the use of wine, women, meat, fish, and mantra in their worship. When I met this lama he was seated in a wooden room surrounded by seven women, who were chanting mantras with him. After a few mantras they would pick up and eat a piece of raw meat which was mixed with certain spices, including chilies, and then continue chanting again.

After fifteen minutes the lama stopped chanting and asked me the purpose of my visit. I smiled and said I had come to see him. He said, "No, no, that's not true. Your name is such and such and you are in disguise. The Sikkim police are searching for you." He said all this in an angry tone because he knew that I despised his way of worshipping and at the same time eating raw meat. He studied my thoughts, which terrified me. But I was not surprised that he could do this, because by this time I had already met several thought-readers and knew the whole process of reading someone's thoughts. I became humble and said I was in his country only to learn more about tantra. This yogi was a tantric and he gave me his book of worship to go through, but I had already read this scripture before. He led me to another lama who was also a tantric. He knew the Hindi language fairly well because he had lived in India at Bodhigaya, the place where Buddha was enlightened.

Much of the literature found in Tibet is a translation of the Puranic stories of the Hindus. Some of that literature is Taoism and Confucianism mingled with Buddhism, but there is nothing systematic or philosophically original. My knowledge of the Tibetan language was very poor, but this lama talked to me in Hindi, so it was easy for me to communicate with him concerning spiritual matters. I could communicate in Tibetan with regard to everyday necessities, but I could not independently go through the piles of handwritten manuscripts which were preserved in the various monasteries of Tibet.

At the monastery where I was staying a Sanskrit manuscript was being worshipped by the lamas. It had a thick crust of sandal dust on the cloth in which it was wrapped. I was told that anyone who read this manuscript would immediately get leprosy and die. Many lamas came to worship it, but no one had ever read it. I had a strong desire to look through the long, handmade leaves of that manuscript, but the lama wouldn't accept any of my persuasions for allowing me to see it. All my efforts failed. I remembered a saying that goes: "The scriptures belong to those who study them, not to those fools who own them but do not know their contents." At three o'clock in the morning I went to the interior of the monastery, where many lamps were burning, and I opened the manuscript, which was wrapped with seven silken cloths. When I began reading it I was surprised to see that it was a part of the *Linga Purana*, one of eighteen books containing thousands of spiritual stories, methods, and practices based on the ancient Vedic literature of India. I rewrapped it quickly and returned to my room.

Since I had disturbed the position of the lamps and was unable to rewrap the manuscript accurately, it was quickly discovered that the book had been opened. I was rightly suspected. I told the lama who spoke Hindi, "I have been assigned by the Himalayan masters to go through this, and if you say anything to me, you will suffer and not me."

Fortunately this stopped the head lama and the other lamas—otherwise they would have beaten me to death. I proved that nothing had happened to me after opening the forbidden book, and convinced them that this substantiated my claim that I was authorized to do so. They started a rumor about me, saying that a young lama had come from Bodhigaya, India, with great power and wisdom. My Tibetan guides advised me to leave, so I proceeded to my destination. Sometimes utter ignorance in the path of spirituality is accepted as secret knowledge; people do not like to examine their blind beliefs. I had encountered fanaticism and blind faith before.

When I finally met my grandmaster he embraced me, saying, "Oh, you are very tired, you have gone through many problems. The path of enlightenment is the toughest path, and that seeking is the hardest task." After he described my whole journey to me, he told me to bathe and refresh myself. I had been very disgusted with the long and tiring journey. All my practices and yoga disciplines had been neglected, and that was the worst thing for my inner condition. But suddenly, upon being embraced by my grandmaster, I forgot all the pains and miseries I had gone through. The way he looked at me was the same as the look of my master. His compassion was indescribable. When great yogis and masters look at their disciples the whole of their being starts radiating that love which is superb and fulfilling.

I had been told by my master that my grandmaster was from a brahmin family, that he had wandered in the Himalayan mountains since his early childhood, and that he came from an unbroken line of sages. He looked very old, but very healthy. He would get up from his seat once early in the morning and once in the evening. His height was five feet nine or ten inches. He was very slim, but very energetic. He had bushy eyebrows and his face glowed and radiated deep calmness and tranquility. He had a perennial smile. He lived on yak's milk most of the time and sometimes barley soup. Occasionally a few lamas would come and study with him. He lived in a natural cave at the height of 7,000 feet and used fire to remove the dampness and to boil milk and water. His students made a wooden portico before the entrance of his cave. It was a beautiful place, from which we could see the long mountain ranges and vast horizon.

During my stay with my grandmaster I asked him questions on many advanced and rare practices, and I received replies to all of my questions. After replying to many of my spiritual queries, he asked me why I was hesitating in not expressing my prime desire. With trembling voice I said, "Please convince me so that I understand the technique of *para-kaya pravesha*." He said, "Okay."

The next morning one of his lama students came to see him. It was about nine or nine-thirty in the morning. My grandmaster said, "I am going to give you wisdom. I am going to demonstrate for you." He said he could leave his body and enter someone else's body, and then come back to his own body again. He said he could change his body at will. The thought flashed in my mind, "He wants to cast off his body and wants me to immerse it or bury it," but suddenly he said, "It's not that." He was replying to all my thoughts. He instructed me to go inside the cave and again check if there was any outlet or hidden door, but I had already lived in that small cave for more than a month and I thought there was no point in checking the cave again. But he ordered me to go and examine that small cave again. I did as he ordered, and as I had seen before, it was a small rock cave with only one entrance, having a wooden portico outside. I came out and sat under the portico with the lama next to me. He told us to come nearer to him and hold a wooden plate which was like a round tea tray. When we held the tray, he said, "Do you see me?" We said, "Yes."

In my ignorance I said, "Please don't try to hypnotize me. I won't look at your eyes." He said, "I am not hypnotizing you." His body started becoming hazy, and that haziness was a human form like a cloud. That hazy cloud human form started moving toward us. Soon in a few seconds' time the cloud disappeared. We found that the plate which we were holding started becoming heavier. After a few minutes the wooden plate again became as light as it was before. For ten minutes the lama and I remained standing holding that plate, and finally sat down, waiting in great suspense and awe for something to happen. After ten or fifteen minutes the voice of my grandmaster told me to get up and to hold that wooden plate again.

When we held the plate it started becoming heavier, and again the cloudy form reappeared in front of us. From the cloudy form, he came back to his visible body.

This amazing and unbelievable experience was a confirmation. He demonstrated this *kriya* [action] once again in a similar manner. Perhaps that day will never come when I can speak about this to the world. I would like to do so, because I feel that the world should know that such sages exist, and the researchers should start researching such secret signs. Miracles like this show that a human being has such abilities, and in the third chapter of the *Yoga Sutras* Patanjali, the codifier of yoga science, explains all the *siddhis*. I do not profess or claim that such *siddhis* are essential for self-enlightenment, but I want to say that human potentials are immense, and as the physical scientists are exploring the external world, the genuine yogis should not stop exploring the inner abilities and potentials.

His way of teaching was very practical and straightforward. When I insisted on knowing about our tradition he said, "In our external way of life we come from Shankara's order, but actually our spiritual tradition is different from any institutional traditions existing in India." I also asked why he lived in Tibet and not in India. He answered, "It does not matter where I live. Here I have a few advanced students, who are prepared and who practice under my guidance. In the future I might come to India." I often showered questions on him, exactly as I did with my master. He spoke very little and answered me briefly with a smile and then he closed his eyes. He would say, "Be still and quiet and you will know without being told verbally. You should learn to see through your inner eye and to hear through your inner ear."

My diary is full of the instructions he gave me. He told me to cultivate more love by serving my disciples and students through meditation, speech, and action. I wondered how one could serve through meditation and wanted to know more. He said, "The sages, yogis, and spiritual masters serve the world by going deep within to the central fountain of love and expressing that love to the students without using any method of communication known so far to modern man. This, the finest of all communication, becomes very active in deep silence, and helps the student to resolve all fears, doubts, and problems. Any selfless wish experienced by the master during that time is always fulfilled." I lived with my grandmaster for several months doing *sadhana,* enjoying his divine presence, and learning a few methods of solar science and advanced techniques of rightist tantra.

Solar science is one of the highest of the advanced yoga sciences which can help humanity today by eliminating suffering. According to my grandmaster it involves a particular type of meditation on the solar plexus, and is very beneficial for removing all obstacles created by physical and mental diseases. The solar system is the largest network in the human body, and its center is called *manipura chakra.* There are various ways of meditating on this chakra, but by including advanced pranayama, solar science brings forward an awareness of a level of energy finer than the pranic level. At this level the energy rhythms are studied by meditating either on the morning sun or on *udaragni,* which is the internal center of fire. [This fire is created by the friction of the upper hemisphere and the lower hemisphere, which in the Upanishads are called upper *arani* and lower *arani.*] This healing science, though described in the Upanishads and known about by scholars, is understood in a practical way by very few. By learning this science one can have absolute control over his three sheaths—physical, pranic, and mental. One who is adept in such knowledge can communicate and heal anyone, regardless of the distance between them.

I also received a few important lessons from my grandmaster on Sri Vidya, the highest of all sciences and the mother

Sri Yantra

of all mandalas found in Tibetan and Indian literature. In advanced practices the student learns how to concentrate on different parts of Sri Yantra, and a few rare students learn to travel to the center. This yantra is considered to be a manifestation of divine power, and the *bindu*, or point in the center, is the center where Shakti and Shiva are united. Even after being initiated in this *vidya* in the Malabar hills of India, my teacher there did not give me the practice of *bindu bhedana* (piercing the point). In this worship of the Divine Mother the final knowledge imparted by the great sages is found. For this knowledge a scriptural study is essential, but most essential is the direct guidance of a master who is adept in this *vidya*. There are very few people who know this, and they can be counted on the fingertips, though I do not know them all. Our tradition alone teaches this *vidya*. If anyone is accomplished in this, then he is from our tradition. Having met my grandmaster and having received this knowledge, my purpose for visiting Tibet was fulfilled.

One day after two and a half months of study with my grandmaster I was sitting outside our cave thinking about the diary in which I used to record my experiences. A thought flashed in my mind: "I wish I had my diary here so I could note down a few experiences."

My grandmaster smiled and beckoned me to come to him. He said, "I can get your diary for you. Do you need it?" Such a possibility was not a great miracle for me anymore, for I had experienced such things before.

I casually replied, "Yes—and a few pencils too." I had left my diary in India at a sanatorium called Bhawali near the Nanital hills in North India. Suddenly three pencils and my diary, which was quite large, containing 475 pages, were before me. I was pleased but not especially surprised. I told him that I preferred him to give me something spiritual.

He laughed and said, "I have already given you that. You

should learn to retain it without resistance or carelessness."
Then he said, "My blessings are with you. Now I want you to
go to Lhasa, and from there you should return to India." I said,
"It is not possible for me to return to India. I will be arrested."
He replied, "India will soon have independence. If you delay,
the heavy snow and glaciers will prevent you from returning to
India this year."

I have not seen my grandmaster again. Some time later I
heard that he bid goodbye to his close disciples and disappeared. Some people say that they last saw him sitting with gar-
lands of flowers around his neck, floating on the current of
Kali Ganga, a river which flows through Tanakpur. I have
asked my master if he is still living in his mortal body. But my
master just smiles in response, and says, "That you will have to
find out for yourself."

Concerned about what would happen on my return, yet
somewhat confident, I went to Lhasa with the help of the lama
who had earlier been my host. I left for India in June 1947.
With the help of two mules and two guides, it took me a month
to cross the snow-blanketed passes and reach Gangtok, the
capital city of Sikkim. Three days before I arrived there India's
independence was declared.

While in Gangtok I lived in a monastery, which still exists
on the northeast side of the city. There I visited a lama who was
a remarkable man. He was a genuine Buddhist yogi and a
learned Sanskrit scholar who had lived for many years in
Bodhigaya in India. Usually the scholars of Buddhism criticize
Shankara, just as swamis from the order of Shankaracharya
criticize Buddhism. But this wise man, citing references from
many texts, taught me a synthesis of Buddhism and Shankara's
advaita system. [Shankara was a great yogi philosopher and a
dynamic young avatar (incarnation of God) who systematized
and organized the *advaita* (non-dualist) system, although the
codifier of this system was Gaudapada Acharya.] He said,

"There is no difference between these systems of philosophy as far as the ultimate Reality is concerned. There are verbal differences, but no experiential differences. Cast off all sectarian influences and attain the highest state of consciousness or nirvana."

He was sad to know that followers of Buddhism in India, Tibet, China, Japan, and the whole of Southeast Asia had forgotten the meditative tradition of self-enlightenment and had again fallen back toward ritualistic patterns, although this was not the way of Buddha. The unalloyed Buddhism which can help the modern world has all been lost. In thousands of temples Buddhist lamas, priests, and monks are performing rituals, while Buddha said, "Ye! Light thy own lamp. No one will give you salvation. Realize thyself. Attain nirvana and thou art Buddha thyself."

The lama also criticized the *advaitins,* the followers of Shankara, for indulging in rituals and for not teaching *advaita* philosophy properly. He said, "Such teachings are creating confusion in the world." Then he explained, "Shankara's philosophy is a synthesis of Vedic philosophy and Buddhism." He quoted the Vedas, saying: *"Asadva idam agra asit . . ."* which means "This visible universe has come out of the void . . ." He quoted several other scriptures and compared the philosophy of the *Mandukya Upanishad* with the *Sankhya Karika* of Ishvara Krishna, who was a Buddhist scholar. After tutoring me for several days he suggested that I leave the monastery and return to my master in the Himalayas.

Preparing to Tear the Veil

◆

Each student has his own image of what a teacher should be. If you come to me, you are not prepared to see me as I am. Since your expectations are not fulfilled, you decide that I am not a good teacher. This is not the proper way to approach a teacher. Approach with determination and a burning desire to learn. Then there will be no problem.

How will you find the right master? There is a saying in the scriptures: "When the disciple is prepared the master appears." If you are not prepared he will be there, but you won't notice or respond. If you do not know what a diamond is, the diamond may be there, but you ignore it and pass it by, taking it to be just a piece of glass. Further, if you do not know the difference, you may acquire a piece of glass, think that it is a diamond, and cherish it your whole life.

During the period of seeking, the student may become too intellectual, ignoring *sahaja-bhava* (spontaneous intuition); or conversely, he may become too emotional, ignoring his reason. An emotional trip is as dangerous as an intellectual trip; each feeds the ego. Those who do not believe in discipline should not expect enlightenment. No master can or will give it to them just because they want it.

A genuine spiritual teacher, one who is assigned to teach according to tradition, searches out good students. He looks for certain signs and symptoms; he wants to know who is prepared. No student can fool a master. The master easily perceives how well the student is prepared. If he finds that the student is not yet ready, he will gradually prepare him for the higher teachings. And when the wick and oil are properly prepared, the master lights the lamp. That is his role. The resulting light is divine.

We should not worry about who will guide us. The important question is: Am I prepared to be guided? Jesus had only twelve close disciples. He helped many, but he imparted the secret wisdom only to those few who were prepared. The Sermon on the Mount is comprehended by only a few, not by the multitudes. Those not on the path do not understand, for example, why one should be meek and poor.

The master's ways of teaching are many, and sometimes mysterious. He teaches through speech and actions—but in some cases he may teach without any verbal communication at all. I have often felt that the most important teachings have their source in intuition and are beyond the powers of verbal communication.

You should do your duty in the world with love, and that alone will contribute significantly to your progress on the path of enlightenment. You do need one who can guide and help you. You need an external guru as a means to attain the guru within you. Sometimes you may become egotistical and decide, "I don't need a guru." That is ego talking. You must tame it.

You'll never meet a bad guru if you are a good student. But the reverse is also true: if you are a bad student, you won't meet a good guru. Why should a good guru assume responsibility for a bad student? Nobody collects garbage. If you are in search of a guru, search within first. To become a yogi means to know your own condition here and now, to work with yourself. Don't grumble because you don't have a teacher. Ask whether you deserve one. Are you capable of attracting a teacher?

Once when I complained to my master that he was not teaching me, he said, "Come on, I'll become your disciple for the time being. You become the teacher. Act exactly as I have." I told him, "Sir, I do not know what to do." He said, "Don't worry; you'll know."

So he came to me with his eyes closed, carrying a bowl which had a big hole in it, and he said, "Teacher, give me something." I asked, "How is it possible for me to give you anything? Your bowl has a hole in it." Then he opened his eyes and said, "You have a hole in your head, and you want something from me."

Increase your capacity. Purify yourself. Acquire that gentle strength within. God will come and say to you, "I want to enter this living temple that you are." Prepare yourself for that situation. Remove the impurities—and you will find that he who wants to know reality is himself the source of reality.

Of the many swamis and teachers of all faiths whom I have known, only a few have been fully enlightened. I once raised this problem with my master. I said, "Sir, so many people are called swami or sage. The people of the world are cheated. Why are there so many inadequate teachers who aren't really ready to be teachers, who themselves should still be students?"

He smiled and said, "Do you know, a garden of flowers often has a fence or a hedge around it to protect it? These people are the hedge created for us by the Lord. Let them pretend. One day they will in fact become fully realized. For now they are only cheating themselves."

If you want to meet a genuine and fully knowledgeable teacher, you must first prepare yourself. Then you will be able to pass through the hedge.

XIII

Mastery over Life and Death

◆

YOU ARE THE ARCHITECT OF YOUR DESTINY. DEATH and birth are merely two events of life. You have forgotten your essential nature, and that is the cause of your suffering. When you become aware of this, you are liberated.

Birth and Death Are
but Two Commas

◆

I used to follow my master because he raised me from my young age, but I was not always convinced of the truth of what he taught. When I was calm and quiet, doubts would often rise from the deeper levels of my mind. I was directed by my master to visit various swamis. At first I thought, "I am wasting my time; these are useless people. They are withdrawn from the world, sitting under trees. Why do they do that?" Slowly I came to realize that first we should learn to doubt our own doubts and to analyze the very doubts themselves.

When I was seventeen I was sent to visit a certain sage who was a disciple of my master, but I did not know that at the time. My master told me, "If you really want to learn from a genuine swami, go to this man and live with him." I was directed to go to a place near Gangotri, where I found a swami sitting in a cave. Never before had I seen such a beautifully formed body. At that age I was interested in body-building and physical strength and was envious of a body like his. He had a broad chest and a very small waist, and his muscles were very solid. I was amazed to learn that he was eighty-five years old.

After I greeted him the first thing I asked was, "Sir, what do you eat here?" I was preoccupied with food. After my experience at the college I had become like a Westerner in the matter of food. Each day a variety of meals was available, and I was always anticipating the various dishes to be enjoyed at pending meals.

The swami asked, "Are you hungry?" I replied that I was. He told me, "Go to that corner of the cave, where you will find some roots. Take one and bury it in the fire. In a few minutes remove it and eat it." I did as I was told, and found the root was delicious. It tasted like milk over rice pudding! I could not eat the entire root. I was satisfied to know I could stay there for some time because there was something good to eat.

After I had eaten, Swamiji said, "I will not teach you through words." I sat by him for three days, and there was no conversation at all. On the third day I decided that it was a waste of time and energy to stay with a man who was silent all the time. He was not teaching me anything. While I was thinking this, he said, "Boy, you were not sent to me to receive intellectual knowledge such as you can find in books. You have come here to experience something. I am going to leave my body the day after tomorrow."

I could not understand why someone would choose voluntarily to leave his body. I said, "Sir, that will be suicide. It is not good for a sage like you to commit suicide." This was the kind of thing I had learned from studying in the college.

He said, "I am not committing suicide. When you remove an old bookcover and replace it with another, you do not destroy the book; when you change your pillow case, you do not destroy your pillow."

At the age of seventeen, I was doubtful. I said, "You have a wonderful body. I wish I could have a body half as beautiful as yours. Why are you discarding it? That is not good; it is a sin." In this way I thought I was teaching him.

He listened for some time without responding. After a while my brother disciple came in, and I exclaimed, "How did you get here? When I last saw you, you were far away from this place." He quietly took me aside and said, "Don't disturb him. You ask him silly questions. You don't understand sages. Let him leave his body peacefully."

But I argued with my brother disciple. I said, "He has such a beautiful body. Why should he leave it? This cannot be yoga; this is a simple suicide case. The police are far away from here or I would have them arrest him. This is an illegal act."

In spite of what my brother disciple said I remained doubtful and disapproving. When we went out for morning or evening ablutions I would say, "This healthy man with such a beautiful body should go and show people how to build and maintain healthy bodies. He says I am only seeing his body, that I should see something more. But what is that?" My brother disciple, who was older than I, replied, "Calm down. There are many things you still must learn. Let us keep our minds open so that we may come to understand. There are many mysteries in life."

The swami wouldn't speak to me, so after twenty-four more hours I said to my brother disciple, "I have not learned anything from silence, so I want to leave this place."

He replied, "Why don't you witness the process by which he leaves his body?"

I said, "This is a silly thing. I would rather die in a hospital, under the care of a good doctor, than die in a cave. What is this foolishness?" My ideas were totally modern and materialistic.

My brother disciple said, "You don't understand. You were asked to come here and sit. If you want to argue in your mind, you can do that. That is your business; I can't stop it—but don't disturb me."

Finally Swamiji spoke up. "Actually I am not doing anything. When it is time for us to leave the body we know it. We shouldn't stand in the way of nature. Death helps nature. We should not be afraid of death, because nothing affects us. Do you understand?"

I said, "I don't want to die, so I don't want to understand."

He said, "Your attitude is not good. Try to understand what death is; don't be afraid of it. We are afraid of many things, and that is not the way to live. Death does not annihilate you, it only separates you from a body."

I retorted, "I don't want to exist without my body."

He continued: "Death is a habit of the body. No one can live in this same body forever. It is subject to change, death, and decay. You have to understand this. Very few people know the technique of gaining freedom from their clinging to life. That technique is called yoga. It is not the yoga that is popular in the modern world, but is the highest stage of meditation. Once you know the right technique of meditation you have command over other functions of your body, mind, and soul. It is through prana and breath that a relationship is established between mind and body. When the breath ceases functioning, the link breaks, and that separation is called death. But you still exist."

I asked, "How does one feel existing without a body?"

He replied, "How do you feel when you go without a shirt? It's nothing."

But no matter what he said, he did not philosophically or logically convince me, for I still had an immature mind in many ways.

The day before he was to depart his body he gave us instructions: "Early in the morning, at five, I will leave my body. I want you to immerse it in the Ganges. Can you both do that?" I replied, "Of course! I can do it alone!" I picked him up by myself to demonstrate. The Ganges was not far away, just a few hundred yards.

Much of that night I remained awake, trying to understand the motives of this man's voluntarily discarding such a good and beautiful body. We regularly got up at three a.m. (From three to six is considered the best time for meditation, so we would go to bed between eight and ten and get up at three.) But that morning we all awoke even earlier, and began talking together.

The swami said, "Tell me, what do you wish? Whatever you wish I promise to fulfill it."

I replied, "You are dying; what can you do for me?"

He said, "Boy, for a genuine teacher, nothing like death really happens. A teacher can guide his students even after his death." Then he turned to my brother disciple and asked, "Isn't he a headache for you?"

My brother disciple replied, "Indeed yes, but what can I do?"

Between five and five-thirty we were still talking, when the swami suddenly said, "Now sit in meditation. In five minutes I will leave my body. Its time is over. This instrument which is called body is not capable of giving me more than I have already attained, so I will leave it behind."

Five minutes later, he sang out, "*Aumm . . .*" and then there was silence.

I checked his pulse and heartbeat. I thought, "He may have suspended his pulse and heartbeat for some time and might start breathing again." Then I checked his body temperature, his eyes, and all that. My brother disciple said, "Enough of that. We have to immerse his body before the sun rises." I told him, "Don't worry. I will do it myself." But he said, "I want to help."

When we both tried to lift him, we found that we could not budge his body. Then we brought a branch from a pine tree and inserted it under his thighs to pry him loose, but we failed. We tried everything we could think of for over an hour, but could not move him an inch.

I often recall what happened next. I shall never forget the experience. A few minutes before sunrise I heard someone say, "Now we will carry him." There was no one around, so I thought, "Perhaps I am imagining it." My brother disciple also looked around. I asked, "Did you hear something?" He said, "Yes, I also heard it." I asked, "Are we hallucinating? What is going on?"

Suddenly the swami's body rose into the air, apparently of its own accord, and slowly moved toward the Ganges. It floated in the air for a few hundred yards, and then lowered and sank into the Ganges.

I was shocked, and could not assimilate this experience for a long time. When people talked of miracles some swami was alleged to have performed, I had always said, "There is some trick in it." But when I saw this levitating body with my own eyes, it very quickly changed my attitude.

When I returned to the monastery several swamis were engaged in a discussion. The subject was: If God really created and watches over this world, then why is there so much misery? One swami said, "This physical universe is only one aspect of existence. We have the ability to know other aspects, but we don't make sincere efforts to realize this ability. Our minds remain focused on the physical aspect only. Man is suffering because he does not know the whole." What they said inspired me. I now began to listen with genuine interest, and found that my uncertainties were gradually resolved by what they were saying.

When I compare the materialistic world with the lifestyle of the sages I find the former concrete, emphasizing that which can be seen, touched, and grasped. But the lifestyle and atmosphere in which the sages live, though non-materialistic, is more realistic as far as the object of life is concerned. The world of means also has some value in life, but without awareness of the absolute Reality everything is in vain. Ordinary men regard certain aspects of life as mysterious or mystical, but such mysteries are easily solved when the veil of ignorance is removed. The technique of dying is not known to the modern scientists, but in yoga science such techniques are described and imparted to those who are prepared to practice them. The mystery of death and birth are revealed to a fortunate few.

The known part of life is a line which is stretched between

these two points, birth and death. The vast portion of one's existence remains unknown and invisible beyond these two known points. One who understands the unknown part of life knows that this life span is like a comma in a vast sentence which has no period. In the ancient yoga scriptures it is said that there is a definite way of leaving the body. Eleven gates are described through which the pranas or subtle energy can exit. The yogi learns to leave through the gate called *Brahmarandhra,* located at the fontanelle, the crown of the head. It is said that he who travels through this gate remains conscious and knows about life hereafter exactly as he knows life here.

Attitudes Toward Dying

Y ou are the architect of your life. You build your own philosophy and construct your own attitudes. Without right attitudes the entire architecture remains shaky. When one starts realizing this fact then he starts looking within, transforming himself and becoming aware of many levels of consciousness. He then finds strength within himself. Inner strength is the source of fulfillment. The sages have proven this fact, but modern man does not understand it. He is still searching and seeking for happiness in the external world.

When I was young I also thought that the source of happiness lay in the external objects of the world. One day my master sent me to the house of a rich man who was on his deathbed. When I arrived this rich man said, "Sir, give me your blessings." He was immersed in sorrow and full of tears.

I asked him, "Why are you crying like a poor and helpless child?"

He answered, "I wish I could be a child. Now I realize that I am the poorest and weakest man in the world. All the comforts and riches are at my disposal, but nothing seems to help me. All is in vain."

I could easily see the effects of inner poverty in that rich man. I have since studied many dying people, including poets, writers, philosophers, and political leaders, but always found that they all were miserable on their deathbed. Their clinging to life and their attachment to the objects of the world made them miserable. Those who are aware of the immortality within are free and unattached to the objects of the world. They leave their mental body in a positive state of mind.

The literature written on the life of Chaitanya Maha Prabhu reveals that the room in which he lived vibrated the chant he repeated after his death. I once had such an experience in the city of Kanpur. There is a family of doctors whose mother was a great devotee of the Lord. She was my initiate. Six months before her death she decided to live in a room by herself, remembering the Lord's name and meditating. After six months she fell sick and became bedridden. The time of her parting seemed imminent. Her older son, Dr. A. N. Tandon, was very much attached to his mother. He wanted to remain by her side. His mother said, "I don't want you to be attached to me. Don't sit next to me anymore! I have done my duties toward you. I have to walk all alone during the journey. Your attachment will not help me in any way."

Ordinarily dying people become lonely and frightened. A sense of false security grows, and they become deeply attached to their children and things they possess. But this woman was constantly at peace, completely absorbed in the name of the Lord. She said to her sons, "I am in great joy. Your attachment toward me has no power to hold me on this mortal plane."

Her son started weeping bitterly. He said, "Mother, I love you immensely. Don't you still love me? What has happened to my dear mother?"

She replied, "That which was expected to happen has already happened. I am a free soul now, in great joy. I am a wave of bliss in the ocean of the universe. I am free from all fears and anxieties. You're still attached to my mortal body, but I have now known that body is just a shell. Do you call it mother?"

I was present there. She wouldn't allow anyone to sit in the room but me. Five minutes before her death she smilingly whispered in my ear, "These people think that I have lost my mind, but they do not know how much I have gained." Then she asked me to call all the family members. She raised her hand and blessed them, and then left for her heavenly abode.

After her death the walls of that room in which she lived vibrated with the sound of her mantra. Anyone who came would feel the sound being vibrated from those walls. Someone informed me the walls of that house were still radiating her mantra. I could not believe it. So I visited the house and I discovered that the sound of her mantra was still vibrating there.

Mantra is a syllable or word or set of words. When consciously someone remembers his mantra, it automatically is stored in the unconscious mind, though ordinarily one does not remain aware of this fact. During the day of parting, when the mind is failing and stops functioning, attachment toward body and other possessions of the world makes one horribly lonely and miserable. During such a period that which one has stored there in the unconscious mind becomes one's guide. This period of separation is painful to the ignorant. This is not the case with a spiritual person who has remembered his mantra faithfully: the mantra guides him through this period of transition, which is frightening to the ignorant. Death is not painful, but fear of death is very painful. The mantra is a powerful support and guide which leads the dying person peacefully through that unknown period of darkness. Mantra then becomes a torchbearer when one goes through the corridor that exists between death and birth. Constantly being aware of the mantra with complete faith is one of the surest methods. All the spiritual traditions of the world use this method. A purified and trained mind with the help of mantra awareness dispels the darkness

416

during the period of transition. Mantra is a rare friend indeed, which helps one whenever it is needed, both here and hereafter. By remembering the mantra constantly, the aspirant creates deep grooves in the unconscious, and then the mind flows spontaneously in those grooves. Mantra is a spiritual guide which dispels the fear of death and leads one fearlessly to the other shore of life.

It is an accepted fact to yogis that the body is like a garment. They believe that when the garment is no longer useful it can be cast off consciously without any fear or misery. This way of casting off the body is not unusual for them.

I was fortunate to have witnessed such a case during the Kumbha Mela at Allahabad. Kumbha Mela is a festival of sages which is celebrated every twelve years. Many sages and learned people assemble on the holy banks of the Ganges to share their experiences and knowledge with all those who attend. This festival lasts for a month. All religious people of India like to enjoy this spiritual gathering.

During this time I was staying in a garden house situated on a bank of the holy Ganges. Early one morning at about three o'clock I was informed that Vinay Maharaja had decided to cast off his body punctually at four-thirty. This swami was a student of my master. I immediately rushed to the hut where he was staying. There he talked to me for half an hour, discussing the higher practices of Yoga-Vedanta. There were six other swamis sitting around him. Exactly at four-thirty, after explaining the technique of voluntarily casting off the body, he bade goodbye to us, saying, "God bless you; we'll meet on the other side." Then he was silent. He closed his eyes and became still. We all heard the sound "tic" come from his skull. This was the sound of cracking the skull. This process is called casting off the body through *Brahma-randhra*. We later immersed his body in the Ganges. There have been many such occasions when I witnessed a yogi casting off the body consciously.

Modern man knows how to eat, talk, wear clothes, and live

Kumbha Mela

in society. He also knows how to prepare the expectant mother to give a safe birth, and has discovered the painless method of labor. But modern man has not yet learned the techniques of casting off the body voluntarily and joyfully. During the time of death he becomes miserable and experiences many psychological pains. Our modern society, though highly evolved technologically, is still ignorant of the many mysteries of life and death. Modern man has not yet discovered the resources which are already within him.

Death is a habit of the body, a necessary change. The dying man should be educated psychologically for this moment. This inevitable change called death is itself not painful—but the fear of death creates miseries for the dying man. There are many aspects of education imparted to modern man for his success in the world, but no one imparts the knowledge which gives him freedom from the fear of death. It is essential for human beings to find out the way of comforting the dying.

The Techniques of
Casting Off the Body

◆

I, along with two friends, started a journey from Gangotri to Badrinath. It was July, the traveling season of the clouds. We took a narrow, zigzagged footpath, an unusual route which was known by only a few yogis and sages. It took four days to travel the twenty-five miles on foot from Gangotri to Badrinath using this route, while it would have taken many more days using the much longer, ordinary route. As we passed through the snow-blanketed peaks at 12,000 feet nature, though it seemed to be cruel, gave us a vision of the beauty of the Himalayas which I had not seen before.

We halted for the night nine miles from Gangotri. On the other side of the Ganges from this place lies Bhoja Basa, where grow the trees whose bark is used for writing the scriptures. The next morning, before we started going toward Gomukh (the source of the Ganges) in an attempt to cross the mountain to Badrinath via this unusual and unknown route, a young swami from Madras, who lived on the other side of the Ganges, met us. His language was Tamil, which is spoken in the southern states of India; he could communicate with us only in broken Hindi. He had studied for several days with

Swami Tapodhanamji, a very learned scholar and austere person of the Himalayas. The four of us continued our journey to Gomukh at the foot of the mountain glaciers from where the Ganges flows. We had a small tent, a few biscuits, and some popped corns. At Gomukh we met a swami called Hansji, and he joined us. Beyond this point no yogi or swami lives. Hansji lived here every summer. He had been a naval officer. He became disgusted with his sailor's life and had gone in search of the yogis and sages of the Himalayas. As a young man of thirty-five years he accepted the life of renunciation and was known in this area for his calm, gentle, and loving nature.

The next day we bade goodbye to Hansji, who was actually not in favor of our adventurous expedition to Badrinath through this unknown route. We camped at the height of 16,000 feet that day, and the next day at the height of 18,000 feet. Traveling became more difficult without any respiratory equipment, because the air is thinner at higher elevations. The three days we traveled were like walking on the space just above the roof of the world, from where you can see the clean blue sky with twinkling stars hung high on the pillars of glory.

Our tent was very small, and with the help of our warm clothing and body-heat radiation we passed this crucial night breathing shallowly in the cold, wind, and snow. At midnight the young swami who had joined us on the way made a decision to cast off his body there high in the Himalayas. He did not do this out of frustration, but perhaps because he knew that his time in the world was over. In deep snows, if one gradually removes his clothing a time comes when the whole body becomes painless and insensitive.

It is true that in the deep snow of the high Himalayan mountains one becomes numb and insensitive. I collected this evidence from various scriptures, sages, and even books written by Westerners who go to the Himalayas for "peak hunting." But the yoga way of casting off the body is done through a proper technique. Letting oneself freeze while in samadhi is a traditional way of dying for a particular sect of Himalayan yogis. It is called *hima-samadhi.*

The word *samadhi* is frequently used by Patanjali's system of yoga for the highest state of tranquility. But according to the Himalayan custom the various methods which are used for consciously casting off the body are also called samadhi. Among themselves yogis and sages usually use this word in the sense of "He has taken *maha-samadhi*," meaning "He has cast off his body."

We did not want to leave this young swami there all alone, and tried to persuade him to come with us. But for lack of the knowledge of Tamil we could not communicate and convince him. We were with him until ten o'clock in the morning, but our advice and persuasion would not work. He had already made the decision to voluntarily leave his body in the land of the *devas.* So, leaving him behind, we went ahead and reached Badrinath after two days. Yudhishthira, a prominent character of the *Mahabharata,* also went to the Himalayas during his last days. He told his wife that he was going to meet the gods and then go on to his final abode. We parted at the shrine, and I went to my mountain home.

This way of casting off the body is one of the ways which many ancients accepted willingly, but there are various other ways of doing this. One is called *jal-samadhi,* and is done inside the deep waters of the rivers of the Himalayas by retaining the breath. *Sthal-samadhi* is done by sitting in an accomplished posture and consciously opening the fontanelle. The techniques of dying which are used by yogis are very methodical, painless, and conscious. This is unusual in the Western world, but not in the Himalayas. It is not like committing suicide, but is an exact process or way of leaving that body which is no longer an instrument for enlightenment. Such a body is considered to be a burden—an obstacle which might obstruct the journey of the dying man when he goes through his vast unconscious reservoir of memories. Only those who are not competent in higher techniques and not self-reliant on their yoga willpower and control accept the normal methods of dying, which are definitely inferior to the yoga methods.

There is another very rare way of casting off the body. By meditating on the solar plexus the actual internal flame of fire burns the body in a fraction of a second, and everything is reduced to ashes. This knowledge was imparted by Yama, the king of death, to his beloved disciple Nachiketa in the *Kathopanishad*. All over the world instances of spontaneous combustion are often heard about, and people wonder about such occurrences. But the ancient scriptures, such as *Mahakala Nidhi,* explain this method systematically.

Birth and death are two events in life which are considered to be very minor according to the yogis and sages of the Himalayas. Modern men tried their best to discover the mystery of birth; they did so, and can now prepare for that pleasurable event. But for lack of a real philosophy behind life they do not understand or know the techniques of dying, and thus cannot prepare themselves. For a yogi, death is a habit of the body and a change like other changes that occur in the process of growth. Modern men could receive this training, and then there would be less misery in old age when they find themselves completely isolated and ignored by the rest of society. I wonder why modern people do not explore other dimensions, ways, and methods of gaining freedom from that fear which is called death. The Western world, in spite of having enough literature on this subject, is still looking for a solution. Nonetheless people have now started talking to the general public on this subject—but no book explains the techniques for dying. Yoga literature and practices, which are neither religious nor cultural, could be verified scientifically and then used to comfort dying and suffering people.

Living in a Dead Body

$\blacklozenge$

A British military commander in charge of one of the commands in Assam, India, started practicing meditation under the guidance of my master, whom he adored highly. He had met my master in 1938 in a place called Rorkee, some forty miles from Rishikesh. One of the Indian officers had praised my master highly, so this commander accompanied him to meet my master on a bank of the Ganges. After that the commander often went to see my master, and even thought of resigning his high military commission to be with him. He also loved me and wanted me to visit Assam, but I preferred to be in the mountains rather than to visit the towns and cities.

When I was sixteen years of age I met an old adept called Boorhe Baba [*boorhe* means "old"], who lived in the Naga hills. He was on his way to Assam. He stopped to see my master while we were staying in Gupta Kashi cave, five or six miles from the town. This adept was very slim. He had white hair and a beard and dressed in white robes. He had an unusual way of carrying himself. He resembled a very straight, unswaying bamboo staff. This adept would often visit my master and consult with him on higher spiritual practices. He would repeatedly talk to my master about the subject of changing bodies. I was young and did not understand very much about this particular practice, which is called *para-kaya pravesha*. No one talked freely to me about this yoga process.

After ten days I was told to visit Assam with this old adept. We went to Assam by train and then stopped to visit the commander, who practiced yoga postures, pranayama, and meditation regularly. The other military officers did not understand their commander. They thought he did odd things; that he was practicing something strange. One of the Indian majors under this commander talked to me about him. He said, "First he asks me to get a chair, and then he sits on it. Next he asks me to remove the chair from under him—yet he remains in the same position, as if he were still seated comfortably on the chair." He would sit in that position without any support at a desk in his office. Another major who had been with him for a long time told me that since having become a yogi three years earlier, his personality had constantly changed. He said, "He doesn't lose his temper anymore. He is very kind and gentle." The commander became a teetotaler. He knew Hindi well and was studying Sanskrit. While we were there I heard Boorhe Baba tell the commander that in nine days he was going to assume another body.

After a few days Boorhe Baba and I left the military camp and went to the Naga hills. Because of the mosquitoes, snakes, and wild animals, including tigers and elephants, in that part of the country, very few yogis live there. The cave in which we stayed was the cave of the late Swami Nigamananda, who wrote three books [*Yogi Guru, Tantric Guru,* and *Vedanta Guru]* on his experiences, which I found very useful. During the time we spent together, this adept would often talk on some profound subject, while I would be preoccupied with flexing my muscles. I told Baba, "I have strong muscles," to which he replied, "Very soon your strength will be tested."

424

I had an inquisitive mind, so I was constantly asking questions of Baba. Finally he said, "No questions anymore. Focus your mind on your mantra." This Baba knew several languages, including Sanskrit, Hindi, Pali, Tibetan, and Chinese. Sometimes he spoke to me in English, but only when he was annoyed with my constant chattering. Then he would say in English, "Shut up!" I loved silence, but in order to know more about the many things I found mysterious, I would put questions to him. In spite of his annoyance I continued pestering him. When the time was approaching for us to leave the cave I asked him why he wanted to assume another body. He replied, "I am over ninety years old now, and my body is not a fit instrument to remain in samadhi for a long time. Besides, the opportunity has presented itself. Tomorrow there will be a dead body in good condition. A young man will be bitten by a snake and then placed in a river thirteen miles from here." I found his talk quite bewildering. He told me that we would leave the cave in the morning and reach our destination before sunset.

When morning came, however, we could not leave the cave. During the night an elephant had inserted its trunk into the outer chamber of the cave. A scorpion, hiding itself in the corner of the cave, had stung the elephant on the trunk, and the elephant died in that position. Its two front legs, the trunk, and the head were inside the cave, and its hindquarters were outside. We obviously could not get out without great effort. Baba caught hold of the scorpion with his bare hands and said, "Bad boy! What a horrible thing you have done."

"Don't do that!" I yelled. "It will sting you." But he replied, "No, it wouldn't dare do that." It was a huge, black scorpion, about five inches long. I wanted to kill it with my wooden sandal, but Baba said, "No one has the authority to kill any living creature. These two got even with each other. You will know what happened when you understand the cause and effect of karma." He wouldn't explain more to me because we had to leave and the distance we had to cover on foot through such a dense forest was long. After two arduous hours of trying to push the dead elephant out of the way I finally made enough space for us to crawl out. Thirteen miles north of the cave we came upon a river, where we camped that night. In the morning I bathed in the river and at four-thirty sat for meditation. When I opened my eyes Baba was gone. I searched for him and waited the whole day, but he never turned up. So I decided to depart for the Himalayas.

The whole journey seemed to be very mysterious and fruitless. Even my way back was a rugged path through thorny bushes. When I reached the Assam headquarters of the British commander, he said, "Boorhe Baba has done it! He has assumed a new body!" I still did not understand the whole thing. Immediately the next morning I left for my Himalayan home. When I arrived my master said, "Boorhe Baba was here last night and was inquiring about you." A few days later a young sadhu visited our cave. He started talking to me as though he had known me for a long time. He described all the events of our journey to Assam in detail and said, "I'm sorry you could not be with me when I changed my body." It was strange for me to talk with someone who had appeared at one time very familiar to me, but now he had a new body.

I found that his new physical instrument did not affect his previous capacities and characteristics at all. He exhibited all the intelligence, knowledge, memories, talents, and mannerisms of the old Baba. I verified this by minutely watching his speech and actions. The young man even had that same strange bamboo-like walk of the old man. Later my master gave him a new name, saying, "The name goes with the body, not the soul." He is now called Ananda Baba and is still a wanderer in the Himalayas. When I see him, even today, I think of him in his previous body and have difficulty in adjusting to the body which is in front of me.

With all the evidence I collected I found out that it is possible for a highly advanced yogi to assume the dead body of another if he chooses to do so and if a suitable body is available. The adepts alone know the process. For the ordinary mind it is only a fantasy.

I feel my life has been fuller and richer for what I have learned from the great sages. If my hands cannot lift the veil of the future nor my eyes penetrate its folds, I can still hear melodies of the music and distinguish their voices. The objects of the world do not pass through my mind, but their voices echo from the depths of my being.

My Master Casts Off His Body

One day in July 1945 my master said that he wished to cast off his body. I argued with him: "It is written in the scriptures that the master who leaves a foolish disciple in the world is committing a sin and goes to perdition." So he said, "Okay, then I will not cast off my body, because you are still a fool and ignorant."

Then in the year 1954, shortly before I was to leave for Germany, I was taking a bath in the Ganges and thought, "That was not right for me to do. I should not have forced him to stay bound to his body, as he has already given me so much."

When I went to my master I didn't tell him of my thought, but he said, "Ask the other swamis to come at five-thirty this evening for the last teachings I want to impart." We were at a height of 11,600 feet near a shrine in the Himalayas. This place is situated between Basudhara and Badrinath.

The witnessing of the death of a yogi is considered to be a worthwhile experience in our tradition; we always try to witness a master's death. It shows that one can die voluntarily whenever he decides. If a master wants to live for a long time he will—but the day he wants to leave his body, he will just cast it off, exactly as a snake leaves his skin.

I asked my master, "Why do you want to cast off your body?" He said, "You were taking a bath and you were thinking that you had no right to hold me back. Now you are strong and you have learned something. You are finally mature and you can stand on your own in the world. I feel free to go on my journey." There were five of us with him on the top of a mountain. He sat in the center surrounded by us and asked all of us if we wanted to learn or know about any spiritual practices. I was in deep sorrow, but at the same time would not express my attachment for him, thinking that the body must go to dust sooner or later. It is inevitable. So I tried hard to compose myself. He looked at me and said, "Do you want anything from me?"

I said, "I want you to be with me whenever I need you, whenever I am in distress, helpless, or cannot deal with a situation."

He promised me that he would, and then he blessed me. We all bowed before him. He sat in the accomplished pose and closed his eyes. Gently he muttered the sound *"Aumm"* and became lifeless.

We all started crying. We did not know whether we should bury the body or immerse it in the river. We couldn't decide. For two hours we discussed this and consoled each other, but could not come to any conclusion. Finally the decision was left to me. We thought of carrying his body to our cave, but since it was sixty-three miles away, it would take several days to reach there. Nonetheless another swami and I started to carry his body toward the cave. In the mountains it was not possible to travel at night, so we stopped in a small cave. We were very quiet and passed the night sitting and looking at each other. I never believed that my master would ever leave me, but he had done so. Next morning after sunrise we started carrying his body again and walked about fifteen miles. We thought of disposing of the body, but we could not decide where and how it should be done. We were afraid that the body would decompose. Two nights had passed, and on the third morning we decided to bury it on the top of the mountain from which we could see our cave far away in the distance. We dug a pit six feet deep and laid the body inside it.

We wanted to cover up the body with boulders and earth, but none of us could move our limbs. We could talk to each other, but all five of us became completely inert and lifeless, as if we were paralyzed. It was an experience which I had never had before. I felt as though my soul were entirely different from my body and I was fully conscious of the separation of body and soul. I felt like jumping out of my body, and the others had a similar experience. There was a small fir tree just five feet away from us, and we all heard the sound of my master saying, "I am here, wake up. Do not be sad. Do you need me in my body again, or do you want me to help you without the body?" I said, "I need you in your body."

With one voice we all cried for his help and begged him to come back. Then I felt a tingling sensation in my body. Slowly the numbness went away and we started moving our limbs. My master got up and came out of the pit. He said, "It's too bad that you still need me in the body. You still worship the form and cannot go beyond it. Your attachment to my body is an obstacle. Now I will see that you are not attached to my body anymore." Then he started teaching me the relationship between the body and the formless soul.

Many times when I lived with him in the cave he would remain in absolute silence for several days without any movement. Whenever he opened his eyes we would go and sit near him. One day he told me that there are three categories of beings: (1) the Absolute Being, the Lord of the universe; (2) the sages who have power over birth and death and who are semi-immortal beings. They are born and die at their will; (3) the ordinary people, who do not have mastery over birth and death. For them death is a constant fear that lurks in their minds and hearts. Such ignorant people suffer.

A sage and a yogi are not bothered by the minor events of death and birth. They are free from all fears. Being free from all fears is the first message of the Himalayan sages. That fearlessness is one of the steps toward enlightenment.

In the course of the conversation my master told us that the highly accomplished yogis and sages are ageless and can live as long as they wish. The individual soul can voluntarily cast off the body and can even enter into another body. It is said that the great yogi and sage Shankara was gifted with such a power. One of the scriptures describes this process as *para-kaya pravesha*. I was intensely interested in experiencing this process of the changing of the body, though earlier I had had a similar experience in Tibet with my grandmaster. My master told me that it is not unusual or impossible for an accomplished yogi to change his body, provided he finds a suitable replacement.

He described three ways of expanding the life span: (1) through highly accomplished yoga powers and a disciplined life, one can live for a long time; (2) by changing the body one can continue to live consciously with all the experiences carried from the previous body; (3) enlightenment is freedom itself, and there is no need of clinging to the garment which is called body.

After studying a few rare manuscripts and learning at the feet of my master, my desire for knowing this science grew stronger.

The sages explored and expounded the deeper truths of life. These truths are the truths of all time and all humanity, and hence the universality of their appeal. Deep down in the hearts of all realized men, no matter what their race and what their color, is the desire to understand and to hold to the truth, to attain to the higher destiny of the human race.

Man has been searching for immortality since the dawn of civilization. If one has done something in the past, the same thing can be done by someone today; and if someone can do that today, the same can be done by all.

Life expresses itself through the medium of the body. Desires seek form for self-manifestation. Desire is the inner soul, and form is the external. Without content, there can be no form—it will be dead matter. Being devoid of rhythmic vibration, neither form nor desire is content and will be eternally homeless. Therefore desires seek embodiment, while forms seek desires.

Many are those who perceive the mere body. Being unable to apprehend the life within, they consider the lines of the picture to be final: they cannot pierce through them. Their realization must ever remain untrue, their knowledge incomplete. To learn more about man's inner life rhythms, one should learn to go beyond desire and to cultivate the inward sensitivity and one-pointedness of that mind which can seek help from the finer forces of rhythmic vibrations.

Life is a rhythm, and one who knows this rhythm can live as long as he wishes.

XIV

Journey to the West

◆

"EAST IS EAST AND WEST IS WEST" IS A PRIMITIVE idea. Modern man has reached the moon! The West is advanced in technology, and the East in spirituality. Why not build a bridge of understanding? That the West has much to share with the East is beyond doubt—but the East also has something to contribute to the West. The flower of the West without the fragrance of the East is a flower in vain.

A Doctor's Recurring Vision

◆

There was a psychiatrist from a small town in Germany. People often called him a crazy doctor because he did not believe much in modern medicine; he was more inclined to search for esoteric knowledge. In 1955 he had recurring visions of my master. He felt that the man who was appearing in his visions was calling him to come to India. The same vision occurred again and again for seven days, so he went to Frankfurt and bought an airplane ticket for India. But while waiting for his flight he fell asleep in the airport lounge and missed his plane.

Shortly before that my master asked me to go to Germany to learn something about Western psychology and philosophy. A businessman from Bombay managed to get my ticket to Frankfurt and gave me a few letters of introduction to his friends there. With further instructions from my master, whom I adored as my gurudeva, I left for Germany. When I arrived in Frankfurt the doctor was at the airport. When he saw that I was a swami from India he approached me and showed me several drawings he had made of the person in his recurring vision. He asked me if I knew of any such man in India.

The first thing he said to me was, "Please help me. The man in this drawing has appeared to me in a vision again and again. I have tried to draw the picture of my vision as well as I could. I'm sure it is not an hallucination. This vision has created such deep grooves in my mind that I cannot do my work. All that I can think of is this image. You are a swami from India. Perhaps you can help."

When I saw the drawings, I said, "He is my master." He insisted that I go back to India with him and take him to my master—but my master did not want me to return right away: he thought that I was attached to his mortal being, and wanted to break the mortal ties to strengthen my awareness of the immortal link between us. He wanted me to remain physically away from him for some time and to become aware of the more subtle bond which exists between us. That's why he sent me to different teachers in different parts of the Himalayas.

I gave the doctor a long letter to show Dr. Chandradhar and Dr. Mitra of Kanpur, India. In the letter I asked them to lead him to Jageshwar, where my master was camping next to the temple and teaching Professor Nixon (Krishna Prem) and Dr. Alexander (Anand Bikkhu).

With the help of the doctors of Kanpur the German doctor met my master, stayed with him for three days, and then returned to Germany. He then arranged for me to visit different institutes and universities throughout Europe. I met with a great many Western doctors and psychologists. After visiting several European countries and studying in many institutions and universities I returned to India. Some time later this doctor again left for India, where he became a *sannyasi* [renunciate]. He now devotes his time to meditation in a small thatched hut in the northeastern Himalayas. Some Westerners call him crazy because he prefers to live in isolation. I have met a few foreigners like him who have become swamis, and I have found them to be more serious than many of the Indian swamis.

A prophetic vision is the rarest of all visions. It flashes from the source of intuition and is therefore beyond the concept of time, space, and causation. Such a vision sometimes is received by laymen accidentally. But those who do meditation and truly have attained the fourth state of mind receive such guiding visions consciously. This unalloyed vision always comes true.

Swami Rama after emerging from the cave

Transformation in the Cave

◆

For eleven months I lived in a small cave. For those eleven months I never saw a single human being. In our tradition this is an essential practice. Usually it is not practiced for less than eleven months, because it is believed that even the most inert aspirant will realize the highest truth through this practice during that period. So the teacher says, "No matter how able you are, I will assume you to be the most inert. You will have to complete eleven months in the solitude of the cave."

You are not allowed to come out and take a bath, but you are taught a vigorous breathing practice which cleans your pores and which is actually better than bathing. You get a very limited amount of food once a day and some water, but that is quite sufficient to maintain life. My food was mostly barley and mountain vegetables, some juices, a glass of milk in the morning and one in the evening. In the limited space of the cave, which was six feet by six feet, I would do a few postures regularly and would sleep for two to three hours only. The rest of the time I remembered my guru-mantra and meditated or gazed. Three times a day I did pranayama vigorously but very cautiously.

The entrance to the cave is closed, but there is an outlet for the waste to wash away and a tiny needlepoint hole in the ceiling of the cave where a single shaft of light can enter. This tiny hole is to aid in concentrating the mind on a single point. This happens spontaneously, even if you don't want it to happen. You don't have to make any effort to concentrate in that situation, because there is only one ray of light and nothing else. In such isolation what will you do the whole day if you don't learn meditation? If you don't do meditation you quickly become imbalanced. You have no choice.

The sages systematically teach you the method of going deep into meditation. They say, "This is the first step, the next, the third," and so on. They will describe certain symptoms that arise out of meditation. When a particular symptom appears then you know you are going to the next step. In this way you attain the highest degree of concentration. They keep a strict watch on you so that you remain undisturbed and do not go through suffering of any sort.

Dwelling in the cave for the first two months was very difficult for me, but later I started enjoying it immensely. The science of raja yoga teaches *samyama*—inner transformation through concentration, meditation, and samadhi. During this training I discovered that without living in silence for a considerable time, maintaining a deeper state of meditation is not possible.

After eleven months I came out of the cave. It was five o'clock in the evening on July 27. I was asked not to stay outside in the sun for the first week. I had difficulty in adjusting to the external world. Everything looked different, as though I had come to a strange new world. The first time I went to the city it took me forty minutes to cross a street corner because I was not accustomed to so much external activity. But gradually I became able to deal with the world. Coming back to the external world I realized that the world is a theater where I could test my inner strength, speech, emotions, thoughts, and behavior.

After the completion of this training I was prepared to come to the West. I did not want to leave my master, but he insisted. He said, "You have a mission to complete and a message to deliver. That message is ours, and you are my instrument." My master then instructed me to go to Japan. He told me that I would meet someone in Japan who would help me come to the United States.

I left for Tokyo from Calcutta by plane with only eight dollars in my pocket. When we stopped in Hong Kong I ordered tea in the airport restaurant, and was surprised to be presented with a bill for four dollars. I left another dollar as a tip, so I arrived in Tokyo with only three dollars and an apple, which I had saved from the meal aboard the airplane.

A man came up to me and asked where I had come from and where I would be staying in Japan. I told him, "I have a friend and I will stay with him." He asked me, "Who is your friend?" I didn't know how to answer him since I didn't know anyone in Japan, so I said, "You are that friend." I stayed with him and he introduced me to Yokadasan, the spiritual head of Mahikari. He has a following of several hundred thousand. Yokadasan had had many visions of a sage of the Himalayas. When I was introduced to him he hugged me with reverence and said, "I have been waiting for you. I hope you will give me the secret teachings of the Himalayan masters."

I lived with him for six months and had occasion to address and teach various spiritual groups in Tokyo, Osaka, and other cities.

After I had imparted the message of my master to Yokadasan he bought me a ticket, and I continued on my journey to the United States. Before I had left India my master had told me that in the United States I would meet my students and associates. He described many details to me which have

Swami Rama with Yokadasan, the spiritual head
of Mahikari, and his successor

since come true. I have still to complete my task. This sometimes makes me pensive but I know that when the Lord gives
me the opportunity I will fulfill the purpose of my life. My purpose is to create a bridge between the East and West by establishing a center of learning from where I can faithfully deliver
the message of the sages.

Ways of East and West

◆

When I left the Himalayas to visit Japan and the United States my master gave me a few instructions. I asked him, "What shall I teach to the students who wish to learn from me? Shall I convert them and teach the religions of India? Shall I ask them to follow the Indian culture?" He said, "You foolish boy."

I said, "Then tell me, what shall I teach them? The culture in the West is entirely different from ours. Our culture does not allow one to get married to anyone without the consent of other family members, while the culture in the West believes in a free social life. A Christian can get married to anyone, and the Jewish people do likewise. Of course their ways of worshipping God are set in a fixed particular style, while we worship the way we like and choose the path of enlightenment we want. We are free-thinkers but we are in the bondage of social laws, and they are in the bondage of certain fixed ideas in their way of thinking and worshipping."

I asked, "These two diverse ways of life seem to be quite apart. How can I deliver your message to the West?"

He said, "Though these cultures live in the same world

Swami Rama teaching in the United States

with the same purpose of life, they are each extreme. Both East and West are still doing experiments on the right ways of living. The message of the Himalayan masters is timeless and has nothing to do with the primitive concepts of East or West. Extremes will not help humanity to attain the higher step of civilization for which we all are striving. Inner strength, cheerfulness, and selfless service are the basic principles of life. It is immaterial whether one lives in the East or West. A human being should be a human being first. A real human being is a member of the cosmos. Geographical boundaries have no powers to divide humanity.

"To get freedom from all fears is the first message of the Himalayan sages. The second message is to be aware of the reality within. Be spontaneous and let yourself become the instrument to teach pure spirituality without any religion and culture.

"All the spiritual practices should be verified scientifically if science has the capacity to do so. Let providence guide you."

With reverence I made a bow and started for my journey. I came to the city of Kanpur, where I stayed a few months with our disciple Dr. Sunanda Bai, who bought my air ticket to Japan.

Dr. Sunanda Bai

Our Tradition

$\diamond$

Shankaracharya established an ascetic order 1,200 years ago, though renunciates had already lived in an unbroken lineage from the Vedic period. He organized his orders through five main centers in the North, East, South, West, and center of India. The entire ascetic order of India traces its tradition from one of these centers. Our tradition is *Bharati. Bha* means "knowledge"; *rati* means "lover." *Bharati* means "he who is the lover of knowledge." From this comes the word *Bharata,* the land of spiritual knowledge, one of the Sanskrit names used for India.

There is one thing unique to our tradition. It links itself to an unbroken lineage of sages even beyond Shankara. Our Himalayan tradition, though a tradition of Shankara, is purely ascetic, and is practiced in the Himalayan caves rather than being related with institutions established in the plains of India. In our tradition learning of the Upanishads is very important, along with the special advanced spiritual practices taught by the sages. The *Mandukya Upanishad* is accepted as one of the authoritative scriptures.

The knowledge of Sri Vidya is imparted stage by stage and

the advanced student is taught *Prayoga Shastra* [which explains the practicality and application of the discipline one has to follow for this knowledge]. We believe in both the Mother and the Father principles of the universe. That which is called maya, or illusion, in our worship becomes the Mother and does not remain as a stumbling block or obstacle on the path of spiritual enlightenment. All of our worship is internal and we do not perform any rituals.

There are three stages of initiation given according to our tradition. First: mantra, breath awareness, and meditation; second: inner worship of Sri Vidya and *bindu bhedana* (piercing the pearl of wisdom); third: *shaktipata* and leading the force of kundalini to the thousand-petaled lotus called the *sahasrara chakra*. At this stage we do not associate ourselves with any particular religion, caste, sex, or color. Such yogis are called masters and are allowed to impart the traditional knowledge. We strictly follow the discipline of the sages.

It is not possible for me to discuss in detail the secret teachings of *Prayoga Shastra,* for it is said: "*Na datavyam, na datavyam, na datavyam*—Don't impart, don't impart, don't impart" unless someone is fully prepared and committed and has practiced self-control to a high degree. These attainments can be verified through the experiences of the sages of the past. In our path, gurudeva is not a god but a bright being who has faithfully and sincerely attained a state of enlightenment. We believe in the grace of the guru as the highest means for enlightenment, but never as the end. The purpose of the guru is to selflessly help his disciples on the way to perfection.

Our tradition has the following orientation:

1. One Absolute without a second is our philosophy.
2. Serving humanity through selflessness is an expression of love, which one should follow through mind, action, and speech.
3. The yoga system of Patanjali is a preliminary step

accepted by us for the higher practices in our tradition, but philosophically we follow the *advaita* system of one Absolute without a second.

4. Meditation is systematized by stilling the body, having serene breath, and controlling the mind. Breath awareness, control of the autonomic nervous system, and learning to discipline primitive urges are practiced.

5. We teach the middle path to students in general, and those who are prepared for higher steps of learning have the opportunity to learn the advanced practices. This helps people in general in their daily lives to live in the world and yet remain above. Our method, for the convenience of Western students, is called superconscious meditation. I am only a messenger delivering the wisdom of the Himalayan sages of this tradition, and whatever spontaneously comes from the center of intuition, that I teach. I never prepare my lectures or speeches, for I was told by my master not to do so.

6. We do not believe in conversion, changing cultural habits, or introducing any God in particular. We respect all religions equally, loving all and excluding none. Neither do we oppose any temple, mosque, or church, nor do we believe in building homes for God while ignoring human beings. Our firm belief is that every human being is a living institution or a temple.

7. Our members are all over the world, and for the sake of communication we also believe in education. Our graduate program imparts the knowledge given by the sages, thereby fulfilling the inner need of intellectuals.

8. We practice vegetarianism. We teach a nutritional diet that is healthy and good for longevity, but at the same time we are not rigid and do not force students to become vegetarians.

9. We respect the institution of the family and stress the education of children by introducing a self-training program and not by forcing our beliefs, faiths, and way of life on them.

10. Our trained teachers systematically impart all aspects of yoga relating to body, breath, mind, and individual soul. Awareness within and without is the key, and the methods of expansion are carefully introduced to the students.

11. To serve humanity we believe in examining, verifying, and coming to certain conclusions regarding the yoga practices, including relaxation and meditation.

12. Our experiments are documented and published for the benefit of humanity.

13. We believe in universal brotherhood, loving all and excluding none.

14. We strictly abstain from politics and from opposing any religion.

15. Of great importance is the practice of non-violence with mind, action, and speech.

The knowledge that is imparted by the sages and masters of the Himalayas guides the aspirant like a light in the darkness. The purpose of this message is to awaken the divine flame that resides in the reservoir of every human being. This flame, when perfectly kindled by spiritual discipline, mounts higher and higher into the vast light of truth. It rises through the vital or nervous mind, passes through our mental sky, and finally enters at the paradise of light, its own supreme home in the eternal truth. Then the illumined practitioner sits calm in his celestial sessions with the highest of powers and drinks the wine of infinite beatitude. This child of immortality is a child of universal parents, protected all the time by the Mother Divine. This rapturous child of bliss remains divine-will intoxicated in delight. He becomes a sage, a sleepless envoy and ever-wakeful guide for those who tread the path. Such a leader on the path marches in front of human people to comfort, help, and enlighten them.

Om, Shanti, Shanti, Shanti

Glossary

Acharya A spiritual adept in charge of a place of special study.

Advaita The philosophy of non-dualism: that is, that the ultimate Reality is non-dual.

Ahimsa Non-violence; abstaining from killing or giving pain to others in thought, word, or deed. It is the expression of universal love.

Anahata Chakra One of the seven spiritual centers. It is also known as the heart center. This spiritual center, which divides the upper hemisphere from the lower, controls the emotional life.

Ashram A hermitage, dwelling, or abode where ascetics practice and live.

Brahman The Supreme Being, regarded as impersonal, transcending manifestation and action.

Brahmachari A student who continues to live with his spiritual guide and vows to lead the life of a celibate.

Chakras Spiritual centers separating one level of consciousness from another.

Darshan Going into the presence of a holy man or a deity to have a glimpse.

Devas The gods or bright beings.

Gurudeva One who dispels the darkness of ignorance; a spiritual guide. Commonly shortened to "guru."

Hamsa The mythical swan that is able to discriminate between the Reality and that which is only apparently real. Also, an order of ascetics.

Kundalini Primal force latent at the base of the spinal column.

Mala A string of beads similar to a rosary, used for counting the number of repetitions of a mantra.

Mantra A syllable, sound, word, or set of words found in the deep state of meditation by the great sages. They are repeated by aspirants to achieve a specific end.

Maya The cosmic illusion by virtue of which one considers the unreal universe as really existent and as distinct from the Supreme Spirit.

Parsis Worshippers of the Divine Fire.

Prayoga Shastra The book of advanced yogic and tantra practices and their application.

Sadhaka A spiritual aspirant.

Sadhana The process of accomplishing the work of self-realization.

Sadhu A renunciate; one who is in the service of the Lord; one who has chosen to devote his life to spiritual practices.

Sankhya The most ancient system of Indian philosophy.

Samskaras Mental impressions created by past actions.

Sankalpa A resolve; a solemn vow to perform an observance.

Satsanga Conversing with the sages or the company of the sages.

Sattva One of the three qualities *(gunas)* of the manifest universe, which has the characteristics of light and purity.

Shakti Power; energy; force; the Divine Power of becoming; the Absolute Power or cosmic energy.

Shaktipata The awakening of higher consciousness through the grace of the guru.

Shiva The Supreme Reality.

Shiva-linga A symbol for the Supreme Reality.

Siddha One who consciously possesses *siddhi.*

Siddhi Psychic or yogic power.

Sikh A follower of Sri Guru Nanak.

Sri Vidya A treatise that establishes the relationship of microcosm with macrocosm. It is an advanced study in that relationship.

Sri Yantra   A symbolic diagram of the human structure and the cosmos, both manifested and unmanifested. The study and knowledge of this diagram can lead one to the highest state of realization.

Sushumna   The central nerve current that passes through the spinal column.

Swami   A monk from one of the ten orders of renunciates established by Shankaracharya.

Swamiji   A respectful form of address used in referring to a monk.

Tantra   A particular path of yoga that lays stress on mastery through synthesizing the dual forces of the universe.

Turiya   The fourth state, beyond waking, dreaming, and deep sleeping; superconscious state.

Upanishads   The later parts of the Vedas, which are the most ancient scriptures in the library of man today.

Vedanta   The philosophy of the Upanishads.

About Swami Rama

ONE OF THE greatest adepts, teachers, writers, and humanitarians of the 20th century, Swami Rama is the founder of the Himalayan Institute. Born in the Himalayas, he was raised from early childhood by the great Himalayan sage, Bengali Baba. Under the guidance of his master he traveled from monastery to monastery and studied with a variety of Himalayan saints and sages, including his grandmaster, who was living in a remote region of Tibet. In addition to this intense spiritual training, Swami Rama received higher education in both India and Europe. From 1949 to 1952, he held the prestigious position of Shankaracharya of Karvirpitham in South India. Thereafter, he returned to his master to receive further training at his cave monastery, and finally, in 1969, came to the United States, where he founded the Himalayan Institute. His best-known work, *Living with the Himalayan Masters*, reveals the many facets of this singular adept and demonstrates his embodiment of the living Himalayan Tradition.

The main building of the Himalayan Institute headquarters near Honesdale, Pennsylvania

The Himalayan Institute

A leader in the field of yoga, meditation, spirituality, and holistic health, the Himalayan Institute is a nonprofit international organization dedicated to serving humanity through educational, spiritual, and humanitarian programs. The mission of the Himalayan Institute is to inspire, educate, and empower all those who seek to experience their full potential.

Founded in 1971 by Swami Rama of the Himalayas, the Himalayan Institute and its varied activities and programs exemplify the spiritual heritage of mankind that unites East and West, spirituality and science, ancient wisdom and modern technology.

Our international headquarters is located on a beautiful 400-acre campus in the rolling hills of the Pocono Mountains of northeastern Pennsylvania. Our spiritually vibrant community and peaceful setting provide the perfect atmosphere for seminars and retreats, residential programs, and holistic health services. Students from all over the world join us to attend diverse programs on subjects such as hatha yoga, meditation, stress reduction, ayurveda, and yoga and tantra philosophy.

In addition, the Himalayan Institute draws on roots in the yoga tradition to serve our members and community through the following programs, services, and products:

Mission Programs

The essence of the Himalayan Institute's teaching mission flows from the timeless message of the Himalayan Masters, and is echoed in our on-site mission programming. Their message is to first become aware of the reality within ourselves, and then to build a bridge between our inner and outer worlds.

Our mission programs express a rich body of experiential wisdom and are offered year-round. They include seminars, retreats, and professional certifications that bring you the best of an authentic yoga tradition, addressed to a modern audience. Join us on campus for our Mission Programs to find wisdom from the heart of the yoga tradition, guidance for authentic practice, and food for your soul.

Wisdom Library and Mission Membership

The Himalayan Institute online Wisdom Library curates the essential teachings of the living Himalayan Tradition. This offering is a unique counterpart to our in-person Mission Programs, empowering students by providing online learning resources to enrich their study and practice outside the classroom.

Our Wisdom Library features multimedia blog content, livestreams, podcasts, downloadable practice resources, digital courses, and an interactive Seeker's Forum. These teachings capture our Mission Faculty's decades of study, practice, and teaching experience, featuring new content as well as the timeless teachings of Swami Rama and Pandit Rajmani Tigunait.

We invite seekers and students of the Himalayan Tradition to become a Himalayan Institute Mission Member, which grants unlimited access to the Wisdom Library. Mission Membership offers a way for you to support our shared commitment to service, while deepening your study and practice in the living Himalayan Tradition.

Spiritual Excursions

Since 1972, the Himalayan Institute has been organizing pilgrimages for spiritual seekers from around the world. Our spiritual excursions follow the traditional pilgrimage routes where adepts of the Himalayas lived and practiced. For thousands of years, pilgrimage has been an essential part of yoga sadhana, offering spiritual seekers the opportunity to experience the transformative power of living shrines of the Himalayan Tradition.

Global Humanitarian Projects

The Himalayan Institute's humanitarian mission is yoga in action—offering spiritually grounded healing and transformation to the world. Our humanitarian projects serve impoverished communities in India, Mexico, and Cameroon through rural empowerment and environmental regeneration. By putting yoga philosophy into practice, our programs are empowering communities globally with the knowledge and tools needed for a lasting social transformation at the grassroots level.

Publications

The Himalayan Institute publishes over 60 titles on yoga, philosophy, spirituality, science, ayurveda, and holistic health. These include the best-selling books *Living with the Himalayan Masters* and *The Science of Breath*, by Swami Rama; *The Power of Mantra and the Mystery of Initiation, From Death to Birth, Tantra Unveiled,* and two commentaries on the *Yoga Sutra—The Secret of the Yoga Sutra: Samadhi Pada* and *The Practice of the Yoga Sutra: Sadhana Pada—* by Pandit Rajmani Tigunait, PhD; and the award-winning *Yoga: Mastering the Basics* by Sandra Anderson and Rolf Sovik, PsyD. These books are for everyone: the interested reader, the spiritual novice, and the experienced practitioner.

PureRejuv Wellness Center

For over 40 years, the PureRejuv Wellness Center has fulfilled part of the Institute's mission to promote healthy and sustainable lifestyles. PureRejuv combines Eastern philosophy and Western medicine in an integrated approach to holistic health—nurturing balance and healing at home and at work. We offer the opportunity to find healing and renewal through on-site wellness retreats and individual wellness services, including therapeutic massage and bodywork, yoga therapy, ayurveda, biofeedback, natural medicine, and one-on-one consultations with our integrative medical staff.

Total Health Products

The Himalayan Institute, the developer of the original Neti Pot, manufactures a health line specializing in traditional and modern ayurvedic supplements and body care. We are dedicated to holistic and natural living by providing products using non-GMO components, petroleum-free biodegrading plastics, and eco-friendly packaging that has the least impact on the environment. Part of every purchase supports our Global Humanitarian projects, further developing and reinforcing our core mission of spirituality in action.

For further information about our programs, humanitarian projects, and products:

call: 800.822.4547
e-mail: info@HimalayanInstitute.org
write: The Himalayan Institute
           952 Bethany Turnpike
           Honesdale, PA 18431

or visit: HimalayanInstitute.org

The Secret of the Yoga Sutra
Samadhi Pada
Pandit Rajmani Tigunait, PhD

The Yoga Sutra is the living source wisdom of the yoga tradition, and is as relevant today as it was 2,200 years ago when it was codified by the sage Patanjali. Using this ancient yogic text as a guide, we can unlock the hidden power of yoga, and experience the promise of yoga in our lives. By applying its living wisdom in our practice, we can achieve the purpose of life: lasting fulfillment and ultimate freedom.

Paperback, 6" x 9", 331 pages
$24.95, ISBN 978-0-89389-277-7

The Practice of the Yoga Sutra
Sadhana Pada
Pandit Rajmani Tigunait, PhD

In Pandit Tigunait's practitioner-oriented commentary series, we see this ancient text through the filter of scholarly understanding and experiential knowledge gained through decades of advanced yogic practices. Through *The Secret of the Yoga Sutra* and *The Practice of the Yoga Sutra*, we receive the gift of living wisdom he received from the masters of the Himalayan Tradition, leading us to lasting happiness.

Paperback, 6" x 9", 389 Pages
$24.95, ISBN 978-0-89389-279-1

To order: 800-822-4547
Email: mailorder@HimalayanInstitute.org
Visit: HimalayanInstitute.org

HIMALAYAN
INSTITUTE®

Perennial Psychology of the Bhagavad Gita
Swami Rama

With the guidance and commentary of Himalayan Master Swami Rama, you can explore the wisdom of the Bhagavad Gita, which allows one to be vibrant and creative in the external world while maintaining a state of inner tranquility. This commentary on the Bhagavad Gita is a unique opportunity to see the Gita through the perspective of a master yogi, and is an excellent version for practitioners of yoga meditation. Spiritual seekers, psychotherapists, and students of Eastern studies will all find a storehouse of wisdom in this volume.

Paperback, 6" x 9", 479 pages
$19.95, ISBN 978-0-89389-090-2

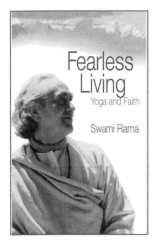

Fearless Living: Yoga and Faith
Swami Rama

Learn to live without fear—to trust a higher power, a divine purpose. In this collection of anecdotes from the astonishing life of Swami Rama, you will understand that there is a way to move beyond mere faith and into the realm of personal revelation. Through his astonishing life experiences we learn about ego and humility, see how to overcome fears that inhibit us, discover sacred places and rituals, and learn the importance of a one-pointed, positive mind. Swami Rama teaches us to see with the eyes of faith and move beyond our self-imposed limitations.

Paperback with flaps, 6" x 9", 160 pages
$12.95, ISBN 978-0-89389-251-7

To order: 800-822-4547
Email: mailorder@HimalayanInstitute.org
Visit: HimalayanInstitute.org

HIMALAYAN
INSTITUTE®